★ ★ ★

"Helmuth von Moltke, the Prussian chief of staff who, together with Bismarck, masterminded the wars of German Unification, was a prolific writer. In this important book we have a wide-ranging collection of his essays orders, ranging from philosophical reflections on the nature of war to instructions for handling wagon trains. The 1869 "Instructions for Large In it Commanders" is along worth the price of the volume: a careful reading of that document helps explain the approach to war and command that helped make the Germans so formidable in the field for almost a century. Moltke molded the Prussian and ultimately the German army at a time of technological and economic change. For that reason as well, this book deserves a much wider audience than those interested in nineteenth-century military history."

—Eliot A. Cohen, *Foreign Affairs*

"This valuable work ably compiles the selected writings on the art of war of one of military history's greatest geniuses. . . . von Moltke laid not only the foundation for Prussian/German military thought, he decisively influenced modern military theory. His impact on American military thinking persists, especially in various military staff college curricula."

—Fritz Heinzen, *Armed Forces Journal International*

"Although, Moltke was primarily concerned with the military problems of his own time, there is an enduring quality to his discussions of the problems of operations and command. . . . I highly recommend this book."

—James S. Corum, *The Journal of Military History*

"[*Moltke on the Art of War* is] a thoughtfully edited, well-translated anthology that merits a place in any serious collection on the craft of war in the modern Western world."

—Dennis Showalter, *War in History*

MOLTKE

ON THE ART OF WAR

Selected Writings

Edited by
Daniel J. Hughes

Translated by
Daniel J. Hughes and Harry Bell

Foreword by
Gunther E. Rothenberg

PRESIDIO
PRESS

BALLANTINE BOOKS • NEW YORK

For Katherine

A Presidio Press Book
Published by The Random House Ballantine Publishing Group

www.ballantinebooks.com

Library of Congress Cataloging-in-Publication Data

Moltke, Helmuth, Graf Von, 1800–1891.
    [Kriegslehren, English. Selections]
    Moltke on the art of war : selected writings / edited by Daniel J.
Hughes : translated by Daniel J. Hughes and Harry Bell : foreword by
Gunther Rothenberg.
      p. cm.
    Selections primarily from v.4 of Militärische werke, entitled
Kriegslehren.
    Includes bibliographical reference and index.
    ISBN 0-89141-484-3 (cloth)
    ISBN 978-0-89141-575-6 (paper)
    1. Military art and science. I. Hughes, Daniel J., 1946–
II. Title.
U102.M6732513   1993
335—dc20   92-43445
                              CIP

CONTENTS

FOREWORD

On June 2, 1866, King William I of Prussia directed that Gen. Helmuth Karl Bernhard von Moltke, Prussia's chief of the General Staff, henceforth was authorized to issue orders directly to the operational commands. The royal order created a command relationship that effectively made Moltke the field commander of the Prussian armies assembled to fight Austria and its German allies. Although Moltke had held his position since 1857, he still was little known in the army. When several days later a Prussian divisional commander received an operations order signed "Moltke," he is reported to have exclaimed, "All this appears to be in good order. But who is this General von Moltke?" His question would soon be answered.

Almost exactly one month later, on July 3, two Prussian armies, executing Moltke's bold and ambitious plan for what has come to be called a "battle of annihilation," fixed the Austrian main army deployed in strength on the heights northeast of Königgrätz with a series of frontal attacks. The battle remained undecided until just before noon, when a third Prussian army arrived to take the Austrian position in the right flank. With his position untenable, the Austrian commander ordered a withdrawal, which was orderly at first but turned into a near rout. Even so, arguably because his subordinate commanders were less willing than he to accept risks, Moltke's brilliantly conceived design fell short of perfection. The Austrian army was defeated but not annihilated. The bulk of it managed to escape, but for the time being it no longer constituted a cohesive fighting force—a fact recognized by the government in Vienna, which lost the will to continue the war and three days after the battle decided to seek peace terms.

Königgrätz ended the struggle for hegemony in Germany and propelled Moltke into the front ranks of the great soldiers. When night fell over the battlefield no one asked any longer who General Moltke was. A campaign of only six weeks had ended with a decisive victory over the army of a major power, a power which at the outset of the war had been widely held to be superior to the Prussians. Moltke's reputation was further enhanced by the equally unexpected and rapid defeat of the Imperial French army in 1870.

These surprising results had been achieved by the application of Moltke's innovative theories. Most experts believe that the firepower of the new rifled weapons and the extended frontages occupied by ever-larger armies transported and supplied by railroads had made frontal attacks futile and flanking maneuver impossible. During the wars of 1859 and 1864, and in the American Civil War, these developments had created a near deadlock on the battlefield with a clear advantage for the defense, pointing toward future wars of attrition. But Prussia, a medium power with exposed frontiers, facing potential enemies on several fronts, could not afford to fight wars of attrition. It needed to achieve a rapid decision.

Moltke's solution, demonstrated in the campaigns of 1866 and 1870, was an adaption of the Napoleonic precepts of offensive war to the realities of the industrial age. His method combined rapid mobilization, transportation, deployment, movement, and combat into one continuous sequence, making every effort to bring superior numbers into the final decisive battle. With his forces initially deployed widely dispersed outside the tactical zone, Moltke intended to place the adversary between converging wings and then, with his own armies concentrating only on the day of battle, destroy him in a complete or at least partial envelopment, the *Kesselschlacht*.

To plan and execute this strategic sequence, Moltke enhanced the role of the Prussian staff officers and created the modern general staff system. No longer confined to administration and planning, this highly select and intensely professional elite was to participate with the commanders in coordinating the actions of the widely dispersed formations, an essential element in Moltke's strategic methods. In war, Moltke held, nothing was certain. "No plan of operations," he wrote, "survives the first collision with the main body of the enemy." Therefore, he concluded, strategy—and in this context he included operations and even tactics—was little more than a "system of expedients." Even so, the first, albeit all important, phases in the strategic sequence—mobilization and transport schedules, and the initial deployment—could be tightly controlled by good staff work on the expanding railroad and telegraph network. But once the armies were deployed, Moltke rarely issued more than a general outline of his plans. Army and major formation commanders were to act within the framework of general directives as opposed to precise orders, with their staff officers providing any necessary interpretation and guidance. Although criticized by some, this approach, a key component of Moltke's methods, provided the necessary flexibility to deal with different and unexpected situations, demonstrated by his use of external lines of operation in 1866 and internal lines in 1870.

Moltke also was prepared to shift his views on such fundamental issues as the question of whether war should be conducted offensively or defensively. Although he had taken the offensive in his wars, he always had favored the tactical defense when possible. After 1870, he became increasingly skeptical about the prospects of the strategic offensive. Looking at the geopolitical situation—especially the mounting threat of a two-front war and the continued improvement in weapons—Moltke's first plan for war against France and Russia, prepared in 1871, warned that large-scale offensive operations could no longer rapidly produce a favorable decision. Instead, he favored a strategy of limited offensive-defensive operations, likely, he conceded, to end in a stalemate to be resolved by diplomacy.

The last, as the editor of this collection, Prof. Daniel J. Hughes, points out in his perceptive introduction, was a major shift in Moltke's view on the relationship between war and politics. Although Moltke considered himself a disciple of Clausewitz, as did almost all German military thinkers, he had rejected the master's contention that policy remained paramount even in war. Instead Moltke had argued that political considerations had no role during war, but after the campaign of 1870–71 he clearly envisaged such an active role even during hostilities.

An accomplished, prolific, and lucid writer, but holding strong views on the unpredictable nature of war, Moltke disliked creating dogma, and it is not surprising that his collected works, some twenty-four volumes, do not contain a comprehensive exposition of his strategic system. It is necessary to gain insight into his thinking by reading his memoranda, instructions, and correspondence. The selections offered here provide an excellent introduction. Overall, they emphasize his writings on the nature of war, the relationship between war and politics, and, above all, the higher direction of war—the subjects which Hughes rightly considers the core of Moltke's teachings and of his influence on generations of German commanders and staff officers.

Moltke was both an exceptionally skilled organizer and a great field commander, employing rarely equaled powers of reasoning and administrative competence to solve an apparently deadlocked strategic or operational situation. This achievement made him the most important military thinker between the fall of Napoleon and the First World War. If Clausewitz was more profound and original, his influence on actual German, European, or American military practice, the "art of war," is extremely difficult to determine. By contrast, all armies, if in modified form, adopted Moltke's staff system, while his concepts of an integrated sequence of mobilization and operations, and his command methods emphasizing individual initiative within an overall objective (today often referred to as *Auftragstaktik*), remained central in Prusso-German operational-strategic theory and practice into the Second World War. His work also influenced American military thinking. Moltke's campaigns were studied in U.S. Army staff colleges at the turn of the century, especially his campaign in Bohemia in 1866, which remains part of the curricula at the U.S. Army's Command and General Staff College at Fort Leavenworth, Kansas, and the U.S. Marine Corps School of Advanced Warfighting in Quantico, Virginia, to this day.

Perhaps not too much should be made of this, however. Moltke was very much a man of his time who tried to find solutions to his own contemporary problems. He was, Hughes writes, "the forerunner, who laid the seeds of modern theory, rather than the creator of a full-fledged modern system." This contention is valid, the more so when one considers that even the greatest contributors to the development of strategic theory have been able to do little more than to outline broad principles, often mere conclusions arising from the circumstances of their time. Moltke would have been the first to agree. Strategic doctrines, he concluded, "do not go much beyond the basic rules of common sense," and decisions of military commanders are based not on rigid theories but on available information—usually imperfect calculations of what *can* be done rather than what theoretically ought to be done. Still, his legacy remains important, an example of what can be achieved by one man. Operating within the ever-present fog of war, contending with difficult, self-willed, and often foolhardy subordinates, and unlike Napoleon never holding supreme command—in Prussia the king and his chief minister took the field—Moltke brought his armies to victory. More than a hundred years later he remains a military thinker whose ideas are applicable to our time. The selected writings from his works presented in this collection give the reader a valuable insight into the mind of a truly great soldier.

Gunther E. Rothenberg

Introduction

Count Helmuth von Moltke is most famous for his accomplishments as a field commander during the Prussian army's victories over the Austrians in 1866 and, with other German contingents, over the French in 1870–71. His celebrated victories have been the subject of numerous studies, including at least two of the best single-volume campaign studies ever written.[1] Moltke's other dimension has been relatively neglected since the Second World War. In addition to being one of the most successful field commanders of the nineteenth century, Moltke was a military intellectual of great importance to Prusso-German military theory. Termed "the ablest military mind since Napoleon" by David Chandler, Moltke laid much of the institutional and theoretical foundation of the modern German military system.[2] Gunther Rothenberg argued that Moltke "may be considered the most incisive and important European military writer between the Napoleonic era and the First World War."[3] Moltke's influence extended far beyond his own times.

---

1. They are by Gordon Craig, *The Battle of Königgrätz: Prussia's Victory Over Austria, 1866* (Westport, Conn.: Greenwood Press, 1975 [1964]); and Michael Howard, *The Franco-Prussian War: The German Invasion of France, 1870–1871* (New York: Collier Books, 1969 [1961]).
2. David Chandler, *Atlas of Military Strategy* (New York: The Free Press, 1980), 198.
3. Gunther Rothenberg, "Moltke, Schlieffen, and the Doctrine of Strategic Envelopment," in *Makers of Modern Strategy: From Machiavelli to the Nuclear Age*, ed. Peter Paret (Princeton, N.J.: Princeton University Press, 1986), 297. Along with the earlier essay by Hajo Holborn, cited below, Rothenberg's majesterial essay is the best introduction to Prusso-German military thought available in English.

Although the army of Molkte's lifetime was a royal Prussian rather than an imperial army, its power was at the core of Prussian dominance of the German Empire and its influence extended to the other armies (those of Bavaria, Saxony, and Württemberg) of Bismarck's federal state. The subsequent armies of the Weimar Republic and of Nazi Germany were truly "German." The continuity in personnel, military thought (much of which was Moltke's), and institutions from the Prussian to the German armies justifies the common reference to a single Prusso-German approach to warfare. This volume has the purpose of making Moltke's thoughts on the art of war available in English to a wider audience.

Helmuth von Moltke was neither a Prussian by birth nor a military officer by basic inclination. His nephew, Helmuth von Moltke (the younger), related that his uncle had told him that he had been forced into the Danish cadet corps and thus had his profession determined for him. He would have preferred, the elder Moltke said, to have studied archaeology and to have become a professor of history. Moltke served in the Danish army until 1822, when he entered Prussian service.[4] This was a risky undertaking, as he had to resign his Danish commission and pass a rigorous examination before being accepted by the Prussians. For the privilege of acquiring his new commission, he thus gave up his Danish seniority and became the most junior lieutenant in the Prussian army.

For the next thirty-five years Moltke pursued a successful if unspectacular career. He gained admittance to the General War School, as the War Academy was then called, in 1823. His application and acceptance were notable because he was allowed to take the entrance examination before he had completed the required three years of service and because his main essay was so good that it became part of the General Staff's research archive.[5]

4. Eberhard Kessel, ed., *Moltke Gespräche* (Hamburg: Hanseatische Verlagsanstalt, 1940), 228–29. The original primary source for this note, Nachlass Schmerfeld, appears to have been lost in the bombing attack that destroyed the German army's archives in 1945. Frequently given the title "the elder" to distinguish him from his nephew, "the younger," Count Moltke may also be differentiated by his noble rank. His nephew was not a count (*Graf*).

5. Eberhard Kessel, *Moltke* (Stuttgart: K. F. Koehler Verlag, 1957), 25. Kessel based his biography, by far the best of many, on many sources that were later destroyed. Unfortunately, it is available only in German.

Moltke's years at the General War School were not particularly noteworthy, although he was quite successful. One of the ironies of those years was that young Moltke, who subsequently was the most important person in incorporating Carl von Clausewitz's basic thoughts into Prusso-German military theory, apparently had no personal contact with the author of *On War*. Clausewitz held a purely administrative position at the General War School, and the two great thinkers probably took no notice of each other. During those years Moltke was a very junior and largely unknown officer, so there was no reason for Clausewitz, who normally had no contact with the students at the General War School, to have taken note of him. Nor would Moltke and other students have known about Clausewitz's ongoing studies of war. Clausewitz, in any case, confided in only a very limited circle of close friends.[6] While at the General War School, Moltke apparently limited his reading in the military literature to the minimum required by the course of study. Instead, he concentrated on geography, literature, and languages.[7]

For the next twelve years Moltke served as a typical junior General Staff officer and spent some time with his regiment (the 8th Life-Infantry).[8] In 1835 he terminated his service with tactical units when he set off for Turkey. Upon his return, Moltke began a long series of assignments in high-level staff positions and acquired important connections with the Prussian royal family. He became well known to the future King of Prussia and German Emperor William I, and to his son, the ill-fated King and Emperor Frederick III. Moltke served as an aide to the latter and accompanied him on several lengthy trips through Prussia's eastern provinces and to England. Moltke also established his reputation as one of the most able General Staff officers in the army. During his long career, in a pattern he later denied to other General Staff officers as much as possible, Moltke never commanded a unit, not even a company.[9]

6. Ibid., 35.
7. Ibid., 47.
8. Ibid., 52–110. Still useful for Moltke's early years is the older biography by William O'Connor Morris, *Moltke: A Biographical and Critical Study* (New York: Haskell House Publishers Ltd., 1971 [first published 1893]), 1–12.
9. In this respect Moltke's career was somewhat similar to that of Count von Schlieffen, whose command experience was limited to command of the 1st Guards-Ulan Regiment. On this see E. G. Blau, "Der ältere Moltke und Schlieffen," *Wissen und Wehr,* no. 1 (1934): 824–34.

When Prince William of Prussia assumed the responsibility of rule from his ailing older brother in 1857, one of his first and most important acts was to appoint Helmuth von Moltke as chief of the Prussian General Staff.[10] Building on the solid foundation established by his predecessors, Wilhelm von Krauseneck and Carl von Reyher, Moltke wasted no time in placing his stamp on the General Staff and, to a lesser extent prior to 1870, on the entire army.[11]

Although Moltke's role in institutional development between 1858 and 1888 is not a major topic of this volume, some mention of it is important for understanding the practical significance of his military philosophy, as well as the overall context of his writing. Prior to Moltke's becoming chief of the General Staff, neither that position nor the institution as a whole enjoyed the power, influence, or prestige which they enjoyed by the end of the campaign of 1870–71.

The emergence of the General Staff began soon after Moltke became staff chief, although this was hardly apparent in the early years. In 1858 he succeeded in gaining substantial control over corps staff rides. New guidelines established two points that became the hallmarks of Moltke's ideas on command. Commanders should order as little as possible (leaving details to subordinate commanders) and they should take care to limit their orders to what was practicable. Similarly, a royal order in 1861 extended the General Staff's influence to the maneuvers of large units.[12] In 1872 Moltke succeeded in placing the War Academy directly under the chief of the General Staff.

Moltke's contributions to Prusso-German military theory can only be outlined in broad terms here. Although he wrote no single integrated

---

10. Hajo Holborn, "Moltke and Schlieffen: The Prussian-German School," *Makers of Modern Strategy: Military Thought from Machiavelli to Hitler* (Princeton, N.J.: Princeton University Press, 1948), 176. This classic essay, slightly modified and substantially shortened by Gunther Rothenberg, also appears in the 1986 edition.

11. Eberhard Kessel, *Moltke*, and Max Jähns, *Feldmarschall Moltke* (Berlin: Ernst Hoffman & Co., 1900), leave no doubt that Moltke's predecessors laid many of the foundations for the success of the General Staff in the wars of German unification. Clearly, however, Moltke's vision of how the General Staff should exploit technological advances and adapt to the changed conditions of modern warfare went far beyond those of Krauseneck (1829–48) and Reyher (1848–57).

12. Kessel, *Moltke*, 245–46, 278.

work on warfare, his views became the foundation of Prussian military thought, particularly in the areas of strategy and large-unit operations. The selections printed in this volume focus on his teachings concerning the nature of war, the relationship between war and politics, and the conduct of war. He wrote many other essays on tactics, and either wrote or directed a number of important historical studies of nineteenth century campaigns. These are beyond the scope of this collection and, in many cases, are already available in English.[13]

Although Moltke did not follow Clausewitz's teachings on the proper relationship between war and politics, on many other points he was the key link between *On War*'s philosophical speculations and the theory and practice of the Prussian army. Writing after the Second World War, General Staff officer Hermann Teske wrote that Moltke was the incarnation of Clausewitzian theory.[14] In the essays printed here, the reader will find ample confirmation that Moltke employed Clausewitzian thinking and specific terms in numerous cases. Both Clausewitz and Moltke emphasized the primacy of battle and annihilation of the main enemy army. Both accepted uncertainty in warfare and emphasized improvisation over permanent or binding doctrine. Both emphasized the need for speed in making and executing decisions rather than lengthy searches for ideal solutions. Both emphasized moral factors in war and the need for independent action by local commanders, although Moltke certainly carried this farther than did Clausewitz.[15] Both rejected the idea that

13. The following portion of this introduction contains more detailed bibliographic information on Moltke's writings. Eventually these came to include 8 volumes of memoirs, 14 volumes of military works, 1 volume of mobilization plans, 1 volume of records of conversations with various people, and a number of smaller items.

14. Hermann Teske, *Die Silberne Spiegel. Generalstabsdienst unter der Lupe* (Heidelberg: Kurt Vowinckel, 1952), 18.

15. On these and other points, see Michael Howard, "The Influence of Clausewitz," in *Makers of Modern Strategy* (1986), 29–30; Kessel, *Moltke*, 507; and Ulrich Marwedel, *Carl von Clausewitz. Persönlichkeit und Wirkungsgeschichte seines Werkes bis 1918* (Boppard: Harald Boldt Verlag, 1978), 130–31. Although Marwedel's penetrating and exhaustive study praises Clausewitz beyond all reason and defines wisdom by the standard of whether or not one accepted Clausewitz's teachings, it is a fundamental work that unfortunately has not received the attention it deserves.

systems could ever replace individual talent, and neither believed that any firm rules were possible in warfare.[16]

Nevertheless, this should not be the only focus in reading Moltke's writings. Some German thinkers argued that his concept of concentric operations conducted by separated armies which converged only during the course of a battle was a radical departure from Clausewitz's ideas. Many of Moltke's tactical concepts differed from those of Clausewitz because of the vast changes in infantry weapons and advances in the application of new technologies to the battlefield. The Prussian general and theoretician Sigismund von Schlichting argued that Moltke's methods marked a radical departure from those of Napoleon and launched an entirely new era in the development of the art of war. Although Schlichting's views were not entirely new, his penetrating analysis touched off a seemingly endless debate within the Prussian army. Schlichting's own concepts, based on Moltke and Clausewitz, later became vastly important in their own right as a main pillar of modern operational thought.[17] Herbert Rosinski concluded that Moltke was the man who applied Clausewitz's pure theory to the sphere of practical action. Waldemar Erfurth, an important German military writer and general in the Second World War, argued that Moltke freed the Prussian General Staff from Jomini's theories, led it into the intellectual world of Clausewitz, Scharnhorst, and Gneisenau, and developed Clausewitz's operational teachings in light of nineteenth-century developments.[18] In any case, a comparative reading of the writings of Clausewitz and Moltke is certainly helpful in understanding the nature of the thought behind the methods and system of the Prusso-German army.

Moltke regarded war both as one of the worst disasters that could befall human societies and as an inevitable part of the divine world

---

16. A point most forcefully and elegantly made by Gunther Rothenberg in "Moltke, Schlieffen, and the Doctrine of Strategic Envelopment," 299.

17. Rudolf von Caemmerer, *The Development of Strategical Science during the 19th Century,* trans. Karl von Donat (London: Hugh Rees, 1905), is the best introduction to the controversy.

18. Herbert Rosinski, *The German Army* (London: The Hogarth Press, 1939), 127. Waldemar Erfurth, *Der Vernichtungssieg. Eine Studie über das Zusammenwirken getrennter Heeresteile* (Berlin: E. S. Mittler, 1939), 35.

order. In a letter written in 1880 to a professor at the University of Heidelberg, Moltke made his famous statement that eternal peace was a dream, and not even a pleasant one. He was equally pessimistic about the possibility that international law would be able to banish war from the earth or even lessen its fearful consequences. The only hope for improving the conduct of armies in war, he thought, lay in the gradual progress of civilization and in bringing the better parts of the population into modern armies through universal military service.[19] He was under no illusions, moreover, that future wars would be won as cheaply and quickly as had been those of 1864, 1866, and 1870–71. Moltke feared a repetition of the popular uprising, the "people's war," which had prolonged the Franco-Prussian War at great cost to both sides, as well as a long struggle between regular armies. Moltke's impatience and frustration with the second phase of the struggle against France emerges clearly in the texts printed here.[20]

Given that war was an inevitable part of the divine order, and even a positive force in developing and disciplining humanity, Moltke developed one-sided views on the relationship between politics and war. While Clausewitz argued that war was merely an extension of politics by other means and that military considerations and men must be subordinate to political factors and leaders, Moltke held the opposite opinion. Although he recognized that political matters were the reason for conducting war and gave lip service to Clausewitz's dictum that war must serve policy, in practice his views were quite different. He believed that once war had begun, political advisors and their considerations should play no role in military strategy and the conduct of operations. Moltke's own statements offer scant support for Eberhard Kessel's efforts to reduce the differences between Bismarck and Moltke to a question of

---

19. This famous letter, published in Moltke's military writings, first appeared in his *Gesammelte Schriften und Denkwürdigkeiten,* 9 vols. (Berlin: E. S. Mittler & Son, 1892–93), vol. 5, 194–97. Its translated text may be found in this volume in Chapter One.

20. Rudolf Stadelmann, *Moltke und der Staat* (Krefeld: Scherpe Verlag, 1950), 324–25. Stig Förster, "Optionen der Kriegführung im Zeitalter des Volkskrieges—Zu Helmuth von Moltkes militärisch-politischen überlegungen nach den Erfahrungen der Einigungskriege" in Detlev Bald, ed., *Militärische Verantwortung in Staat und Gesellschaft* (Koblenz: Bernard & Graefe, 1986), is also important.

which office should retain ultimate responsibility for advising the head of state during war.[21] Moltke's efforts to prevent political leaders and their interests from determining military strategy were consistent with his written views that upon mobilization the king's political advisor should step into the background and remain there until the conclusion of the war. As Rudolf Stadelmann demonstrated, in 1871 Moltke, despite all his comments about the importance of political considerations in military questions, attempted to exclude all political influence from Prussian decision making.[22] Michael Howard pointed out in his introduction to *On War* that Moltke refused to accept Clausewitz's insistence on the subordination of military means to political ends.[23] The result was Moltke's celebrated conflict with the minister-president of Prussia and chancellor of the German Empire, Otto von Bismarck.[24] In subsequent years Moltke at times seems to have been in favor of preventive war against France, although his efforts to influence national policy cannot be compared with those of his successor, Count Alfred von Waldersee.[25]

21. Kessel, *Moltke*, 508–09, argues that Moltke's views were similar to Clausewitz's and that the extended conflict between Moltke and Bismarck during and after the Franco-Prussian War was largely a question of personalities or of bureaucratic politics.

22. Stadelmann, *Moltke und Der Staat*, 206–13. These efforts failed.

23. Michael Howard, "The Influence of Clausewitz," 30–31. Howard also refers the reader to Stadelmann's analysis, cited above. Jehuda Wallach, *Kriegstheorien. Ihre Entwicklung im 19. und 20. Jahrhundert* (Frankfurt am Main: Bernard & Graefe, 1972), 84, makes the same point with reference to Moltke's essay "On Strategy," which is included in its entirety in this book.

24. The relationship between politics and the military establishment in Prussian and Imperial Germany has been one of the most prominent themes of modern German history. For an introduction to the issues involved, see Gordon Craig, *The Politics of the Prussian Army, 1650–1945* (New York: Oxford University Press, 1956) and the same author's *Germany 1860–1945* (New York: Oxford University Press, 1978). Still useful is Gerhard Ritter's *The Sword and the Scepter: The Problem of Militarism in Germany*, 4 vols., trans. Heinz Norden (Coral Gables, Fla.: University of Miami Press, 1964–1973). Despite the controversy over Ritter's definition of militarism, his research on this question remains important.

25. One of the most recent presentations of Moltke's thoughts on the question of national policy and strategy is Stig Förster, "Facing 'People's War': Moltke the Elder and Germany's Military Options after 1871," *Journal of Strategic Studies*, no. 2 (June 1987): 209–30.

Moltke's views on the art of war established the basic principles of the Prusso-German way of war and endured, with some changes, to the end of that tradition in 1945. First and foremost, like Clausewitz, Moltke had no faith in systems of any kind. His system consisted of a pattern of thought rather than a series of procedures to be followed or successive tactical acts to be performed under all circumstances. Moltke placed his faith in the ability of Prussian officers to use their education and judgment to adjust to concrete situations as they came up. His famous statement that strategy was a system of expedients typified his belief that no simple rules or formulas existed for determining military plans. Moltke's statements should be taken against the background of the detailed systems of the eighteenth century and may be seen as a rejection of such systems. Strategy, Moltke believed, was based on concrete situations rather than upon mathematical or other rules to be applied in every case. This line of thought extended to his concepts of campaign planning and tactics, as the texts included here demonstrate.[26]

Despite his aversion to systems, which could too easily degenerate into dogma, Moltke believed in a few fundamental principles to guide an army's conduct of war. He never reduced these basic principles to lists of slogans or catchwords so familiar to modern American officers. One must therefore read his works carefully to find those concepts that he stressed or mentioned repeatedly. For this, his 1869 *Instructions for Large Unit Commanders* is probably the most important single document.[27]

One of Moltke's most fundamental points was that battle was both the means of winning wars and the dominant consideration in conducting war. In this he laid the foundations of German theory through

---

26. Kessel, *Moltke*, 506, 511–12, discusses these issues.

27. This was his *Verordnungen für die höheren Truppenführer vom 24 Juni 1869*. It was reprinted with only minor changes in 1885. The Prussian army's final pre–World War I version of the manual, published in 1910, followed Moltke's basic principles very closely. See Prussia, Kriegsministerium, *D.V.E. Nr. 53. Grundzüge der höheren Truppenführung vom 1. Januar 1910* (Berlin: Reichsdruckerei, 1910). The manual maintained Moltke's wording as much as possible. Both Hajo Holborn and Gunther Rothenberg quote the 1869 edition extensively in their *Makers of Modern Strategy* essays cited previously.

the end of the Second World War. His views on this drew upon Clausewitz's ideas on the necessity of fighting great decisive battles and of annihilating the main enemy force. Moltke endorsed these articles of faith and carried them further than did Clausewitz. Moltke argued that the decision by force of arms was the most important means to reach the goal of a war and the most important part of war. His writings frequently discuss the need to annihilate the enemy's armed forces in a rapid campaign. Moltke clearly contributed to the Prusso-German emphasis on annihilation as much as did any other man.

Although Moltke thus further elaborated the principles of decisive battles and annihilation, which had become commonplace in the 1830s, by the end of his life he had developed doubts that a rapid decision would be possible under the conditions prevalent by the century's end. His mobilization plans written after 1871 contain many passages indicating his growing doubts about the prospects of achieving quick victories by annihilating opposing armies. Nevertheless, Moltke should receive credit or blame for the basic concept of annihilation, which some writers have wrongly attributed exclusively to Count Alfred von Schlieffen.[28]

As a natural consequence of belief in the necessity of seeking a rapid and decisive battle, Moltke emphasized the offense over the defense, even though he fully recognized the advantages afforded the defender by modern firearms. In stressing the importance of mobile operations and conducting wars offensively, Moltke reversed Reyher's emphasis on using fortresses to defend railroads and other important installations.[29] Not a system of fortresses, Moltke argued, but a mobile field army was the nation's best defense. Nevertheless, he never lost sight of Clausewitz's dictum that the defense was the stronger form of war.

28. Kessel, *Moltke,* 108–09, and 243–44; Stadelmann, *Moltke und der Staat,* 326–27, and Peter Rassow, *Der Plan Moltkes für den Zweifrontkrieg* (Breslau, 1938), 10; Count Helmuth von Moltke, *Die deutschen Aufmarschpläne 1871–1890,* ed. Ferdinand von Schmerfeld (Berlin: E. S. Mittler, 1929), passim. Jehuda Wallach's study of the annihilation idea in the German army attributes the development of this "dogma" entirely to Count Alfred von Schlieffen. See his *The Dogma of the Battle of Annihilation* (Westport, Conn.: Greenwood Press, 1986 [German edition, 1967]), passim. Stig Förster has rightly criticized Wallach for overlooking the annihilation idea in Moltke's theory.

29. On this point see Kessel, *Moltke,* 239.

Both men favored the offensive, even though it was more difficult and more costly, because only the offensive offered prospects for a decision. Moltke's early writings in particular stressed the need for taking offensive action at all levels.[30]

In the sphere of tactics, Moltke had always warned of the devastating effects of defensive firepower and the necessity of finding appropriate ways to overcome them. His second major concern, closely related to the first, was the role of cavalry, whose traditional function in delivering the final decisive attack had become obsolete because of improvements in firearms. Moltke saw the cavalry's primary utility in the areas of reconnaissance and exploitation of victories already won by the infantry and artillery.[31] Although this selection of readings does not reproduce the bulk of Moltke's writing on defensive firepower, his views are evident even in his essays on other topics.

It was in the area of large-unit operations that Moltke made his most lasting contribution to German theory and practice. One of his most controversial innovations, whose newness many denied at the time and later, was his concept of separated armies. The German term most frequently used was *getrennte Heeresteile,* literally meaning "separated parts of the army." Moltke himself occasionally used this precise term, which later became the shorthand reference to his entire system of moving and concentrating armies before and during battles. Moltke argued that large concentrations of units had become inherently disadvantageous, even disastrous, because of the size of modern armies and the resulting difficulties of moving and provisioning them. In the tactical sphere, moreover, modern weaponry had virtually eliminated turning movements within the range of the enemy's artillery or even rifle fire.[32] Thus, in order to conduct operations (in the German sense)

30. As several authors have pointed out, Moltke's later writings emphasized defensive over offensive tactics. See Wallach, *Kriegstheorien,* 74–76.

31. Kessel, *Moltke,* 248.

32. Here one must bear in mind the difference between *Umgehung,* a turning movement on a large scale, and *Umfassung,* which normally meant a flank attack. The former belonged to the realm of strategy, the latter to tactics. One should also note that German theorists, including Moltke, did not insert an "operational level" between strategy and tactics. The Prusso-German army recognized no hierarchical divisions of war as do many modern armies.

and to strike deep into the enemy's flank, concentration of separated parts of the army should take place only on the battlefield after the battle had begun. Moltke thus added a new dimension to Scharnhorst's old dictum "march divided, fight united."[33]

Separating one's armies in this manner and in immediate proximity to a strong enemy presented the great danger of defeat in detail if the enemy were able to mass the bulk of his forces to crush one of the smaller parts of the divided army. Moltke recognized this danger but thought the potential gain, a decisive victory, to be well worth the risk.[34]

Under such a system, the supreme command had to allow its subordinate commanders considerable independence to exercise their own judgment. The primitive communications means of the time frequently could not overcome the distances separating armies from their main headquarters. Commanders of far-flung detachments had to make important decisions without consulting with the high command. Moltke turned this necessity into a virtue by emphasizing the advantages of developing commanders who could exercise initiative within the framework of the high command's overall intent. He did this by leading his army commanders primarily through directives (*Weisungen*) rather than detailed orders, although he was quite prepared to issue very detailed and strict orders if necessary. Moltke frequently issued such restrictive orders in 1866 and 1870–71. The reader will find references to some of these instances in the selections printed here. Moltke was willing to allow subordinate commanders to deviate from the details of his directives so long as their actions were consistent with his overall concept. Like almost everything else in Moltke's approach, however, this was dependent upon the situation and the personalities involved. In 1866, for example, Moltke would have preferred to command the Prussian forces opposing Hesse and Hanover with general directives. The incompetence of the Prussian commander, Maj. Gen. Eduard Vogel von Falkenstein, forced Moltke to interfere in the details of that campaign.[35]

---

33. Siegfried Mette, in his *Vom Geist deutscher Feldherren. Genie und Technik 1800– 1918* (Zurich: Scientia A. G., 1938), 155, was among the few writers to caution that Scharnhorst and Moltke meant different things by this common phrase.
34. Erfurth, *Vernichtungssieg,* 44. See also Egon Freiherr von Gayl, *General von Schlichting und sein Lebenswirk* (Berlin: Verlag von Georg Stilke, 1913), 247.
35. See Craig, *Königgrätz,* 40.

Moltke consistently taught his subordinates to "march to the sound of the cannon" and join in local battles. He believed that a tactical success was to be seized whenever possible—even if it came about in a largely unforeseen manner. He was remarkably tolerant of the resulting disruptions of his plans and refused to modify his position—even after very serious problems both in 1866 and in 1870 had jeopardized everything. Moltke held firmly to his original view, which became a fundamental basis of German theory through the Second World War.

Here again, Moltke's views were similar to Clausewitz's teachings. In book six, chapter eight of *On War*, Clausewitz wrote that all strategic planning rested on tactical success alone, because only tactical successes could produce a favorable outcome. Wilhelm Balck's multivolume work on tactics, the most comprehensive statement of German thought before the First World War, used Moltke's phrase that strategy grows silent in the face of the need for a tactical victory.[36]

Moltke's insistence that the supreme commander must allow his local commanders such freedom of action later became one of the most controversial aspects of his methods. A number of subsequent writers, most notably John F. C. Fuller, harshly criticized Moltke for unleashing his commanders and abdicating his own responsibilities. Most German authors defended Moltke's command methods by arguing that the large armies of his and later eras made such a loose system of command necessary. Nearly all Prussian and German capstone regulations published after 1869 contained versions of Moltke's statement that hesitations in reaching decisions and inaction were worse than mistakes in choosing means.[37]

Linking the original mobilization with the deployment and the opening moves of a campaign was another of Moltke's innovations. His famous

36. Wilhelm Balck, *Taktik*, 6 vols. (Berlin: R. Eisenschmidt, 1908–12), vol. 1, 7–8.

37. Brian Holden Reid, *J. F. C. Fuller: Military Thinker* (New York: St. Martin's Press, 1987), 109; J. F. C. Fuller, *A Military History of the Western World*, 3 vols. (New York: Minerva Press, 1956), vol. 3, 134. The editor of this volume has analyzed the issue in greater detail in "Auftragstaktik," an article in the forthcoming *Brassey's International Military Encyclopedia*. Some German authors defended Moltke's command methods by arguing that the large armies of his day made such a loose system necessary. See Jähns, *Moltke*, 583–84; and Rothenberg, "Moltke, Schlieffen, and the Doctrine of Strategic Envelopment," 300–01.

statement that a mistake in the original deployment could hardly be made good in the entire course of a campaign reflected his concern over flexible deployments linked to the subsequent campaign. This did not mean, however, that Moltke thought that a campaign could be planned in detail before it began. On the contrary, he insisted that no plan lasted beyond the first encounter with the enemy's main army. Only a layman, he argued, would believe that a commander developed a plan and followed it exactly, foreseeing all developments, to its successful conclusion. Although Schlieffen has received most of the credit for inventing this process of inextricably linking deployment to the campaign plan, the concept definitely began with Moltke.[38]

In making his original plans and deployments, Moltke relied upon the new and expanding system of railroads in Prussia. This was in marked contrast to his predecessors, who had shown but little interest in railroads. Although General Reyher noted how much more skillfully the Austrians had exploited railroads during the mobilizations of 1850 than had the Prussians, he moved very slowly and made little effort to establish a basis for full use of the railway system in wartime. Moltke substituted vast energy and diligence in exploiting railroads in place of Reyher's lethargy. The General Staff's greatly increased involvement in planning for and utilizing railroads was one of the hallmarks of Moltke's term as chief of the General Staff.[39]

A large portion of Moltke's literary legacy has been published. Translations of some of his letters have appeared in various editions.[40]

---

38. Michael Geyer, "German Strategy in the Age of Machine Warfare, 1914–1945" in *Makers of Modern Strategy* (1986), 527–97, blames Schlieffen. Dennis Showalter, *Railroads and Rifles: Soldiers, Technology and the Unification of Germany* (Hamden, Conn.: Archon Press, 1986 [1975]), 60–61, and Stadelmann, *Moltke und der Staat,* 37–38, stress Moltke's reliance on the initial mobilization and deployment.

39. See Showalter, *Railroads and Rifles,* 38–39 and Arden Bucholz, *Moltke, Schlieffen, and Prussian War Planning* (New York: Berg, 1991), 31–43.

40. Representative samples are Mary Herms, trans., *Field-Marshal Count Helmuth von Moltke as a Correspondent* (New York: Harper & Brothers, 1893); Mary Herms, trans., *Essays, Speeches and Memoirs of Field-Marshal Count Helmuth von Moltke,* 2 vols. (New York: Harper & Brothers, 1893); and *Letters of Count Helmuth von Moltke to His Mother and His Brother,* trans. Clara Bell and Henry W. Fischer (New York: Harper & Brothers, 1892). His letters to his wife written while he accompanied Crown

Sections of his historical and official writings have also appeared in English, notably his one-volume history of the Franco-Prussian War.[41] In 1974, Greenwood Press assembled three selections from Moltke's military works under the title *Strategy; Its Theory and Application: The Wars for German Unification, 1866–1871.* This volume actually contained a short selection of early planning papers from prior to the war of 1866, a selection of his correspondence from that war, and excerpts from Moltke's very extensive correspondence during the Franco-Prussian War. None of these books contain any of Moltke's theoretical writings.[42]

The selections of Moltke's writings published here are a fair representation of his views on the art of war. The reader must use them with caution, however, because they are but a small part of his diverse writings.[43]

More serious is the question of the texts' authenticity. The Prussian General Staff edited and published Moltke's official writings in a series of volumes released between 1892 and 1912.[44] Since Moltke

---

Prince Frederick to Russia in 1856 were published as *Field-Marshal Moltke's Letters from Russia,* trans. Robina Napier (London: Kegan Paul & Co., 1878). His short sketch of conditions in Poland appeared as *Poland: An Historical Sketch* (London: Chapman & Hal, 1895).

41. Helmuth von Moltke, *The Franco-German War of 1870–71* (New York: Harper & Brothers, 1892). This originally appeared as volume 3 of his *Denkwürdigkeiten.*

42. The volume assembled the following previous publications: Great Britain, General Staff, ed. and trans., *Moltke's Projects for the Campaign of 1866 Against Austria* (London: His Majesty's Printing Office, 1915); and Capt. Harry Bell, trans. and ed., *Extracts from Moltke's Correspondence Pertaining to the War, 1870–71* (Fort Leavenworth, Kans.: The Army Service Schools Press, 1911).

43. Helmuth von Moltke, *Gesammelte Schriften und Denkwürdigkeiten,* 8 vols. (Berlin: E. S. Mittler & Son, 1892–1918), is primarily a collection of nonmilitary letters, essays, and a few speeches. It has some military writings. Moltke's *Militärische Werke,* 14 vols. (Berlin: E. S. Mittler & Son, 1892–1912), draws from a wide range of published and archival sources. Generalfeldmarschall Graf von Moltke, *Ausgewählte Werke,* 4 vols., ed. Ferdinand von Schmerfeld (Berlin: Reimar Hobbing, 1925), is a condensed version of the *Militärische Werke* with some private writings in volume 4. Schmerfeld was one of the General Staff officers who edited the military works.

44. Cited as Moltke's *Militärische Werke* above.

had left no definitive collection of his writings, the military history section of the General Staff assembled his works from a variety of sources. These included his previously published memoirs, the official histories of his campaigns, previously published books and articles, documents from the archives of the General Staff, and a scattering of other sources.[45] In assembling these volumes, the General Staff frequently printed an essay by Moltke, followed by historical examples illustrating the principles discussed in the text. These historical examples may or may not have been written by Moltke. Those that Moltke did not write personally came from the official histories written by the General Staff under his close personal supervision. The fact remains, however, that the resulting product reflected what the General Staff wanted the Prussian officer corps and others to regard as Moltke's teachings. Moltke himself, who resisted the writing of any such collections of his teachings or theories, might have assembled such volumes quite differently.

Some doubt exists as to the authenticity of at least one of the texts. Gerhard Ritter, who had access to the Prussian military archives before their destruction in the Second World War, challenged the accuracy of Moltke's essay titled "On Strategy."[46] Ritter argued that the General Staff made serious alterations in those sections of Moltke's writings dealing with the relationship of politics and military strategy during war. Nevertheless, the views presented in the essay seem quite consistent with Moltke's other writings, the authenticity of which is not in question. There seems to be no reason to doubt that the es-

---

45. Moltke had a strong prejudice against memoirs, which he considered inaccurate attempts at self-aggrandizement, and insisted that everything that anyone might wish to know about his part in the wars of unification could be found in the General Staff's archives. Nevertheless, in 1887 he finally began writing his own history of the Franco-Prussian War, which became volume 3 of the *Denkwürdigkeiten* and provided important sections of the text printed in the *Militärische Werke*. Notes at the beginning of each section more precisely indicate the source of the text of that chapter.

46. Ritter, *Sword and Scepter*, vol. 1, 303–04. The essay appeared in the *Militärische Werke*, in volume 2, part 2, 287–93. It also appeared in volume 13 of the series *Kriegsgeschichtliche Einzelschriften*, published by the General Staff before the First World War (Prussia, Grosser Generalstab, *Kriegsgeschichtliche Einzelschriften*, vol. 13 [Berlin: E. S. Mittler, 1890], 1–4).

say is at least broadly representative of Moltke's views on the relationship of war and policy. The differences between the various versions of the essay are minor.[47]

The selections in this volume come primarily from volume four of the *Militärische Werke,* which consisted of three book-length parts.[48] The chapter titled "Instructions for the Commanders of Large Units" appeared in volume two, part two of the *Militärische Werke.*[49] To the best of the editor's knowledge, these volumes have not previously appeared in English, although collectively they are among the half-dozen most fundamental documents of the Prussian army's theory of war. Captain Harry Bell of the Army Service Schools at Fort Leavenworth, Kansas, prepared rough translations of the three parts of volume four between 1912 and 1916. The current editor has retranslated selected portions of these three volumes for publication here. Although scarcely a sentence of Bell's original translation remains intact, it seems only proper to include him as joint translator.[50]

Excellent maps of the Austro-Prussian and Franco-Prussian wars that will help the reader follow the discussions found in the historical examples are contained in Gordon Craig's *Königgrätz* and Michael Howard's *Franco-Prussian War.*

47. The version of the essay "Strategy" in Schmerfeld, *Generalfeldmarschall Graf von Moltke: Ausgewählte Werke,* vol. 1, 241–42, is much different than the version in Grosser Generalstab, ed., *Kriegsgeschichtliche Einzelschriften,* vol. 13 (Berlin: E. S. Mittler, 1890). Neither represents a great departure from the other versions or the overall views presented elsewhere in Moltke's writings.

48. Volume 4's overall title was *Kriegslehren* (Teachings on War). The three parts were, respectively, *Die operativen Vorbereitungen zur Schlacht* (Operational Preparations for the Battle); *Die taktischen Vorbereitungen zur Schlacht* (Tactical Preparations for the Battle); and *Die Schlacht* (The Battle). They were published in 1911 and 1912.

49. Part 2 of volume 2 was titled *Moltkes Taktisch-strategische Aufsätze aus den Jahren 1857 bis 1871.* The section of the *Verordnungen für die höheren Truppenführer vom 24. Juni 1869* (first published in 1900) appeared in pages 165–215.

50. This volume has not used the older partial translations by H. R. G. Crauford, *Observations on the Influence that Arms of Precision Have on Modern Tactics* (London: W. Mitchell & Co., 1871), or the unpublished piece by Commander A. G. Zimmerman, "Moltke's Works: Precepts of War," 2 parts (typescript, U.S. Naval War College, 1935). The editor is indebted to Gunther Rothenberg for bringing this to his attention.

Each chapter contains a brief introduction and a number of explanatory footnotes. I have tried to hold these to a minimum, but some commentary is unavoidable given both the texts themselves and the nature of the historical questions involved. Many of Moltke's statements will make no sense to readers who are not at least broadly informed about German history. Many of his comments about politics and political leaders, for example, should be understood in the context of his lengthy and bitter conflict with Otto von Bismarck.

Moltke's writings, especially his letters and unofficial essays, have long been regarded as classics of German prose. Certainly he was a gifted writer, military thinker, and field commander. Still, he was human, as the selections printed here make clear. His views on society reflected both the social prejudices of his aristocratic profession and the social Darwinism so prevalent in Germany and Europe during his lifetime. His preference for the unreformed Prussian monarchical form of government added a further fundamental bias to much of his writing, both theoretical and historical. Despite the depth of the research and thought that stood behind much of his work, Moltke was above all a practical nineteenth-century German soldier rather than an objective historian. The reader must bear this in mind.[51]

The reader should not allow concern for Moltke's personal idiosyncrasies to obscure the most fundamental fact about his writings: Moltke's views, as taught in the Prussian army and printed in his publications, formed one of the pillars of Prusso-German theory. His *Instructions for Large Unit Commanders,* written in 1869 and revised slightly in 1885, remained largely in effect in 1914. In 1910 the army's new version of that regulation correctly noted that its text preserved Moltke's exact words wherever possible.[52] Many of Moltke's basic concepts carried over into the new German army after the Imperial army's defeat and the nation's collapse in 1918.

---

51. Thus, in Moltke's writings one finds profound insights into the nature of war side by side with extreme examples of conservative and nationalistic prejudices of all types. Moltke frequently couples objective analysis of military situations with one-sided political statements and greatly distorted historical accounts.

52. Prussia, Kriegsministerium, *Grundzüge der höheren Truppenführung* (Berlin: Reichsdruckerei, 1910), 5.

Moltke left an enduring legacy in that vague area known as the "art of war." Although it might be going too far to say, as one recent author has, that Moltke's methods in such areas as orders bore "a striking resemblance" to modern American methods, there is no doubt that much of modern military theory bears the mark of the Prusso-German system, to which Moltke was probably the most important contributor.[53]

Nevertheless, this comparison must not be taken too far. The modern concepts of "operational level of war" and "operational art" contain many points of view, definitions, and assumptions that would have been foreign to Moltke. Moltke was a forerunner who laid the seeds of modern theory, rather than the creator of a full-fledged modern system. To find the origins of that, one must turn to Schlieffen, Schlichting, various theorists of the Imperial and Soviet armies, and to the growth of American technology and systems analysis.

---

53. See, for example, Arthur T. Coumbe, "Operational Command in the Franco-Prussian War," *Parameters* 21, no. 2 (Summer 1991): 86–99. Other, much less sophisticated, arguments of the same general nature may be found in recent U.S. Army and Marine Corps literature.

CHAPTER ONE
THE NATURE OF WAR

This chapter consists of several essays written separately by Moltke and printed together in volumes two and four of the *Military Works*.[1] Moltke here expresses the opinion that war is an unavoidable and even positive aspect of human existence. Another theme that emerges clearly in these pages is Moltke's rejection of Clausewitz's thoughts on the subordination of warfare to the requirements of national policy. Moltke appeared to accept Clausewitz's dictum that war was an extension of politics, but in practice Moltke acted quite differently. He insisted that political considerations came into play only before and after the war, not during the course of operations and combat. Moltke's opinion triumphed completely over Clausewitz's views throughout the German army, with fateful consequences in the First World War.

The General Staff used a variety of sources in assembling the following essays. Most important among these were the previously pubished *Memoirs* and the official histories of the campaigns of 1866 and 1870–71.[2] The latter sections on offense and defense came from

1. Prussia, army, Grosser Generalstab, *Moltkes Militärische Werke*, 14 vols. in 4 (Berlin: E. S. Mittler & Son, 1892–1912), vol. 4, part 1: *Moltkes Kriegslehren. Die operativen Vorbereitungen zur Schlacht* (1911), 1–15. The essay "On Strategy" is in vol. 4, part 2, 287–93.

2. Helmuth von Moltke, *Gesammelte Schriften und Denkwürdigkeiten des General-feldmarschalls Grafen Helmuth von Moltke*, 8 vols. (Berlin: E. S. Mittler & Son, 1892–1918). The campaign studies are Prussia, army, Grosser Generalstab, *Der Feldzug von 1866 in Deutschland* (Berlin: E. S. Mittler & Son, 1867); and *Der deutsch-französische Krieg, 1870–71*, 5 vols. (Berlin: E. S. Mittler & Son, 1874–81). Moltke's

several sources. In addition to previously unpublished documents from the General Staff's archives, the editors relied on the General Staff's official studies of the campaigns of 1864, 1866, and 1870–71. Thus, some of the texts on historical examples may not have come directly from Moltke's pen, although he certainly had closely supervised their writing.

These latter selections, taken from volume four, part three of the *Military Works*, provide an overview of Moltke's thoughts on the relationship between offense and defense, flank attacks and turning movements, and on when one should go on the offensive. Moltke adopts the Clausewitzian point of view that defense is the stronger form of war, but that only the offense produces a favorable decision. Thus, every war—and most battles—regardless of how it began, should end with an offensive operation. In these passages Moltke develops the idea that frequently the best method of conducting a strategic offensive is to drive into the enemy's territory with the aim of forcing him to take the tactical offensive against one's own defense.

Where known, dates of authorship are in parentheses after the section title. A precise determination was not possible in every case.

WAR AND PEACE (c. 1880)

Eternal peace is a dream, and not even a pleasant one. War is a part of God's world order. War develops man's noblest virtues, which otherwise would slumber and die out: courage, self-denial, devotion to duty, and willingness to make sacrifices. A man never forgets his experiences in war. They increase his capability for all time to come.

On the other hand, who can deny that every war, even a victorious one, inflicts grievous wounds on all involved? Neither territorial gain nor billions in indemnity can replace the dead nor offset the mourning of families. War is a rough and violent business (*Handwerk*).

But who in this world is able to avoid the misfortune or to evade the necessity? Are not they both conditions of our earthly life in accordance with God's directions? Adversity and misery are merely

---

own account of the war against France, drawn primarily from the offical history, appeared as volume 3 of the *Gesammelte Schriften und Denkwürdigkeiten.*

unavoidable elements in the world's order. What would have become of humanity without these hard spurs to thinking and action? Our renowned poet [Schiller] allows not Wallenstein, but Max, to say: "War is horrible like heaven's plagues. Still, it is good; it is a destiny the same as plagues."[3]

A humane effort to lessen the suffering that accompanies war is to be fully valued. However, whoever knows war will agree that it cannot be restrained by theoretical chains. Lessening its horrors is rather to be expected from the gradual advances in general civilization that promote the humanity of each individual. This is because the conduct of war reflects the progress of civilization. Only such general progress, and not laws of war, can lead to the goal. Every law requires an authority who watches and regulates its execution; but this power is lacking in the observance of international agreements. Acknowledgment of certain established rules does not secure adherence to these rules. That a flag of truce must not be fired upon is a well-known rule of war. Yet, we saw it violated in several instances in our latest campaign—for instance, at Metz on August 19, 1870.

By the same token, no paragraph learned by heart will convince the soldier that he must see a lawful enemy in the unorganized populace which resorts to force of arms on its own initiative and from which his life is not secure for a moment, day or night.[4]

Thus, not much weight should be attached to international agreements. What third power will resort to arms solely because one or the other of two belligerents has violated the laws of warfare? There is no earthly tribunal. Success is to be expected from the religious and moral education of the individual. It also stems from the sense of honor and justice of the leaders. They lay down the law and act accordingly as far as possible under the abnormal conditions of war, where everything must be considered individually. We see now that humanity's conduct of war has not kept up with the general improvement in morals.

---

3. These words were spoken by Max Piccolomini in Friedrich von Schiller's "The Death of Wallenstein," act 2, scene 2. See *Wallenstein: A Historical Drama in Three Parts,* trans. Charles E. Passage (New York: Frederick Praeger Publishing Co., 1958), 161, lines 728–29.

4. These comments refer to the popular uprising that occurred after the encirclement of Napoleon III's regular forces at Metz and Sedan.

Simply compare the horrors of the Thirty Years' War with those of the most recent campaigns.

The introduction of universal military service, which enrolls the better educated classes in the army, has been an important step in reaching the desired objective. Of course the rougher and more violent elements remain. No longer, however, do they form the entire establishment of an army. In addition, governments possess two effective means: discipline inculcated in time of peace, and provisions for feeding the units in the field. Without the latter, discipline can be maintained to only a limited degree. The soldier endures hardships and privations, fatigue and danger. He not only *can but must* take from the resources of the land what is necessary for his existence. The superhuman must never be required of him.

Rapid conclusion of a war undoubtedly constitutes the greatest kindness. All means not absolutely reprehensible must be used to accomplish this end. This involves both weakening the hostile fighting forces and making use of all the resources of the hostile environment: finances, railroads, provisions, and even prestige. The last war against France was conducted with this view and energy, but still with greater moderation than ever before. It produced neither the plundering of earlier campaigns, with their commanders who were intent only on enriching themselves, nor the horrors of oriental struggle, and was decided after just two months. The battles assumed a more embittered character only when a revolutionary government continued it for some additional months to the detriment of its own country.[5]

One hopes that with advancing civilization war will be less frequent, but no state can entirely dispense with it. Human life, even the entirety of human nature, is nothing but war of the future against the present. The lives of the various peoples are no different. As long as different nations lead separate existences, there will be disputes that

---

5. After the destruction of the major French field armies at Sedan and Metz in the early weeks of the Franco-Prussian War, the revolutionary government continued the war both by resisting within the fortresses at Paris and by raising new armies. This prolonged the war and frustrated German hopes for a rapid victory. The standard English account of the war is Michael Howard's *Franco-Prussian War*.

can be settled only by force of arms. I consider war the *last,* but entirely justifiable, means to uphold the existence, the independence, and the honor of a state.

Some have proposed to replace diplomacy with a permanent assembly of deputies chosen by different nations to adjust the various international disputes and interests and thus to prevent all future wars. This will certainly never suit the way of international negotiations. A world-historical transformation of German conditions, such as that which occurred in 1866, could not have come about by peaceful conventions and decrees.[6] Action was required—pressure on the inside, war on the outside. One of the many German states had to become powerful enough to carry along the rest of them. It was King William who, through the reform of the Prussian army, created the power that secured unity and resulting liberty for Germany.[7] There can be no thought of freedom if there is no power to uphold it. The road to that objective led to Königgrätz and Sedan and may possibly lead to future battlefields.

I have more confidence in the judgment and power of governments than in the Areopagus of delegates selected by the peoples and international brotherhood or what has been proposed in this direction, which is suited only to create Babylonian confusion.

I believe that all governments are today honestly endeavoring to maintain peace. The only question is if they are strong enough to be able to do so. I also believe that in all countries the largest majority of the population desires peace. Nevertheless, the people do not decide, but the parties they have placed in control.

6. In 1866 Prussia defeated Austria and assumed political and military primacy in Germany, thus destroying the old German Confederation. The Prussian-dominated North German Confederation excluded Austria from most German affairs. The standard English work on the war is Gordon Craig's *Königgrätz.* Craig's *Germany, 1866–1945* (New York: Oxford University Press, 1978), 3–22, discusses the long-term consequences of Prussia's victory, which surprised most of Europe.

7. King William I, who ruled Prussia from 1861 until his death in 1888, was also the first German emperor, ruling from 1871 until his death. Under the German constitution established in 1871, the king of Prussia was automatically the German emperor. William I was the grandfather of Emperor William II, the infamous kaiser of the First World War.

Times have passed when, for dynastic purposes, small armies of career soldiers took the field to capture a city or a certain section of territory, and then went into winter quarters and concluded peace. The time of cabinet wars lies behind us; it belongs to the past.

Modern wars call whole peoples to arms. Hardly a single family escapes the common suffering. The full financial power of the state comes to bear. No change of season halts the ceaseless action. Peace is endangered by the opinions of peoples, by desires for annexation and revenge, by the endeavor of related peoples to effect a consolidation, by dissatisfaction with domestic conditions, and by pressure of the parties (especially their spokesmen). The momentous decision for war is more easily arrived at by an assembly in which no single individual bears full responsibility than it is by one individual, no matter how high a position he occupies. One more frequently encounters a peace-loving sovereign than a national assembly of wise men. Today, cabinets alone no longer decide the question of war and peace. Nor do they govern the affairs of the populace. On the contrary, in many instances the people are the ones who direct the cabinets. In this way an incalculable element has been introduced into politics. The money market also has today gained an influence that can call the armed forces into the field for its interest. European armies have occupied Mexico and Egypt to meet the demands of high finance.[8]

The war of 1870–71 started from similar circumstances. A Napoleon on the throne of France had to justify his position by political and military successes. Victories by the French on distant battlefields satisfied public opinion only for a short time. The successes of the German armies created jealousy.[9] These successes were considered arrogant challenges, and revenge was demanded for Sadowa.[10] The liberal tendencies of the times rebelled against the autocracy of the emperor.

---

8. Here Moltke refers to the involvement of the French in Mexico and of the British and French in Egypt. Moltke was a conservative monarchist with no confidence in parliamentary democracy, as these passages make clear.

9. Here Moltke clearly means the victories of the armies of Prussia and Austria, acting under the auspices of the German Confederation, over Denmark in 1864 and of the Prussians over Austria in 1866.

10. Sadowa was the name frequently used in some German sources for Königgrätz, the decisive battle of the Austro-Prussian War of 1866.

He had to make concessions. His domestic policy was weakened, and one fine day the nation learned that its deputies desired war with Germany.[11]

Our earnest wish is that in the future all governments may be strong enough to curb the warlike passions of their populations. The value and blessing of a strong government cannot be overestimated.[12] In Germany, many consider the government as a sort of hostile power that cannot be sufficiently restricted or curbed. I believe our governmental power should be strengthened and protected as much as possible. A weak government is a misfortune for the country and a danger to its neighbors. "The best of men cannot live in peace if such does not suit his bad neighbor."

Only a strong government can carry out beneficial reforms and assure peace. Peaceable assurances by our neighbors are of course very valuable, but we can find security only in ourselves.

I believe that a powerful yet peaceful state in the heart of Europe is the best guarantee of permanent peace in this part of the world. Germany has shown that it is a peace-loving nation, one that does not need war to achieve glory and which does not want war to make conquests. I really do not know what we would do with a piece of land wrested from Russia or France. Germany's principal strength rests in the homogeneity of its population. It is true that on our frontiers we have citizens who are not of the German nationality.[13] This is the result of

11. Moltke's version of the origins of the Franco-Prussian War was neither accurate nor complete. Numerous historians have examined this question in great depth. Craig's *Germany, 1866–1945*, summarizes a very complicated story. Still of use are Otto Pflanze, *Bismarck and the Development of Germany: The Period of Unification 1815–1871* (Princeton, N.J.: Princeton University Press, 1963), 433–57; and the classic account by Robert H. Lord, *The Origins of the War of 1870* (Cambridge, Mass.: Harvard University Press, 1924). These accounts should be supplemented by recent research on Bismarck, too voluminous to be listed here.

12. This passage is highly reminiscent of Leonard Krieger's proposition that the Germans developed a peculiar notion of freedom, defining the latter as freedom from various types of danger and unrest rather than individual freedom in the Anglo-American sense. See Leonard Krieger, *The German Idea of Freedom: History of a Political Tradition* (Boston: Beacon Press, 1957).

13. The German Empire was not homogeneous ethnically or linguistically. Major minority groups included Poles in some of the eastern provinces of Prussia, and Frenchmen in Alsace and Lorraine.

centuries of war, of campaigns and peace treaties, of victories and defeats. The frontiers of a large state cannot be constructed according to scientific principles. These non-German citizens, however, fought alongside Germans with the same joy and bravery. But it is well known that not all their interests are the same as ours. How could we now be expected to be so foolish as to weaken, instead of strengthen, ourselves by enlarging our territories? Did the German Michael ever draw his sword for any purpose other than to save his hide?

As a matter of fact, since 1871 Germany has pursued a peaceful policy, one as never before found in world history. A mighty state, in addition to solving its domestic social problems, made its power, its prestige, and its predominance felt by all peoples. It did this not in order to encroach upon its neighbors, but only to assure peace with them. It also sought to assure peace among its neighbors themselves.

But such a policy can be carried out only if based on a strong army ready for war. If that powerful driving wheel in the state's machine is lacking, the machine will come to a standstill and the notes sent by our foreign office will have no weight. The army has been the foundation upon which such a policy could be constructed. It is the army that gives weight and support to diplomatic action, but only so long as it is actually ready and able to intervene when objectives cannot be attained peacefully.

To be sure, one can sincerely regret that iron necessity imposes increased sacrifices for the army on the German nation. Nevertheless, we have become a nation at all only through sacrifice and work. The wish to save the enormous sums spent annually for the military system, to relieve the taxpayers from them or to utilize those sums for peaceful purposes, is undoubtedly perfectly justifiable. Who can deny that? Who does not love to figure out how many good, useful, and beautiful things could be created with those sums? But we must never forget that the savings of a long series of years of peace can be lost in a single year of war. Our elderly citizens have personally experienced the entirely different sacrifices imposed by a hostile invasion. The enemy in the country! We suffered that for years at the beginning of the nineteenth century. I call attention to what the years 1808 to 1812 cost our nation after an unfortunate campaign. Those were years of peace when the active strength of the army was small and the term of service was as short as could be desired. Still, Napoleon could boast that he had squeezed a billion out of small and poor Prussia. We saved on our army because we had to, and paid tenfold for a foreign one. The enemy occupying our nation would hardly ask if a bank were state-owned or private. He would make short shrift of our finances.

The credit of a state rests above all on its security. What a panic would break out on the stock exchange, how greatly would all property relationships be shaken, if the permanency of the German Empire could even be doubted!

We should not forget that since the downfall of the old German Empire,[14] Germany was the battlefield and the decisive object for the affairs of all others, or that Swedes, Frenchmen, and Germans transformed Germany into a desert for more than a century. Are not the large ruins on the Necker, the Rhine, and far into the interior permanent monuments to our past weaknesses and to the insolence of our neighbors? Who desires to recall the days when, on the command of a foreign monarch, German contingents had to march against Germany? A lost war also ruins the best financial establishment; finance has to be secured by the army. Should a war break out now, its duration and end cannot be foreseen. The largest powers of Europe, armed as never before, would take the field. None could be so completely defeated in one or two campaigns that it would declare itself vanquished and that it would have to accept the hard peace conditions imposed upon it. None would promise not to rise up again, even if only after years, to renew the struggle. Such a war could easily become a seven years' or a thirty years' war. Woe to him who applies the torch to Europe, who is the first to throw the match into the powder cask![15]

Such a great question involves preserving what we have achieved with such great sacrifices and the existence of the state. It may involve the continuation of the social order and civilization, as well as

14. Here Moltke refers to the Holy Roman Empire of the late Middle Ages rather than to the shadow of that empire which Napoleon destroyed. The following reference is to the destruction of the Thirty Years' War, 1618–48.

15. This well-known section stands in stark contrast to the predominant belief of most European military leaders prior to 1914. The common wisdom of the day was that modern wars would have to be short. Moltke made this statement in a speech to the Reichstag on May 14, 1890. Its text is in the *Gesammelte Schriften und Denkwürdigkeiten*, vol. 7, 137–40.

hundreds of thousands of human lives. In such a case financial questions can be considered only secondarily, and every monetary sacrifice appears justified in advance. If we did not have to expend large sums of money for military purposes our finances would, of course, be on a more favorable basis. But the most brilliant financial condition would not have prevented the enemy from being in our nation today if our defense establishment had been inadequate. For some time past, and even today, only the sword keeps other swords in their scabbards.

The best pledge for peace is to be armed for war. This object cannot be attained with weak forces, nor with volunteer armies. The fate of every nation rests in its own power. An alliance is certainly very valuable, but it is not good, even in normal life, to rely on foreign assistance. Our best security therefore lies in the excellence of our army.

We must not allow a weakening of the inner efficiency of the army; otherwise we will have a militia. Wars carried on by militia armies have the peculiarity of lasting much longer. For that reason, if for no other, such conflicts cost more in sacrifices of money and blood than all other wars. I will merely call attention to the American War of Secession, conducted by both sides with militia armies. No one desires to transplant the horrors of that war to European soil. Of special interest is the statement by Washington, the man who carried out the first war for freedom in America. According to Bancroft's excellent history of the United States, Washington spoke thus: "Experience, which is the best teacher for action, so clearly and decisively condemns confidence placed in militia, that no one who values order, regularity and economy and who loves his own honor, character and inner peace will put any confidence on the outcome of anything undertaken with militia." And again he said: "Short service and unfounded confidence in the militia were the causes of all our misfortunes and the increase in our debt."[16] It is well known that the war was finally ended only

16. Here Moltke refers to George Bancroft, *History of the United States of America from the Discovery of the Continent,* revised edition, 6 vols. (New York: D. Appleton & Co., 1888 [1882]), vol. 5, 51. Washington said this in a statement to Congress in September 1776. Moltke does not mention that Bancroft went on to present the opposite viewpoint, that the militia had performed well in the American War of Independence.

by the appearance of a small corps of but six thousand men, all of whom were real soldiers.

France tried militias twice. The first thing the French revolutionaries did was to disband the hated army. The nation itself was to protect its youthful freedom. Patriotism was to take the place of discipline; courage and mass were to replace military training. A certain halo still surrounds the volunteers of 1791. Still, there is a nonpartisan history concerning them, written by a Frenchman and based on the archives of the French War Ministry (Rousset, *Les Volontaires de 1791–1794*, Paris, 1870).[17] One reads there on each page how useless, how costly, and what a scourge to their own country these volunteers were. Only after experiences lasting for thirteen years did the French finally desist from placing the armies under volunteers and place the volunteers in the army. When thereafter a man like the First Consul[18] and other excellent generals placed themselves at the head of this army, these volunteers traversed all of Europe victoriously. By that time, they had become soldiers.

The above-mentioned work made its appearance in March 1870 and only six months later we saw France resort to the same means—of course in extreme distress.

From a broad humanitarian standpoint, one might desire only to see proof that the firm decision of an entire people makes its subjugation impossible, that a "people's" army suffices to protect the country. Of course our point of view is different. We have shown that the rebellion, even of a nation with such inexhaustible means and of such patriotism as France, could not withstand the onrush of even a small but

17. The reference is to Camille Rousset, *Les Volontaires 1791–1794* (Paris: Librarie Academique, 1870). For a more recent study of the revolutionary army, the interested reader should consult John Lynn, *The Bayonets of the Republic: Motivation and Tactics in the Army of Revolutionary France, 1791–1794* (Urbana: University of Illinois Press, 1984).

18. "First Consul" was the title Napoleon gave himself under the Constitution of the Year Eight (1799). This constitution ended the three-consul system that had brought Napoleon his early victories. See Georges Lefebvre, *Napoleon*, 2 vols., trans. Henry F. Stockhold (New York: Columbia University Press, 1969), vol. 1, 71–75. Lefebvre's classic study first appeared in 1936. Stockhold's translation is that of the fifth edition, published in 1965.

well-trained and courageous army. We experienced it all and became convinced that even the most numerous collection of the best, most patriotic, and bravest men could not resist a real army. Those who preach the arming of the populace should study the slight success that the armed populace gained in the years 1870–71. An armed mass of people is far from being an army. Leading such a mass into battle is pure barbarism.

The French *Garde mobile* prolonged the war several months.[19] They caused bloody sacrifices, great destruction, and much misery. But they were unable to change the course of the war, and in the peace they gained nothing for France. It was probably only due to the reign of terror of their advocates that it was possible to raise such badly organized armies, without trains, exposed to inclement weather, without field hospitals and surgeons. With all their patriotism and bravery, these unfortunate men were unable to resist our brave, well-organized units. The misery of the bivouac decimated them without mercy. The wounded lay by the hundreds along the roads without any assistance until picked up by our field hospitals and ambulances. Even the disorder of the *Franctireurs* did not delay our operations a single day.[20] Their gruesome work had to be answered by bloody coercion. Because of this, our conduct of the war finally assumed a harshness that we deplored, but which we could not avoid. The *Franctireurs* were the terror of all the villages; they brought on their own destruction.[21]

That such conduct of war was a cruelty for the country, causing it the deepest of wounds, was of little concern to those who above all

---

19. The *Garde mobile* was a politically unpopular and only partially successful effort to create a third-line reserve behind the active army and the regular reserve. Its men had very limited training, and that mostly as individuals rather than as units. In 1870 the half-million men in the *Garde mobile* were, as Michael Howard states, "unorganised, unequipped and untrained." See Howard, *Franco-Prussian War*, 31–35. They formed the hard core of the French resistance in the "people's war" phase after the destruction of the regular French army in the first months of the struggle.

20. *Franctireurs* were guerrilla fighters who opposed the German armies after the defeat of the regular French army. This text capitalizes German nouns as is the practice in that language.

21. This passage should be seen as a rationalization for the reprisals taken by the Prussians in areas where *Franctireurs* were active. Similar rationalizations may be found for much more extensive atrocities in both world wars.

else desired power, the legality of which the nation did not dare to question.

The lawsuits which arose after the war in France give a picture of the confusion and horrors that are the natural consequences of arming the population. If we arm the nation, we arm the good and the bad elements at the same time, and bad elements are to be found in every nation. Of course, the former are in the preponderance. But have not we ourselves had the experience, in arming the national guard (*Bürgerwehr*), of seeing how soon the better element becomes tired of the matter, disappears, and leaves the field to the unreliable elements? Arms are quickly distributed but not so quickly taken back.[22]

The history of the Paris Commune teaches us what it means when the government allows the reins of power to slip from its hands, and when power is transferred to the masses. There the opportunity was offered for democracy to transform its ideas into actuality. There democracy could establish a government, at least for a time, according to its ideals. But nothing was created; a great deal was destroyed. French reports, confirmed by official documents, concerning this deplorable episode of French history give us a chance to see the depth of the depravity existing then. These reports describe conditions and events that one would have thought unbelievable had they not occurred before the very eyes of our astonished and horrified units of occupation, who would soon have made an end to them had they not been forced to observe with rifles at rest.

Probably we ourselves have elements like those that came to power in Paris after the war. If we do not have any, proper care undoubtedly will be taken to supply them to us from the outside. Behind the honest revolutionary will then appear dark phantoms: the so-called Basserman phantoms of 1848, the *professeurs de barricades* and the incendiaries of the Commune of 1871. It may have been imported heroes who destroyed the monuments of French glory in Paris. God prevent

---

22. As a conservative monarchist who strongly opposed the socialist and democratic movements of the nineteenth century, Moltke recalled the Revolution of 1848 with apprehension. The social prejudices of the officer corps had a pervasive influence on all aspects of the Prussian army. This entire section should be seen as part of the efforts of the officer corps to combat and discredit those movements.

us from ever arming such people. The inner cohesion of our army must never be allowed to become questionable.

No nation has trained its whole strength as far as has ours by the introduction of the universal military obligation. The task is to make a soldier out of a recruit; that is, a man who not only practices the parade step or mounts guard, but who is expected to act independently, thoroughly knowing his arm and having the fullest confidence in it, under the most difficult conditions. Such a man has learned how to obey and how to command—for even the very lowest private becomes a superior as soon as he takes his post on guard or leads a patrol. That task is not quite as easy as it appears to be at the writing table. The question is not merely one of tactical, I might say artisan-like, training of the man. With that we create material which can be incorporated into the solid framework of the army. However, such material can never form the nucleus of an army. The Austrians lost the campaign of 1859 mainly because they lacked experienced soldiers.[23] At the outbreak of the war they had not yet completed their reorganization, and consequently were forced to enlist a relatively large number of recruits who greatly undermined the reliability of their units. The young Austrian soldiers lacked the endurance possessed by the French because of their longer term of service and campaign experience.

As mentioned above, with us the question involves far more than technical training; the main question is of training and stabilization of moral qualities, the military upbringing (*Erziehung*) of youth to manhood. That cannot be drilled into the recruits; it must be acquired by long years of service.

Of course military service is not productive work. Yet it makes the state secure. Without that security, any productive work is impossible. Military service is a school for the growing generation in regard to order, punctuality, cleanliness, obedience, and loyalty—attributes that underpin subsequent productive work.

It has been said that the schoolmaster won our battles. Mere knowledge,

---

23. This reference is to the War of 1859, which pitted the Austrian army against the forces of France and the kingdom of Sardinia. The defeat of the Austrians was an important milestone toward the unification of Italy, which finally was completed in 1870.

however, does not elevate a man to the point where he is ready to risk his life for an idea—for duty, honor, and the fatherland. For that, the entire education of a man is necessary. Not the schoolteacher, but the educator (*Erzieher*), the military class, has won our battles, has educated the nation in regard to corporal vigor and mental freshness, love of fatherland, and manliness. We therefore cannot do without the army for the domestic purposes of educating the nation. For external purposes, the army is indispensable.[24]

The army is not a makeshift. It cannot be improvised in weeks or months; it requires long years of training because the foundation of all military organization rests on permanency and stability. The army is the most noble institution in the nation; it alone makes possible the existence of all other arrangements, all political and civil liberty, all creations of culture and finance. The state stands or falls with the army.[25]

The better organized our fighting force on land and sea, the better equipped, the more prepared for war, the sooner may we hope to safeguard peace or to carry out an unavoidable war with honor and success.

WAR AND POLITICS

Reciprocal Effect between Policy and Strategy

War is the violent action of nations to attain or maintain purposes of state. It is the most extreme means of carrying out that will and,

---

24. The idea that the Prussian army was the nation's school for values was a popular theme among conservative politicians and other leaders through much of the nineteenth century. See Reinhard Höhn, *Die Armee als Erziehungsschule der Nation. Das Ende einer Idee* (Bad Harzburg: Verlag für Wissenschaft, Wirtschaft und Technik, 1963).

25. As things turned out, Moltke's statement was as true for the German Empire's end as for its beginning. Created in large part by their armies, neither the kingdom of Prussia nor the Second German Empire survived the military defeat of 1918. For careful considerations of the army's important role in the monarchy and the constitutional structure of Bismarck's empire, see Manfred Messerschmidt, *Militär und Innenpolitik in der Bismarckzeit und im wilhelminischen Deutschland* (Darmstadt: Wissenschaftliche Buchgesellschaft, 1975), 32–34, and Wolfgang Sauer, "Das Problem des deutschen Nationalstaats" in *Probleme der Reichsgründungszeit 1848–1879*, ed. Volker Berghahn (Köln: Kiepenheur und Witsch, 1968), 448–80.

during its duration, abolishes international treaties between the belligerents. War, as General von Clausewitz says, "is the continuation of policy with other means." Thus, and unfortunately, policy cannot be separated from strategy, for politics uses war to attain its objectives and has a decisive influence on war's beginning and end.[26] Policy does this in such a manner that it reserves to itself the right to increase its demands during the course of the war or to satisfy itself with minor successes.

Given this uncertainty, strategy can direct its endeavors only toward the highest goal attainable with the means at hand. Strategy thus works best in the hands of politics and only for the latter's purposes. But, in its actions, strategy is independent of policy as much as possible. Policy must not be allowed to interfere in *operations*. In this sense General von Clausewitz wrote in his tactical letters to Müffling: "The task and the right of the art of war, as opposed to policy, is mainly to prevent that policy from demanding things which are *against the nature of war,* and out of ignorance of the instruments from committing errors in their use." Military considerations are decisive for the course of war. Political considerations are decisive only insofar as they do not demand something impossible in a military sense. In no instance must the military commander allow himself to be swayed in his operations by policy considerations *only.* He should rather keep military success in view. What policy can do with his victories or defeats is not his business. The exploitation of his victories or defeats is exclusively the business of policy.

Coalitions

A coalition is excellent as long as all interests of each member are the same. But in all coalitions the interests of the allies coincide only

---

26. Gerhard Ritter has disputed the authenticity of this passage. See *The Sword and Scepter,* vol. 1, 303. In some versions, the word "unfortunately" does not appear. Ritter's objections seem excessive to this volume's editor. Ritter cited only two examples of questionable sentences in this essay and offered no archival source for his objections.

up to a certain point. As soon as one of the allies has to make sacrifices for the attainment of a large common objective, one cannot usually count on the coalition's efficacy. Coalitions never readily perceive that the large objects of a war cannot be attained without such sacrifices.

For this reason an offensive and defensive alliance is always an imperfect form of mutual assistance. It has just as much value as, and no more than, what each ally is able to perform in the matter of offense and defense. Thus, in mere coalitions, we cannot demand what is most desirable from a military standpoint, but only that which is advantageous to both allies. Every strategic agreement on the part of allied armies therefore is a sort of compromise in which special interests have to be considered. Such special interests can be silenced only in a unified state.

Neutrality

Considered from a purely theoretical standpoint, the line of the frontier of a neutral country is quite immaterial. Since it cannot be attacked, it need not be strong militarily. Its extension and situation are more important to the non-neutral states than for the neutral country itself. Thus, for instance, until 1860 the neutrality of Northern Savoy covered Switzerland more than Piedmont, and in 1870 Belgium protected almost all of our Rhine provinces.

In reality, one must consider the fact that neutrality can probably be violated, provided that this step does not entail very definite disadvantages for the attacker that far offset his advantages.

These disadvantages will consist in the resistance offered by the neutral country itself and in the support offered by the guarantors of its neutrality. Of course its own resistance is the main point, for outside assistance will be furnished only to the degree required for the direct interests of the guarantors.

Ritter himself cited numerous other sections of the *Military Works* as uncritically as did those whom he criticized for citing these passages. Rudolf Stadelmann, who also had access to the now-lost archives, relied on the version printed here.

HISTORICAL EXAMPLES

The Campaign of 1870–71[27]

Fortunately, the experiences of the campaign of 1866 had an enlightening effect on the minor German states, so that in the Franco-German War particularism was not as important as four years previously.[28] Even in the confidential preliminary discussions between 1866 and 1870, the south German states recognized that a separate defense, for instance of the Black Forest, could not count on the help of Prussia. Rather, south Germany would best be protected by an offensive into Alsace from the direction of the central Rhine, which could be permanently supported by the main force to be concentrated there. The fact that the governments of Bavaria, Württemberg, Baden, and Hesse had their contingents join the main concentration of forces and placed them under the command of King William I, thus denuding their countries of units, shows the full confidence these states had in Prussia. The German army, under a single command, went from victory to victory.

Unfortunately, policy disputes in our own camp created difficulties for strategy in this campaign. Thus, during the lengthy bombardment of Paris, the politicians blamed the chief of the army General Staff for creating the danger of a break with other powers because of

27. The General Staff assembled these historical examples from a variety of sources, primarily from the military writings cited in note 2 above. The historical examples for the most part reflect the General Staff's efforts to validate the preceding theoretical section. Although these no doubt reflect Moltke's views, he did not necessarily write them.

28. "Particularism" refers to the continuing local pride of the citizens of the various German states and their reluctance to see themselves as part of a greater Germany. In 1866 some smaller states declined to join Prussia against Austria, whereas others fought alongside the Austrians. After the victory over France in 1871, many smaller states valiantly and persistently tried to defend their local institutions, values, and customs against what many regarded as the Prussianism of the new German Empire. This remained an important social issue in the Prussian army right up to the First World War. See the editor's *The King's Finest: A Social and Bureaucratic Profile of Prussia's General Officers, 1871–1914* (New York: Praeger, 1987), 26–28.

our advance on Paris. The politicians wanted the German armies to halt at the Lorraine frontier.[29]

After the battle of Sedan there could be no doubt that our operations had to be directed against Paris, the seat of the new government and the center of gravity of the country. To be sure, one encountered a more uncertain course of the war than if the old government and a real army had been present. We would have beaten such an army even if we would have had to advance as far as the Loire, and would have turned against the capital only afterwards. But there was no longer an enemy army in the open field. Paris had to be the new objective, not as a fortress but as the capital of the country. Its capture was the military and political object. Shortly before the fall of the capital, the king's chief military counselor was able to say: "Should we now, with the experiences we have gained, return to the day of Sedan, I would not know what better to recommend to your majesty than what we have done: to continue our operations against Paris."

At the end of November, the same politicians who had spoken against an advance on Paris argued that the beginning of the bombardment of the city was a political necessity and that otherwise intervention of neutral states was to be feared. They said: "The delay in the fall of Paris is seen in foreign countries, as well as in France, as a weakness on the part of Germany," and that this opinion was tied to the tendency of foreign powers to intervene as an encouragement to France to resist.

The chief of the army General Staff needed merely to reply that in the question of the bombardment of Paris, only the military point of view counted. The political viewpoint counted only insofar as it did not demand things that were militarily not allowable. Hence, strategy had the task and right "to prevent politics from demanding things that are against the nature of war; to ensure that ignorance of the workings of the instruments of war did not produce mistakes in their use."

29. This passage may be regarded as part of Moltke's lengthy feud with Bismarck. The best introductions in English to the conflict between Bismarck and the General Staff are Craig, *Politics of the Prussian Army,* and Ritter, *Sword and Scepter,* especially volumes 1 and 2.

(Clausewitz: *Letters to Müffling,* 1827). It would in fact have been a mistake to abandon the point of view of the military authorities. The bombardment could commence only when sufficient ammunition was available for its execution. The army leadership would have been in danger, because poor communications with the home country portended delays in the transport of ammunition. On the whole, the chief of the General Staff did not want to devote the main effort to a bombardment of the hostile capital, but rather to starving it out, and wanted to use the first means only in furtherance of the latter. From a strategic point of view, this had to be adhered to all the more since the political view started from a far different conception of the general military situation. The king's principal political counselor[30] believed that he could make peace after the fall of Paris. The chief of the General Staff also held this view—as long as there were no hostile armies in the field. But since such armies had again appeared, the situation was quite different. The decision of the campaign no longer lay at Paris, but in defeating the armies operating in the field.

The view of the king's principal military advisor proved to be correct. Not the bombardment, but hunger alone conquered the hostile capital. On the other hand, the fall of Paris did not necessarily conclude the war. We were in full readiness to defeat the fighting forces still in the provinces as soon as the armistice had run its course. Acceptance of the German terms by the National Convention in Bordeaux made this unnecessary.

It must be considered as good fortune that the political and military demands were brought into consonance by the presence of the head of state in Versailles.[31]

On the enemy's side, politics played a fateful role from the very commencement of the war. While French diplomacy could have prevented the outbreak of war until France was ready to fight, the French declared war even before the government was in a situation to follow up that declaration immediately. Thus it happened that the French armed

30. Bismarck.
31. Here Moltke refers to King William I.

forces, even before being fully concentrated and ready for offensive operations, were attacked by the German armies on their own ground. It is true that Emperor Napoleon, when in full command of the armies at the outbreak of the war, started an offensive because public opinion in Paris demanded victories. Public opinion, as was seen in 1866, counts for more in France than in any other country. However, on the French side, the presence of the head of state in the field did not produce harmony between military and political requirements. The attempt at offensive operations failed.

After the double defeats of Wörth and Spicheren the [French] intended to fall back to Chalons. However, foreign policy and domestic political considerations made it very hazardous to open a campaign by abandoning the country halfway back to Paris. There would undoubtedly have been no lack of speakers in the National Assembly forcefully denouncing the poor leadership. They would have been greatly applauded for that denunciation. This circumstance overcame all mere military considerations and the French turned again to the idea of opposing the German armies east of Metz.

Considering this dependence of the army's leadership on domestic politics, it is not surprising that in the second half of August Marshal [Patrice] MacMahon considered not the mere military factors, but acted under the continuing pressure of political opinions in Paris and directives from there in his Quixotic effort to relieve Marshal [François Achille] Bazaine. In the beginning, and in proper perception of the situation, he had declined the order of the empress and the Ministerial Council to undertake that relief and had declared that he would march to Paris. There he could risk a battle advantageously because the fortifications of Paris protected his retreat in case of a defeat and precluded any pursuit. When reports from Metz allowed him to see that Bazaine intended to fight his way through Montmédy, Sedan, or Mézières to Chalons, MacMahon turned at Riems, not toward Paris, but to the east, at first in the direction of Stenay. In this he concluded with certainty that the movement of the Army of the Rhine had already begun. He in no case wished to abandon his companion in arms. During this march to the east, the marshal learned in Le Chesne that nothing was to be seen of Bazaine's army in Montmédy and that it was still at Metz. MacMahon again decided to retreat, issuing orders to that effect for the following morning, and reported his intentions to Paris.

During the night, the most urgent remonstrances came from Paris. The Minister for War telegraphed: "If you leave Bazaine in the lurch, revolution will break out." The ministry sent direct demands for him to relieve Metz. MacMahon gave in. Thus, in this case, politics won out in the end over all military reservations. MacMahon then issued renewed orders for the march to Metz.[32]

At Sedan, the Army of Chalons was overtaken by its fate.

There is no doubt whatever that the unfortunate Bazaine acted not only according to military but also political considerations. It is questionable if he could have acted differently, considering the confusion that had arisen in France. His conduct during the battles at Metz demonstrated a decided disinclination to leave the fortress. Under its walls, the marshal could keep his large army intact until the decisive moment. At the head of the only intact army in France, he might have attained power unlike that in any other country. But of course that army had to be freed from all the bonds holding it. A forceful breakout through the German lines, even if successful, would have weakened the army.

It was not entirely unthinkable that the marshal—as the strongest authority in the nation—might offer a prize which would induce the opponent to allow his departure. Then, after the fall of the empire, the Germans would have had to ask themselves what authority could conclude peace and if it would be strong enough to honor its negotiations. It is neither proved nor to be assumed that Bazaine would have acted otherwise than in the interests of France had his plans materialized.

But soon a number of men assembled in Paris. Without asking the nation, they proclaimed themselves the government and assumed control of affairs.[33] Of course Marshal Bazaine, supported by his army, might oppose these men as a rival and could even act as their enemy. He could have restored the authority of the emperor, to whom he had sworn allegiance, but that would have been a crime in the eyes of the Paris government. It remains an open question if by doing so he would have saved the country from additional suffering and greater sacrifices. He

32. Howard, *Franco-Prussian War*, 196–97, substantially confirms this account.
33. Here Moltke refers to the leaders of the revolutionary government in Paris.

was subsequently accused of treason, probably because French national pride absolutely required a "traitor" to explain why they were defeated.

The provisional government repeatedly attempted to conclude peace with us. As early as September 1870, Jules Favre, the minister for foreign affairs, arrived at royal headquarters in Ferrieres to discuss peace terms based on his program of giving up "not a single foot of the country." He believed that he could satisfy the Germans with a sum of money after all their victories and sacrifices. We, of course, could not consider such terms—no matter how much we sought the end of the war, the continuation of which had to bring more sacrifices without producing successes greater than those that had already been attained.[34] At the same time, there was no power in France that appeared capable of coming to final and lasting terms. The self-appointed government in Paris had sprung from the revolution and might be deposed any day by another revolution. Had there been a legitimate monarchy, France undoubtedly would have been granted peace as early as September (1870). But as conditions had developed, only an assembly freely elected by the people could offer the required guarantees. Thus in the discussions, an armistice could be considered only to give the French nation an opportunity, by free and regular elections, to establish a government with which peace terms could be arranged. This would also have been in the political interests of the Germans.

An interruption of operations, however, offered only disadvantages from the military point of view. It would have given the opponent time to continue his armaments and, if it halted the siege of Paris, the capital a free hand to provision itself fully.

An armistice could therefore be granted only on receipt of corresponding compensation. For instance, Strassburg and Toul, which still blocked the railroads, had to be delivered to us to secure the subsistence of our armies. The state of war had to continue at Metz. The siege of Paris had to continue. If it were discontinued, we would have had to occupy one of the dominant forts. Delegates of the people would have had to assemble in Tours in complete freedom.

---

34. By "we," Moltke can legitimately have meant only the General Staff. Bismarck had an entirely different conception of peace terms.

The French declined to accept these conditions, especially the surrender of fortifications, and broke off negotiations.

The journey of [Louis Adolphe] Thiers, the former minister, lasting for seven weeks during the months of September and October, to London, Saint Petersburg, and Vienna, failed to induce those courts to take steps in the interests of France. After his return to Paris, the provisional government again opened negotiations with royal headquarters to make possible elections of popular delegates. Conversations for that purpose took place in Versailles between Thiers and Count Bismarck. They again led to no result because the French not only demanded an armistice of four weeks but also made unacceptable demands that the capital be provisioned.

Peace preliminaries arranged in February 1871 were approved only in March by the new National Assembly in Bordeaux. Only then could the transport of German troops to their homes commence. After the capitulation of Paris, the absence of a real government in France made it seem possible for weeks that operations might be resumed.

The commencement of the war was precipitated by the faulty foresight of the French diplomats. Its conclusion was delayed by the absence of reliable governmental organs.[35]

ON STRATEGY (1871)[36]

Policy uses war for the attainment of its goals; it works decisively at the beginning and the end of war, so that indeed policy reserves for itself the right to increase its demands or to be satisfied with a lesser success.[37]

---

35. No objective historian would concur in these sweeping and simplistic judgments. They probably were indicative, however, of the attitude of much of the Prussian military community.

36. This section comes from *Militärische Werke*, vol. 2, part 2, 33–40.

37. This passage constitutes a clear rejection of Clausewitz's arguments on the proper relationship between politics and the conduct of war. It was written in 1871 while Moltke's memories of his continual conflicts with Bismarck over policy and strategy were still fresh.

In this uncertainty, strategy must always direct its endeavors toward the highest aim attainable with available means. Strategy thus works best for the goals of policy, but in its actions is fully independent of policy.

The first task of strategy is the final assembly (*Bereitstellung*) of the fighting forces, the first deployment of the army.[38] Here, multifarious political, geographic, and national considerations come into question. A mistake in the original assembly of the army can scarcely be rectified in the entire course of the campaign. But these arrangements can be considered long in advance and—assuming the war readiness of the units and the availability of the means of transport—must unfailingly lead to the intended result.

Also included in the broader tasks of strategy are the combat employment of the assembled units, thus operations. Here one will soon encounter the independent will of the enemy. We can limit this only if we are prepared and decisive in taking the initiative. But we may not be able to break the enemy's will except with the means of tactics, with combat.

The military and moral consequences of every great engagement are of such a far-reaching kind that they usually create a fully transformed situation, a new basis for new measures. No plan of operations extends with certainty beyond the first encounter with the enemy's main strength. Only the layman sees in the course of a campaign a consistent execution of a preconceived and highly detailed original concept pursued consistently to the end.

Certainly the commander in chief (*Feldherr*) will keep his great objective (*Zweck*) continuously in mind, undisturbed by the vicissitudes of events. But the path on which he hopes to reach it can never be firmly established in advance. Throughout the campaign he must make a series of decisions on the basis of situations that cannot be foreseen. The successive acts of the war are thus not premeditated designs,

---

38. *Bereitstellung* had a technical meaning in German military terminology beyond mere preparation. It meant the positioning of units for immediate action. See Lt. Col. (Dr.) Friedrich Stuhlmann, *Wehrlexikon, was jeder Deutsche von der Wehr wissen muss* (Berlin: Carl Heymanns Verlag, 1936), 36. The term deployment (*Aufmarsch*) had a broader meaning.

but on the contrary are spontaneous acts guided by military measures. Everything depends on penetrating the uncertainty of veiled situations to evaluate the facts, to clarify the unknown, to make decisions rapidly, and then to carry them out with strength and constancy.

To the calculation of a known and an unknown quantity, one's own will and that of the enemy, enter yet other factors. These are the fully unforeseeable: weather, illnesses, railway accidents, misunderstandings, and disappointments—in short, all the influences that one may call luck, fate, or higher providence, which mankind neither creates nor dominates.

Nevertheless, the conduct of war does not lapse into blind, arbitrary action. A calculation of probabilities shows that all those chance happenings are just as often to the detriment or advantage of the one side as they are to the other. The supreme commander, who must in each case order at least what is reasonable, if not the best possible course of action, always has a prospect to reach his goal.

It is obvious that theoretical knowledge does not suffice for this. On the contrary, both mental faculties and character are necessary for this free, practical, artistic activity, schooled obviously by military training and guided by experience, either from military history or from life itself.

Success, above all, obviously determines the reputation of a supreme commander. How much of this is really earned is extraordinarily difficult to determine. Even the best man fails against the irresistible power of circumstances, and even the average man must endure this power. Nevertheless, in the long run only the intelligent have good luck.[39]

From the beginning of operations, everything in war is uncertain, except for what the supreme commander brings in his own will and ability. Universal rules[40] and the systems built upon them therefore can have no possible practical value.

Grand Duke Charles declared that strategy is a disciplined body of knowledge and tactics an art. He assumed that this "disciplined knowledge

---

39. Moltke borrowed this phrase from Clausewitz.
40. "Doctrine" might be an alternative rendering of the German term *Lehrsätze*. The Prussian sense of doctrine was quite different from that of most modern armies.

of the highest commander determines the course of wartime undertakings," and that the art of tactics merely executes strategic designs.[41]

General von Clausewitz, on the other hand, said "Strategy is the use of the engagement for the goal of the war."[42] In fact, strategy affords tactics the means for fighting and the probability of winning by the direction of armies and their meeting at the place of combat. On the other hand, strategy appropriates the success of every engagement and builds upon it. The demands of strategy grow silent in the face of a tactical victory and adapt themselves to the newly created situation.

Strategy is a system of expedients. It is more than a discipline; it is the transfer of knowledge to practical life, the continued development of the original leading thought in accordance with the constantly changing circumstances. It is the art of acting under the pressure of the most difficult conditions.

DEFENSIVE, OFFENSIVE, AND BAYONET FIGHTING (1861–65)

The defense is able to select its positions so that the enemy will be compelled to cross open ground. It will almost always have time to determine the distances of certain terrain sectors or single objects. It will be able to bring its fire into fullest effect.

The advantages of the offense are clear and permanent. He who acts on his own decision lays down the law to which the waiting party must conform his countermeasures. The attacker has a clear objective

---

41. The reference is to Archduke Charles, *Ausgewählte Schriften weiland seiner Kaiserlichen Hoheit des Erzherzogs Carl von Oesterreich,* edited by his sons Albrecht and Wilhelm, 6 vols. (Vienna: Wilhelm Braumüller, 1893–94), vol. 1, 235–36. The translation above renders *Wissenschaft* as "disciplined body of knowledge." Moltke's actual text reads: "Erzherzog Carl zwar erklärt die Strategie für eine Wissenschaft, die Taktik für Kunst. Er muthet der 'Wissenschaft der obersten Feldherrn' zu, dass sie 'den Gang der kriegerischen Unternehmungen,' die Kunst habe nur die strategischen Entwürfe auszuführen." The citation appears on page 293 of Moltke's *Militärische Werke,* vol. 2, part 2.

42. *On War,* book 3, part 1, "Strategy," 155 (1867 edition).

before his eyes. He chooses the way in which he desires to reach it. The defender must guess at the opponent's intention and must estimate the means for defense. The attacker has the prior decision (*Entschluss*) and confidence of action, while the defender waits in uncertainty and expectation. The defender must take the offensive if he desires to bring about the final decision (*Entscheidung*). It is another question, however, whether we should first fully utilize the obvious material advantages of the stationary firefight before we ourselves take the offensive.

An infantry detachment which, while withholding its own fire and possibly masking that of its batteries, and, while out of breath, hastens out halfway to meet the attacking enemy, surely has lesser prospect of success than a detachment that receives the enemy with its fire at long range and then stands in readiness with fully fresh strength to use the bayonet should the enemy actually come to close quarters. If, on the other hand, the enemy's attack comes to a halt and turns into a retreat, then firing on the enemy or employing cavalry kept available for that purpose will complete his defeat more certainly than a pursuit with the bayonet.

The prerequisite for waiting for the enemy's offensive is, of course, that one's firm decision not to give way is set against his firm decision to attack. It will be easy to make the soldier understand that nothing is more dangerous than to turn around, and that great losses first occur when retreat makes a reply to the enemy's fire impossible. The enemy's fire will become annihilating at short range even if he is armed with inferior rifles.

On the whole, the offensive is not only tactical. Skillful leadership will in many cases succeed in selecting defensive positions which are strategically of such an offensive nature that the opponent will be forced to attack them. We will then take the tactical offensive only after casualties, loss of cohesion, and exhaustion have weakened him. Thus is the strategic offensive united with the tactical defense. But even when we are absolutely compelled to advance offensively against a hostile position, the advantage of stationary firing may be fully utilized if we know how to bring our battalions up to the range most suited for that. Thus, in practice, one may most frequently see the kind of offensive that Frederick the Great recommended and used, which the terminology of our time likes to designate "forward with bayonets."

But if one views this phrase not as figurative, but in its literal meaning of individual struggle of man against man, we will find but very few examples of it since firearms took the place of the short saber and the pike.

The advance with the bayonet is the means finally to overcome the enemy. No army can do without the bayonet. The confidence of the man in his bayonet cannot be sufficiently fostered, but its employment must first be made possible by the course of the battle and must be prepared by the effects of fire. The leader should always remember that even the most brilliant bravery fails against an insurmountable obstacle. He should see that the bayonet attack is not the first, but the final act of the individual parts of the battle, whose sum is the conquest of the battlefield: victory.

DEFENSIVE POSITION, ENVELOPMENT, AND BASE OF OPERATIONS (1865)

The defense has to seek open terrain; the attack seeks broken terrain. A gentle rise in the land with an open field of fire, behind which one can place the reserves under cover, assures the defense of a strong position because of the effects of modern firearms. A direct advance has little hope of success against such a strong position.

Obstacles to the front are desirable where the main point is to offset the enemy's numerical or moral superiority, as, for instance, in the cases of advance guard and rear guard positions, where one seeks to gain time rather than a victory.

If, however, we feel ourselves equal to our opponent, and if we intend to have him exhaust his strength against our defense in order then to attack him, a front without obstacles is preferable. The same obstacle that supports the defense makes an advance difficult. An unobstructed front is strong enough for the defense and is most advantageous for an immediate transition to the offense.

The lesser is the prospect of success in a frontal attack, the more certainly will the enemy turn against our flanks and the more important is their security. Resting one's flanks on terrain only generally covered and difficult no longer corresponds to conditions [of the battlefield], for the attacker will seek out just such terrain to avoid the effects of superior fire. Other than entirely impassable sectors (extensive marshes, rivers, or inland lakes), villages or clumps of woods no larger than can be completely occupied and beyond which an open field of fire is to be found, furnish the most desirable flank support.

Such favorable localities are not available everywhere. When the question is neither one of blocking a defile nor of advancing on a rear guard, but of battle positions in which one seeks a decision, an army will find suitable positions more easily than will smaller detachments.

Smaller detachments must never allow the anchoring of their flanks to draw them into an extension of their wings that is disproportionate to their strength. If a detachment succeeds in anchoring only one of its flanks on a terrain obstacle, strong artillery will serve the same purpose for the other flank.

The smaller the formation (*Truppenkörper*) and the more narrow its front, the easier will be the envelopment of its defensive position. A slight change in direction of the leading element suffices to lead the attacking column into the flank or against one of the wings. Security against this danger lies only in the depth of the position. The range of the artillery and the rapidity of infantry fire, which doubles the effect, allow one to occupy the selected front only lightly so as to hold stronger reserves in the rear until the enemy's intentions are clear. Still, at the start we will always assure ourselves of possession of the most important points of the front by occupying them with artillery. That artillery must be so positioned that it can reach the enemy at the greatest possible range and, without changing position, remain active throughout the battle.

The difficulties of envelopment increase as the front is extended. An example of this is the front of an army corps operating by itself.

Concern for our own communications will prevent us from establishing a new front against a continuous envelopment and an attack in the flank, except in the rarest of cases. One must avoid envelopment either by a retreat or by an attack. From this it follows that the defense can never dispense with its own offensive. This latter encounters the opponent while on the march. It does not have to attack a strong position chosen with care. The enemy has to deploy no matter how he finds the terrain.

The position of a field army can no longer be enveloped tactically. Such an army occupies a front of four miles or more. Such an envelopment becomes a march whose execution leaves no time for combat on the same day.

Should the enemy be so exceptionally favorably based that a flank movement would not endanger his communications, then our position may be strong tactically but strategically unfavorable. We ought not to accept a decisive battle in such a place without absolutely compelling necessity. As a rule, a flank march directly in front of the enemy will endanger the communications of the side that undertakes it and will compel him to select a new line of operations and give up the previous one, unless that side should be so superior as to be sufficiently strong on both lines.

But such a change is a very serious and difficult matter, which one will not easily undertake in actual war. The road on which an army moves is filled with vehicles bringing up replenishment and supplies. Magazines are established on that road. Hospitals and supply stations, detachments and provision columns move along it, as well as field mails and couriers. All these would have to be shifted to another road in a very short time. All authorities charged with sending supplies would have to be notified immediately before we could risk giving up such a line.

One will almost always be compelled to leave a strong detachment for protection of the lines of communication, thus weakening the means for the attack following the envelopment.

Whoever suddenly decides to undertake an envelopment for tactical reasons should make it clear to himself what he intends to subsist on for the next few days and where he can hope to find a rallying position, protection, and reinforcements in case of a reverse.

There are undoubtedly situations that will absolutely force us to attack the opponent in his chosen position, which is advantageous to him and probably fortified.

We know how difficult that problem is. All the above shows that a direct advance across an open front cannot succeed, and that the attack, if possible, must be directed against the defender's flanks and must seek out covered and broken terrain to allow the attacker to bring his fire into effect and enable him to advance gradually.

As a rule, only the proximity of a broad and secure base allows an actual envelopment of a flank. For instance, an army deploying through Cologne may envelop an enemy standing opposite it either on the right or on the left, since it can base itself either on Wesel or on Coblenz. But when it has advanced into the enemy's country it would do better to allow itself to be attacked in a chosen position, for which the opponent, in the necessity of defeating an invasion, has a compelling motive.

The strategic offensive combines well with the tactical defense. Vice versa, the strategic defense finds the necessary freedom of movement for the offensive battle in the vicinity of its supporting points and resources.

DEFENSIVE AND OFFENSIVE (1874)

I am convinced that improvements in firearms have given the tactical defense a great advantage over the tactical offense. It is true that we were always on the offensive in the campaign of 1870 and that we took the enemy's strongest positions. But with what sacrifice! Taking the offensive only after having defeated several enemy attacks appears to me to be more advantageous.

RECIPROCAL ACTION BETWEEN OFFENSE AND DEFENSE (1869–85)

The question of whether combat is to be conducted offensively or defensively cannot be answered in a universally valid way. Only one thing is certain: if one desires to attack, one should do so with decisiveness. Half measures are out of place; only force and confidence carry the units along and achieve success.

The foremost and most evident indication of victory is that at the conclusion of the battle we are in possession of an area held by the enemy when the battle began and which he would not have given up had he not been more or less defeated. Therefore, every victorious battle must end with an offensive advance. It is questionable, however, whether the battle should commence with such an advance.

The advantages of the offensive are sufficiently known. Through the offensive we lay down the law of action to the opponent. He has to conform his measures to ours and must seek means to meet them. But he can find those means.

The attacker knows ahead of time what he wishes and has all moral factors on his side. The defender is suspended in uncertainty and can only guess at his opponent's intentions.

If we are able to take up a position that the enemy probably will attack for political or other reasons, it may become advisable first to utilize the advantages of the defensive before going over to the attack.

However, one should consider if even a brief delay of the decision by arms (*Entscheidung*) entails disadvantages that fully offset the advantages of the tactical defensive. The terrain is but one element of these considerations. The entire situation must be considered in this regard.

Defensive with Subsequent Offensive

We will occasionally desire that the enemy attack us, and in that case we will not choose unassailable positions. If we intend to take up the attack ourselves subsequently, we would not want a difficult obstacle in our front. The element of the effects of fire, which has now assumed such a preponderance, attains its highest development in the open field. A slight swell in the terrain, previously hardly noticed, becomes a strong position if it has a long, open field of fire to its front and if it protects our reserves from the enemy's fire. It also assures the three [combat] arms the greatest degree of effectiveness.

But if a frontal obstacle is unnecessary, and even disadvantageous for decisive battles, a flank support always remains highly desirable. Covered terrain in front of the wings or in front of the flank is dangerous to a great degree. In open terrain one can easily recognize enveloping movements. Batteries posted on the wings force the envelopment back to great distances. Echeloned reserves furnish the means for countermeasures.

The defense's tactical advantages decrease as the masses involved increase. On the one hand, terrain conditions favorable for defense are hardly found everywhere in battle lines extending for miles. Furthermore, support of an attacked flank by the other flank is usually not possible before the former is shattered by a concentrated attack and its retreating masses are thrown against the supporting [units] as they rush forward. In addition, concentrated masses awaiting a hostile attack will usually suffer from the difficulties of obtaining quarters and provisions, while the opponent, on the other hand, need not concentrate any sooner than when he decides to proceed to the attack.

It will therefore be advisable, when very large formations are involved[43] and if one does not possess the means for a general advance, not to be satisfied with a fixed defense. A combination of the two forms of combat is always preferable. Only through a war of movement (*Bewegungskrieg*) can one hope to resist a superior enemy for a long time and to hold terrain. One will scarcely find a position that offers security against envelopment for more than a day and which can save us from a catastrophe if we conduct an immobile defense.

An excessive extension of the front brings the danger of a breakthrough. Too little an extension brings the danger of being enveloped or outflanked.[44] The leader must use his insight to find the correct means between the extremes.

How far one may extend the front to envelop the enemy or to secure a flank depends on many circumstances and cannot be stated in numbers. One can only say that a very great extension contains a direct danger but also the germ of great success.

Villages and woods will more seldom than previously be points around which protracted struggles will sway back and forth. Present-day ranges [of weapons] enable the attacker to bring an overwhelming fire to bear on them. Thus one would act wrongly to exhaust oneself by capturing villages (as at Grossgörschen in 1813).

On the whole, engagements in forests last for a long time. The advance is made step by step by overlapping movements. Such engagements are rich in surprises, but seldom give any assurance of great decisions.

Rises in the ground, on the other hand, afford better cover and in many cases a broader and more open field of fire. They will therefore determine the strength of a position more than villages and clumps of woods. Nevertheless, one must immediately prepare supporting points

---

43. Moltke's term was "*in grösseren Verhältnissen,*" literally, "in large relationships" or "situations."

44. In Prussian terminology, a flanking attack (*Umfassung*) is usually related to a tactical action on the battlefield itself. An envelopment (*Umgehung*) relates to a wider movement turning the entire enemy position but not necessarily concluding in a battle.

captured in an engagement for defense in order to thwart the enemy's efforts to recapture them.

Artful strengthening of that part of the battle line on which a defensive fight is to be conducted has become more and more important and frees other units for other purposes. This strengthening should be considered in every case where one has not yet decided to take up the offensive at once.

Fortresses *forward of* and on the flank are advantageous. *Behind* the front they are often dangerous because they easily induce weak characters to seek protection therein in case of a defeat—where they usually find nothing but destruction.

Deploying one's forces in depth in order to be able to meet hostile enveloping movements is especially necessary in the defense. Concentric fire is difficult to endure. Enveloped central positions are always dangerous and occasionally are more hazardous than the risk of having our lines temporarily pierced.

Reserves must be kept farther in the rear than previously. Of course they must also be able to come into action in a timely manner. Nevertheless, distance facilitates their employment in the most appropriate direction.

A forceful and apt defense must not be satisfied with a simple repulse of a hostile attack. It should strive to make that attack so costly that the enemy will decline to repeat it.

The destruction of attacking units by massed fire will have a moral importance far beyond the confines of the individual. We should never allow the opportunity to take the offensive to slip by when the enemy offers us the possibility of success by dividing his units.

Offensive with Envelopment

The first consideration in an attack will be to use favorable positions to attain fire superiority. The use of strong artillery will enable this most easily. At the same time, this saves infantry strength that one can use at another point.

The effects of heavy fire on the hostile front will, in most cases, require us to direct the attack against a wing of the hostile position. If that is to be done with undivided forces, a slight change of the direction of march will suffice for the purpose if the force is small. On the other hand, armies of a hundred thousand and more occupy a space of more than four miles. An envelopment of their flanks becomes a day's march, delays the decision of arms to the subsequent day, gives the opponent an opportunity to evade it, and, as a rule, endangers the communications of those forces threatening the enemy's communications.

Another means is to fix the enemy's front with part of our strength and to envelop his flank with the other part. In that case it is necessary for us to remain strong enough opposite the hostile front so as not to be overpowered before the flank attack can become effective. We must also be very active in his front to prevent the opponent from throwing himself with superior numbers on our flank attack.

The moral effect of a flank attack is sooner apparent in small detachments and thus more important than is the case with armies. On the other hand, the latter, because of greater difficulties of movement, cannot avoid the consequences of an envelopment as easily.

Frontal and flank attacks stand in reciprocal relationship to each other—the main thing is to achieve correct coordination. Which attack is to be viewed as the main attack and which as the secondary attack will depend on the general operational intention, the disposition of hostile forces, and the terrain. One should group one's forces accordingly. One must be as strong as possible where one intends to seek the decision. If one lacks a general superiority, the only means of attaining superiority at the decisive point of the battlefield is to employ economy of force at other less important points. A main part of the art of good combat leadership consists of distributing forces in accordance with the tasks to be accomplished.

DEFENSE AND ATTACK (1882–86)

All things being equal, the defender has a decisive advantage over the attacker. This advantage decreases to the extent that the attacker has an opportunity to act suddenly and surprisingly because of the extension of the position and protective terrain. Nevertheless, even under less favorable terrain conditions, the advantage still rests with the defender. Yet military history and personal experience demonstrate that the attack has often succeeded against equal and even superior forces.

There is no other explanation of this apparent contradiction between theory and practice except the fact that in such cases the superior energy and skillful leadership of the attacking units offset all material advantages of the defense. Under the same circumstances, of course, such units themselves would have been entirely victorious in the defense.

But if we desire to arrive at correct conclusions in the abstract consideration, we must start with the assumption that the morale of both sides is the same. There remains then only to examine the value of numerical superiority, all other things being equal, and to what extent this can overcome the advantages of the defense.

An attacker who has superiority in numbers can increase his reserves in deep formation, can repeat his attacks, and can thus attempt to shake his opponent's power of resistance. But he cannot use a wider deployment for simultaneous effects in every attack. Each repeated attack costs new sacrifices and success will remain doubtful.

Surplus strength becomes effective simultaneously only in a more extended area on a more extended front, be that an envelopment or a flanking attack.

A turning movement (*Umgehung*) falls out of the scope of tactics into the realm of strategic operations.

If the defender of a strong position sees his vital communications with his base threatened by a hostile turning movement, he has but two choices: either to attack out of his position or to evacuate it. In either case he gives up his defensive advantages. If he, being the weaker, wishes to counter this turning movement by dividing his forces, he would probably be doubly beaten.

A bold opponent will usually select the first method. From this, it follows that the attacker, in order to turn the defender, must remain strong enough opposite the enemy being turned to be able to withstand the latter's most powerful attack. Should the enemy be successful in an attack against our main force, the fate of our flanking element would probably be decided at the same time.

A flanking attack (*Umfassung*) on the enemy is a turning movement in the sphere of tactics. The former works morally and directly, the other materially and directly.

A flanking attack against both flanks of the hostile position will seldom succeed. It presupposes a superiority in the face of which the enemy as a rule would not await an attack (Danish fortifications).

How strong we must be to outflank only one of the enemy's flanks cannot be determined theoretically, but depends wholly on circumstances. It is easily perceived that the attempt can succeed, even if we are but slightly superior, if we ourselves hold a strong position opposite that of the enemy.

An attack on a hostile flank commences with a turning movement outside his fire zone. It therefore involves a march of several hours in most cases, which, under certain circumstances, may last until the evening of the day of battle (Saxon Corps at Saint-Privat).

During the entire course of this march our main force not only has to maintain itself opposite the enemy, but also has to occupy and fix him so that he cannot substantially strengthen his threatened flank.

At first we should conduct a delaying action at a distance. The available room will allow a greater deployment of artillery than that of the opponent. To the extent to which the fire of his batteries is silenced, the infantry will gain terrain in front. The batteries gradually move to within the most effective range, protected against hostile infantry fire by forward skirmishers.

The enemy, seeing himself threatened on the flank, must either go over to the offense immediately with all his strength against our main force, or reinforce his wing by extending his front, bending it back, or attempting to envelop our flank attack. In the former case he assumes all the difficulties of the attack and leaves to us the advantages of the defense; in the latter, he weakens his front and facilitates our advance there.

The detachment making the flank attack turns inward as soon as it arrives on a line with the enemy. With a broad deployment, its greater number of rifles offsets the disadvantage of firing while in motion. Without halting and without taking an intermediate position, it charges the enemy.

This is the moment for the main force to proceed to the offensive.

Because of the range of modern firearms, an isolated advance of a brigade, for example, would not only draw the fire of the hostile detachments directly opposite it, but also that of the neighboring ones. Therefore ours must be a general advance, even if it comes to a halt at a few points. Even [if it halts at points] it will occupy the enemy. If the artillery has once reached an effective range, it will follow the infantry farther only if it would otherwise be unable to fire on the hostile positions until the infantry fire on both sides becomes annihilating. If one has approached this close to the enemy, then the crisis can last but a few moments.[45] If the assault of our infantry then takes place, the batteries, which remained in their positions, keep up a continuous fire but direct it against the probably oncoming hostile reserves and especially against his endangered wing.

The best guarantee of success of an attack over the defense lies in a flanking attack and the simultaneous advance of all our forces against the enemy's flank and front.

HISTORICAL EXAMPLES

1866

During the advance of the three Prussian corps on July 3, 1866, it was the intention to drive the hostile army toward the Elbe to cut it off from the two fortified crossings and, if possible, totally annihilate it.

The First Army stood in Horitz opposite the hostile concentration on the Bistritz and had orders to fix the enemy's front. The Army of the Elbe and the Second Army had started against the enemy's flanks. The former stood at Smidar, the latter behind the upper Elbe on the other side of Königinhof. Thus, they had to march thirteen and a half miles before they could enter the engagement.

In accordance with the intentions of army headquarters, a delaying action ensued on the Bistritz. The enemy held an extremely strong position on the heights beyond Sadowa behind the Bistritz and replied with numerous batteries. It was not our plan to bring about a quick decision with large sacrifices at this point. We had no interest in breaking through here at all costs. The mere advance of the two wings forced the evacuation of the Austrian position opposite the First Army.

---

45. By the "crisis," Moltke means the last 100–300 meters to the enemy infantry's position. This "crisis of the attack" was the subject of frequent discussion in German military literature between the Franco-Prussian War and the First World War.

By 11:00 A.M. the First Army, advancing by divisions in echelon, executed a one-eighth turn to the right onto the terrain occupied at the start by the enemy. It stood on the line forest of Maslowed (Swiep Forest; 7th Division)—forest of Sadowa (Hola Forest; 8th and 9th divisions)—Mokrowous (3d Division).

The Army of the Elbe formed itself behind the line Hradeck-Lubno on the right bank of the Bistritz.

The Austrians did not commit themselves to a lasting defense of this sector. The Prussians had not yet reached their main position on the heights beyond. The Austrian right wing offensively met the attack directed against it with great superiority of numbers. In the center and on the left wing, the Austrians utilized the advantage of the greater fire effect that the defensive has as a matter of course. The Austrian artillery, well known to be excellent, fired from a series of favorable positions on the first approach of the enemy, whose batteries arrived singly and which had to go into position under fire and had then also to cross the Bistritz. By 11:00 A.M., only twelve Prussian batteries were on the right bank, of which only seven could fire, with a total of forty-two guns. On the Austrian side, on the other hand, the batteries of the II, III, and X corps, as well as one Saxon battery, stood in readiness. The fire of these nearly 250 guns formed an imposing obstacle to any further advance of the First Army.

But, as stated, a further advance was not included in the battle plan. Enough had been done fully to occupy the enemy in front. The flank attack by the Army of the Elbe had to become effective very shortly.

The Prussian center was not endangered. An offensive against it had not yet been attempted. One infantry corps (consisting of the 5th and 6th divisions) and one cavalry division, as well as the strong artillery reserve, stood in readiness to meet such an attempt. We could easily await the intervention of the Second Army.

It is true that the left wing of the First Army, the Division Fransecky (14 battalions, 24 guns), was sorely pressed. But the larger were the Austrian masses deployed here (40 battalions, 128 guns of the Austrian II and IV corps; 11 battalions, 24 batteries in reserve), the more decisive would be an attack from the north between Trotina and the Bistritz.

By this time the leading elements of this army, the Guard Corps and the VI Corps, had reached Trotina, but were still more than two miles from the hard-pressed wing of the First Army. The rear elements of the I, Guard, and V corps reached back as far as the Elbe.

En route to Choteborek, the crown prince had become convinced that the battle had now spread along the entire First Army front. His first dispositions had concentrated the Second Army, which up to then stretched out over a space of twenty-two miles, onto the line, hardly ten miles long, Bürglitz-Jeritschek-Choteborek-Welchow.

There then was no doubt that a simple advance of the various corps would lead directly into the flanks and rear of all those forces which the enemy had already thrown into the engagement. But it could hardly be foreseen that the Austrians would fail to notice the Second Army crossing the Elbe and the approach of that army, or that they would be taken by surprise. It was, rather, much more to be expected that the enemy would have posted his units designated for flank protection behind the heights of Horenowes, where then a single battery was visible. If this had not yet been done, the opponent easily could have sent his reserves to that point. In any case, Second Army headquarters was firmly convinced that the decision of the day would depend on a struggle around the heights of Horenowes.

No one, of course, dreamed that most of the units that the enemy had to place for protection against an attack from the north, and thus to cover his right flank, were already engaged on the line Cistowes-Maslowed-Horenowes, and that his main reserve was at that time farther from Horenowes than were the leading elements of the Prussian Second Army.

The effect of the mere approach of the Prussian Second Army was that the Austrian II (and later on the IV) Corps no longer thought of annihilating the 7th Division, but of the salvation of their own army.

By 3:00 P.M. the right wing (II and IV corps) of the Austrian army was beaten and in retreat to Wsestar, Sweti, Prodmeritz, and Lochenitz.

Of the Prussian Second Army, five brigades had fought, and ten had not come into contact with the enemy. The former fought on the line Rosberitz-Nedelist-Lochenitz. The 1st Guard Division, which had pressed farthest forward, had driven the Austrian IV Corps out of its fortified position at Chlum.

In the center of the battle line on the Bistritz, in the meantime, the Prussian reserves (the 5th and 6th divisions) had been deployed on the other bank. Shortly after 12:00 P.M. six divisions were thus ready for the attack as soon as the wing armies came up.

But the moment for the attack had not yet arrived and the artillery duel continued without interruption.

The headquarters of the First Army remained firm in its conviction that only direct action on the wings of the hostile position could assure an advance against the front without too many bloody sacrifices. That some isolated attacks were made out of the forest of Sadowa against the hostile position, despite that conviction, was due to the fighting lust of the units and to a certain disquiet caused by the passive attitude to which they saw themselves condemned. These attacks were not easily prevented and they could not lead to success. They only increased the losses, which on the whole were very great.

Toward 11:00 A.M. the Army of the Elbe had begun to pass through Nechanitz under protection of its advance guard.

It was less important that General von Herwarth should reinforce the First Army front than to take action as soon as possible against the flank of the enemy opposite First Army.[46]

Of course only a small portion of the units had so far been able to traverse the difficult defile at Nechanitz. Nevertheless, half of the day had already passed and First Army had been in combat since early morning. The large obstacle opposing its advance, the formidable Austrian artillery position, could best be removed by an advance through Problus.

The current state of the battle did not require action as early as this against the Austrian army's line of retreat, nor were forces available for that on the left side of the Ufer.

General von Herwarth issued orders for an attack against both flanks of the enemy position at Problus (occupied by the Saxons), so as not to encounter the full fire effect of the Saxon-Austrian artillery in the open area in front of the position. Opposite that front, the Prussian batteries on the hill near Lubno were to be reinforced as much as possible and a reserve, consisting of the detachments that crossed the Bistritz last, posted behind them.

---

46. This was General Karl Herwarth von Bittenfeld, commander of the Prussian Army of the Elbe in 1866.

Successful attacks of the Saxons in the front could not permanently stop the Prussian flank attack (*Umfassung*). The capture of Ober-Prim endangered the position of the Saxon corps at Problus, and at 2:30 P.M. the attack on this, the enemy's last supporting point, began.

The crown prince of Saxony, on the hill at Problus, was fully aware of the continuous advance of the Division Canstein against his line of retreat, as well as the appearance of the Second Army at Chlum, where the retreat of the Austrian right wing plainly was visible. Because the X Corps, alongside of that wing, soon started a retrograde movement, further holding of the position appeared inadvisable. Orders were therefore issued around 3:00 P.M. to commence the retreat.

By the time General von Herwarth received the report of the crown prince's intervention on the left wing, and at the same time received orders from army headquarters (at 1:45 P.M.) to advance against the opposite wing, he had already taken steps to accomplish that.

At the same time the Second Army occupied Chlum, the Army of the Elbe occupied Problus. The double envelopment of the enemy had succeeded.

The concern then was to annihilate him.

The 16th Division could have been utilized for that purpose; it could have been sent ahead against the route of the enemy's retreat. Unfortunately, it was not at hand, for it was still busy crossing the Bistritz at Nechanitz. Had it utilized the bridge at Kuntschitz, it would have been on the battlefield six hours earlier.

1870–71: Wörth

When the crown prince assumed command on the battlefield at 1:00 P.M., he found two of his corps embroiled in a fierce engagement. Both of these corps had so far sent but a part of their infantry across the Sauer, the remainder being held in reserve on the other bank. These purely frontal attacks, executed without cohesion against the extremely strong position of a far superior enemy, had so far no result other than to hold the enemy—which of course was important in itself.

The advance of the Bavarian 4th Division against the hostile flank had been interrupted, but its resumption had been ordered. Another Bavarian division had come up so close that it could very soon intervene and effect direct connections with the Prussian right wing.

The XI Corps assembled on the left wing. A considerable part of the Württemberg Division was expected to arrive from the rear within a very short time.

In addition, the arrival of the Bavarian 3d Division was expected at any moment, while the remainder of the Third Army could not be expected to be available until late in the day.

It is true that no real reserves were then available behind the front between Görsdorf and Gunstett, a distance of two miles. But with the support of a powerful artillery contingent of about two hundred guns, the strength of the V Corps was sufficient to give security against any enemy attempt to break through. Between thirty thousand and forty thousand men became available on each of the wings during the course of the afternoon.

If Marshal MacMahon had united, as the last reports seemed to indicate, the four divisions of the I Corps and one division of the VII Corps and probably also the Division Lespart of the V Corps, the total strength of the French army could not have exceeded sixty thousand men.

Disregarding the fact that the battle could then not be broken off at all, one could scarcely hope to fight later on under conditions as favorable as those at that moment. It was much more to be expected that the marshal would perceive the danger of his situation and would evacuate his position immediately upon the cessation of the sharp attacks which the V Corps had directed against the position without interruption. Considering all these circumstances, the crown prince decided to fight the battle to the finish.

The main point then was to bring the attacks of the first line into consonance with each other and to direct the arriving reinforcements to those points where they probably could join the battle to the best advantage. Consequently, the crown prince issued the following order at 1:00 P.M.:

> The Bavarian II Corps will press against the left flank of the enemy in such a manner that it will come to a halt behind it in the direction of Rheinhofen. The Bavarian I Corps, leaving one division behind as a reserve and hastening its march to the utmost, will take position between the Bavarian II Corps and the V Corps. The XI Corps will proceed via Elsasshausen past the Niederwald to Fröschweiler, acting energetically in this advance.

The Württemberg Division, of the Corps Werder, will follow the XI Corps to Gunstett and across the Sauer. The Baden Division will proceed for the present as far as Surburg.

The V Corps was informed of these orders. It was ordered, however, to delay its attack against the opposite heights because the action of the Bavarian I Corps and the XI Corps could become effective only after an hour or two, and that of the Corps Werder only after three hours.

These orders expressed the intent to double envelop the enemy.

Before receiving a copy of these orders, General [Hugo] von Kirchbach had continued his attack against the opposite heights and by 1:30 P.M. Prussian skirmish lines had outflanked the entire upper edge of the vineyard hills projecting toward Wörth.

But in order to be able to hold the dearly purchased terrain against the repeated energetic attacks of the French, the commanding general was forced to bring up his last reserves from the east bank of the river.

Thus all V Corps's forces were then engaged in gaining a firm foothold on the west bank of the Sauer and in occupying the opponent in front until the neighboring units could make a decisive attack on the flanks.

The entire struggle up to then had consisted of a series of repeated offensive thrusts by both sides. The terrain and the enormous effects of fire in each case caused the attacker to suffer heavy losses, while the defender usually held his position. Only laboriously and gradually did the Prussian units make any progress. Their battalions were decimated, with the larger part of the officers dead or wounded, while the enemy continually brought up fresh reserves. Holding the terrain so far taken took the entire confidence of the commanding general and of all other commanders, as well as the utmost self-sacrifice of the units.[47]

Finally, the first successful attack by the XI Corps against the hostile right wing brought the desired support. Here success was attained

---

47. Here Moltke meant that the commanders had to maintain their resolution and stick to their decisions even in unfavorable circumstances. This was a fundamental tenet of Prussian officer education throughout the period 1860–1945. This was, in fact, a direct continuation of Clausewitz's statements that defined "character" as the ability to stick to one's decisions when their execution became difficult.

in capturing the Albrechtshäuser farm and Morsbronn and holding them in spite of repeated French attacks. Thereafter the Niederwald fell and Elsasshausen was seized from the enemy. Counterattacks by the French infantry and cavalry failed to recapture the villages.

Shortly after the failure of the great French attack on Elsasshausen, the lead elements of the Württemberg Division's 2d Brigade arrived. At the same time the Bavarian 1st Division, as we will see later, had entered the battle on the other wing. For the high command it was then a question of conducting the final decisive attack against Fröschweiler.

In a struggle lasting several hours, the two Prussian corps had succeeded in driving back the French army to the nucleus of its position at Fröschweiler, in annihilating the larger part of the French cavalry, and in threatening the line of retreat toward Rheinhofen from the south. But these corps gradually suffered tremendous losses[48] in their separate struggles against the stubborn resistance of their brave enemy, who was able to turn all his forces against them. After that, the Bavarian 4th Division, following its failure at Nehweiler, had been thrown on the defensive and the units of the Bavarian I Corps were delayed by the swollen Sauer.

The arrival of the German comrades in arms with their fresh forces became more and more desirable in order to secure the success of the assault against the enemy's last bulwark.

From his location on the hill between Wörth and Diefenbach, the crown prince could clearly view the course of the battle, especially the progress made by the XII Corps against Elsasshausen. As early as 1:30 P.M. he had therefore sent orders to General von der Tann to advance across the Sauer to support the V Corps.[49] Meanwhile, orders were sent to the commander of the Württemberg Division, General von Obernitz, to march from Gunstett to Reichshofen and block the French retreat.

The newly appearing units produced for the present—at 3:00 P.M.—no decision on the right wing. Numerous bayonet attacks collapsed

---

48. Moltke's precise term was that the corps had *verbluteten,* literally "nearly bled to death." This was a common expression to indicate extremely heavy casualties.

49. The reference is to Ludwig Freiherr von der Tann-Rathsamhausen, usually referred to as "von der Tann," commander of the Bavarian I Corps.

under the defenders' murderous fire. However, they were successful in renewing the engagement on the Fröschweiler plateau's edge and in driving the pursuing enemy back to his entrenched position.

Although up to then the engagement on the right wing of the German army on the edge of the Fröschweiler heights had either been stationary or wavered from side to side, soon after 3:30 P.M. progress was made on the plateau in the direction of Fröschweiler. This was mainly due to the flanking advance of the right wing under General von Orff (2d, 9th, and 4th Jäger battalions, and the 1st Battalion, 2d Regiment) and the Prussian detachment (5th Jäger Regiment).

In the center, in the meantime, the V Corps had pressed farther forward and had gained contact on the right with the Bavarians and with XI Corps on the left. Between 3:00 and 4:00 P.M., the entire German battle line made a flanking advance against Fröschweiler.

The village was taken by assault and the French units of the Army of Alsace had great difficulty escaping annihilation in a panicky retreat.

Gravelotte–Saint-Privat-la-Montagne

As at Königgrätz, the high command attempted a double envelopment of the enemy at Gravelotte–Saint-Privat. The directive (*Weisung*) of 4:00 A.M. on August 18 to the commander in chief of the First Army pointed out that in the coming fighting the VII Corps should, for the present, retain a defensive position and that it could expect contact with the VIII Corps only toward its front. The directive stipulated the basic thought of the royal headquarters' intent to outflank the hostile left wing. When, at 10:30 A.M., it appeared certain that the enemy intended to establish himself between Point du Jour and Montigny-la-Grange, the intention of the double envelopment was expressed in the directions that the First Army's right wing was to advance from the south, from the Bois de Vaux; that the Second Army's left wing would advance from the north; and that the inner wings of both armies were to advance frontally from Gravelotte against Vernoville.

The attacks were to be made simultaneously, which meant that it was necessary for the First Army to advance only when the Second Army was in readiness to cooperate on its left wing.

As we know, the IX Corps attacked prematurely. The flanking attack [by the Saxons] succeeded only on the left wing, at Saint-Privat.

Even here, success came only after the Guards sustained severe casualties in their advance in the center and after the enemy suffered severe losses from the employment of strong artillery in the main supporting point of this wing—Saint-Privat.

STRATEGIC OFFENSIVE AND DEFENSIVE (1882–86)

Whoever does not feel himself stronger than the enemy and has to choose between defense and offense may be in doubt as to which to choose, for that question mainly depends on the enemy's circumstances, which are not always known. But if we gain the conviction that we are strong enough for the offensive, we should resort to it under all circumstances.

If, for instance, we are able to protect our frontier for months by mere defense, then no security would be thereby attained against continually recurring threats as long as our attacks did not destroy the enemy's forces.

From this it does not at all follow that war should always and everywhere be conducted offensively. We will not always and everywhere be capable of that, if only for the reason that terrain conditions, fortifications, and climatic conditions protect even a numerically weaker enemy against attacks. Considerations of politics and of neighboring states and avoidance of the appearance of aggression may frequently make it advisable to begin the war defensively, with the intention of taking the offensive later on. But an aggressive advance obviously will have every advantage when we have accomplished our concentration before the enemy.

To state the above in one sentence: The tactical defense is the stronger, the strategic offensive the more effective form—and the only one that leads to the goal.

But since the strategic advance is entirely based on tactical successes, the commander in chief (*Feldherr*), to arrive at a choice, has to compare his fighting means with those of the enemy. If he finds that his means are equal to the enemy's, he will choose the strategic offensive without question, which does not preclude his taking the stronger tactical form—the defensive—in the course of the campaign, according to circumstances.

If our strategic offensive has forced the enemy into a situation where he sees his communications threatened, sees himself deprived of his means of support, and sees his capital endangered—in short, where he himself has to assume the offensive, we may of course utilize the advantages of the tactical defense in order later to advance aggressively.

Under certain conditions the strategic offensive may be necessary where we dispose of fewer fighting forces than does the enemy—for instance, if the enemy has invaded our country and where the population's patriotism supports us. In any case, being stronger at the decisive point, even if we have smaller forces, always depends on more skillful leadership.

The strategic offensive retains the right to designate the time for the decision. Thus, it also in most cases robs the tactical defensive of the choice of the place where it will accept that decision.

But one must never deceive oneself as to the fact that the strategic offensive becomes weaker as it progresses, that in the same measure in which it has to employ a large part of its forces in holding its communications, in holding down the hostile population, and in creating security in all directions, it is forced to look for replenishment of its forces. It will be weakened if those replenishments do not materialize.

Therein also lies the hope of the party which is originally forced to retreat. That hope is that, once forced back on its own sources of support, it finally will be able to take up the offensive and may thus expect the situation to turn in its favor.

One may say, in short, that the strategic offensive is the direct way to the objective; the strategic defensive the roundabout way.

HISTORICAL EXAMPLES

1870–71

In the campaign against France, there could be no other procedure for us than the offensive, considering our superiority in numbers at the start. The operation against France (wrote the chief of the General Staff on May 6, 1870, to his section chiefs) will consist merely in our executing—concentrated as much as possible—a few marches into French territory until we meet the French army and then offering battle. The direction of that advance was generally toward Paris, because in that direction we could most certainly expect to meet our objective: the enemy army.

The difficulty lay only in the execution of this very simple plan with very large masses.[50]

In the face of the possibility of a strategic surprise by the French, the tactical defensive was but casually considered; that is, a previously reconnoitered position at Marnheim in the Palatinate where, presuming that the start of a French advance would be made on July 28, 133,000 French could stand opposite 194,000 Germans (Second Army) on August 5, 1870, while on that day the First Army, with 50,000 men, could be opposed by 27,000 French at Trier—Wadern, and the Third Army, 125,000 men, by 44,000 French at Landau.

But that fear was soon overcome. The victorious offensive of the German army stopped only at the gates of the capital.

The French were aware of the great numerical superiority that a unified Germany could mobilize against their fighting forces. Starting with the view that the number of actual forces in the field never is more than one-half of the total strength of the army, France figured on 550,000 Germans in the field against their own 300,000 men.

The French emperor had hoped not only to paralyze this almost double superiority of the opponent by the rapidity of his movements, but also to change the fortune of war in his favor. The requirement for this was that he would succeed in making a surprise crossing of the upper Rhine and in separating southern Germany from northern Germany.[51]

An isolated Prussia was estimated to have a fighting force of 350,000 combatants. It was expected that Austria and Italy would join France as the result of initial successes.

---

50. This is one of the very few cases where Moltke used the word "plan" to describe his operational ideas.

51. Germany at that time was still more of a cultural and geographic expression than a political entity. Allied with Prussia in the North German Confederation were most of the states within the confines of the Old German Bund except, of course, Austria. Many of the south German states, particularly the larger ones of Bavaria, Baden, Württemberg, and Hesse, had great misgivings about the alliance with the Prussians. It was this still relatively weak unity that Napoleon III hoped to overcome by separating the southern states from Prussia, whose territory lay primarily, although not exclusively, in northern Germany.

In accordance with his plan, which the emperor had divulged in Paris only to Marshals MacMahon and [Edmond] Leboeuf, the first concentration of the army was to be made with 150,000 men around Metz, 100,000 men at Strassburg, and an additional 50,000 men in the camp at Chalons.

The emperor then intended to bring the French army from Metz closer to the one at Strassburg and to cross the Rhine at Maxau with 250,000 men.

After this had forced the south German states into neutrality, the Prussian army was to be sought out and fought.

During these operations the reserve corps in Chalons, in the meantime having been sent to Metz, would have the task of covering the army's rear and watching the northeastern frontier. At the same time, the French expected that the appearance of their fleet in the Baltic Sea would hold a part of the German army in defense of the coastline.

Of course this plan was based on the correct view that the enemy's numerical superiority could be offset only by rapid movement. But France deceived herself as to the solidarity of the relationship between southern and northern Germany, just as she underestimated the independence and the numbers of the Prussian fighting forces.[52] The latter was the more remarkable because France must have known that Prussia had fielded 350,000 men in 1866 and that her fighting forces had been substantially increased since that time.

In addition, France did not correctly perceive how little the French army, in its condition at the time, was suited for a quick opening of the campaign and for rapid execution of operations.

In regard to the former, the existing French railroad net did not at all favor a concentration to the degree to which it was generally expected. It is true that the single lines allowed a primary concentration of forces on the Moselle River and around Strassburg, but since the Verdun-Metz road was still incomplete, the various lines ran with only four tracks into the frontier territory, terminating at Diedenhofen, Metz, Nancy, and Strassburg.

---

52. Here Moltke used the word *Selbstätigkeit* of the Prussian army, meaning the ability of its parts to act quickly on their own initiative.

Only one was available on the stretch from Mézières to Diedenhofen. On the other hand, the Vesoul-Nancy road could be used, alternatively, for transports both to Alsace and Lorraine.

But it was entirely wrong to assume that one could effect the concentration on the railroads with order and precision without very thorough and extensive advance preparations.

To this came the difficulties, already mentioned, of completing armaments and equipping the units, establishing depots for supplies at concentration points, and the completion of internal organization of the newly created headquarters, staffs, and units, as well as providing them with the necessary trains. All this could not remain without serious consequences to the entire period of concentration, as well as to the consolidation of the domestic situation.

In spite of all the fervor noticeable in the bureaus of the War Ministry, and in spite of the utmost endeavors put forth by the railroad administration, the concentration could not be accomplished without great interruptions and reductions in the army's mobility, at least in the opening period. The ability to make rapid movements had been the basis of the plan of operations. It was even more necessary because bringing up the large masses of the army from Metz to Strassburg could be made only on a single track, or else had to be accomplished by marching on the few roads leading through the Vosges.

In addition, the French experience in the last war with Italy by no means demonstrated any considerable marching achievements by French units in large masses. At least in Prussia we well remembered that the emperor's army, numbering at that time only a hundred thousand men, covered after the victory at Magenta up to the day of Solferino an average of four miles per day.

French diplomacy could have delayed the outbreak of the conflict at least until France was in readiness for fighting, but France declared war even before the government was in position to act immediately on this declaration. Thus France's forces were attacked by German armies on their own ground even before they were fully concentrated and in readiness to take up offensive operations.

In spite of our numerical superiority at the commencement of the campaign, we did not overcome the disadvantage inherent in most offensive operations. Our fighting means decreased with the progress of the operations. We arrived in front of Paris with only 150,000 men. Although the investing army could be increased to two hundred thousand men by corps coming up from the rear, still the forces required to oppose the relieving units on the Loire had to be taken from the investing army in October. Only by November were the armies at Metz available for operations to the north and south of the capital. But in the middle of December the high command was forced onto the strategic defensive. Thus the successes achieved over the French armies coming up for the relief of the capital could not be exploited. The German forces were insufficient prior to the fall of Paris to extend the operations very far to the south and east. We were unable to follow the enemy to his very last supporting points, such as Lille, Le Havre, and Bourges. Nothing remained but to concentrate our main forces at a few points [Beauvais, Chartres, Orléans] in order to oppose the newly formed hostile armies by short offensives. On the other hand, our opponents, after their armies had either capitulated in the open field or were closed up in Strassburg, Metz, and Paris, absolutely had to undertake offensive measures, and they utilized this method in an excellent manner, worthy of emulation, in their attempts to relieve their capital.

CHAPTER TWO
HEADQUARTERS, OPERATIONS, TECHNOLOGY

In the essays presented in this chapter Moltke sets forth his views on a variety of subjects centering around command arrangements, goals of operations, and the application of technology to the art of war. One dominant theme in his discussion on command was that only a few individuals, preferably only one, should directly advise the commander on important decisions. A second was that of allowing local commanders the freedom to act as their situations demanded. In his consideration of fortresses, Moltke stresses that mobile field forces offer more protection to the modern state than do immobile fortifications. In this, he established a fundamental principle, sometimes carried to extremes, that dominated in the Prusso-German army until the end of the Second World War. Moltke is famous for placing both railroads and telegraphs at the service of the Prussian army. His essays on these topics are especially interesting in view of the importance of railroads and communications to the conduct of modern war. Moltke recognized, however, that the telegraph was a threat to one of the Prussian army's most hallowed principles: the independence of subordinate commanders.

The Prussian General Staff selected this material from essays written at various points in Moltke's career. As in the previous chapter, the years in which the material was written are given at the head of each section. The examples came from the historical works of the General Staff, cited in detail in the previous chapter, on the campaigns of 1866 and 1870–71.[1]

---

1. Here the reader might profitably consult the suggestive, if brief, section on Moltke in Martin van Creveld's *Command in War* (Cambridge, Mass.: Harvard University Press, 1985).

THOUGHTS ON COMMAND (1859–70)[2]

The composition of an army's headquarters is of an importance that is not always sufficiently recognized. There are supreme commanders who need no counsel, who themselves estimate situations and come to decisions. Their staffs merely execute. But these are stars of the first magnitude not found in every century. Among these was Frederick the Great, who never asked advice and who always acted on his own. In most cases the commander of an army will not wish to do without advice. This advice may well be the result of the collective deliberations of a smaller or larger number of men, whose education and experience make them competent to judge correctly. But of that number, never more than *one* opinion must gain prevalence. The military's hierarchical organization must assist both subordination and thought. Only *one* authorized person may submit to the commanding general this *one* opinion. The supreme commander chooses that person not according to rank but according to confidence placed in him. Even if the recommendation is not always absolutely the best, as long as one acts correctly and consistently along the same lines, the matter at hand will be brought to a successful conclusion. In the face of the impeding elements of war, one will but seldom attain the ideal. But even an average decision can attain the objective. The commander, not the advisor, has the infinitely more hard-won merit: to have assumed responsibility for carrying out the decision.

If one surrounds the supreme commander with a number of independent men, the situation will worsen both as their numbers increase and the more distinguished and intelligent they are. The commander will hear the counsel of the one, then of the other. He will carry out one proper measure up to a certain point, then a better one in another direction. Then he will recognize the entirely justified objections of a third and the proposals of a fourth advisor. We will wager a hundred to one that with the very best-intentioned measures he will probably lose his campaign.

---

2. The German title was: "*Zusammensetzung der Hauptquartiere—Wahl des Feldherrn—Freiheit des Handelns.*"

In a deliberative body, the pros and cons are explained with such good and incontrovertible reasons that the one offsets the other. The positive recommendation has against it the most undoubted drawbacks. The negation remains in the right, and everyone agrees to do nothing. In every headquarters there are men who know how to demonstrate with great perception all the difficulties attending every proposed enterprise.[3] The very first time something goes wrong they prove conclusively that they had "said so." They are always right. Because they never counsel anything positive (much less carry it out), success cannot refute them. These men of the negative are the ruination of senior commanders (*Heerführer*).

But the most unfortunate of all supreme commanders is the one who is under close supervision, who has to give an account of his plans and intentions every hour of every day. This supervision may be exercised through a delegate of the highest authority at his headquarters or a telegraph wire attached to his back. In such a case all independence, rapid decision, and audacious risk, without which no war can be conducted, ceases. An audacious decision can be arrived at by *one* man only.

It is always extremely dangerous to issue positive orders from a distance. If the highest military authority is not with the army, then it must allow the commander a free hand. War cannot be conducted from the green table.[4] Frequent and rapid decisions can be shaped only on the spot according to estimates of local conditions.

Thus, once war has been declared, the highest commander in the field must be left complete freedom to act according to his own judgment. His selection is a question of the most far-reaching importance,

---

3. Here Moltke's word was *Unternehmung*, literally, "undertaking." German writers from Clausewitz on consistently used the term to describe military measures without a specific reference to their precise nature.

4. The "green table" refers to the commander's headquarters, far from the fighting front. Here, of course, Moltke's views clashed with those of Schlieffen, who on many occasions said quite the opposite. Of course the two men faced quite different situations, ranging from the size of their respective armies and the distances involved to the changes in weapons.

which unfortunately is determined in many cases by conventional and personal considerations. A heavy responsibility rests on him, responsibility to his God and conscience—beside which responsibility before a court of law disappears. The army commander who is about to launch an enterprise the consequences of which are never certain, or the statesman who has to conduct high policy, will never be deterred from action by the fact that they may have to face a court-martial on the one hand or a civil court in Berlin on the other. A commander carries a far different responsibility before God and his conscience for the lives of thousands of his men and the welfare of the state. He has more to lose than merely his freedom and wealth.

For this reason, the only proper commander in chief in any country is the monarch, who in theory is not responsible, but who in reality carries the heaviest responsibility. Who risks more than he, where the question is of his crown and scepter?

HISTORICAL EXAMPLES

The Campaign of 1870–71

In the war with France, Prussian royal headquarters left the capital on July 31, 1870, fourteen days after the mobilization. At this time, the middle and the center of gravity (*Schwerpunkt*) of the German forces was already southwest of Mainz.[5] The advanced wings were only a few miles from the French frontier. During this period of deployment, Mainz offered the best communications between the advancing armies and the following corps, in addition to all other rearward services. The king established his headquarters there for that reason.

During this campaign, the high command (*Heeresleitung*) usually

---

5. Here Moltke used the German term *Schwerpunkt* to mean the main mass of the German armies. For other interpretations of this term, from Clausewitz to the U.S. Army of the 1980s, see the editor's article titled "Schwerpunkt" in Brassey's forthcoming *International Military Encyclopedia*. German usage of the term was quite different from that prevalent in modern American theory and doctrine.

limited itself to general directives for operations.[6] These guiding principles left execution to the army commanders. However, in circumstances where a great decision could be expected any day, the royal headquarters believed—just as in 1866—that it could not issue directives extending beyond the immediate future. In such crises, it was deemed correct and necessary to link the movements of the large parts of the army by definite orders from royal headquarters, even though this curtailed the independence of the army commanders to some extent. At the same time, the high command recognized how important it was that the army headquarters understand the motives behind the king's orders. This concession was made to General Steinmetz, the First Army commander, particularly in the first weeks of the campaign.[7] It is well known that a certain difference of opinion and intentions existed between General Steinmetz and royal headquarters.

On August 3, the First Army stood south of the line Wadern-Losheim-Saar River. There it received the order to concentrate near Tholey on August 4. General von Steinmetz did not approve of this retrograde movement to get closer to the approaching Second Army and complained to the chief of the General Staff and to the king. On August 5, the chief of the General Staff explained, as he already had done in

---

6. Moltke never defined precisely what he meant by a "directive." The General Staff's official history of the Franco-Prussian War stated that "directives are communications from a higher authority to a lower one, which convey guidelines (*leitende Gesichtspunkte*) rather than definite orders for immediate action. These guidelines should serve as a precept (*Richtschnur*) for subsequent decisions that must be made independently." See Prussia, General Staff, *Der deutsch-französische Krieg 1870–71,* 5 vols. (Berlin: E. S. Mittler, 1874–81), vol. 1, 155. Also useful is the discussion in Colmar Freiherr von der Goltz, *The Nation in Arms: A Treatise on Modern Military Systems and the Conduct of War,* 5th ed., trans. Philip A. Ashworth (London: Hugh Rees, 1906 [German ed. of 1899]), 112–18.

7. On Karl von Steinmetz, one of the most ill-fated of William I's generals, see Maj. E. W. Shephard, "Little Known Soldiers of the Past, IV: Field Marshal Karl Friedrich von Steinmetz, 1798–1877," *Army Quarterly and Defense Journal,* 85, no. 1 (October 1962): 100–06. In addition to being relieved of his command, Steinmetz was subjected to the semilegal censorship of the Prussian army after the war. Emperor William I personally intervened to prevent publication of his memoirs. On this and related subjects, see the stimulating article by Michael Salewski, "Zur preussischen Militärgeschichtsschreibung im 19. Jahrhundert," in *Militärgeschichte in Deutschland und Oesterreich vom 18. Jahrhundert bis in die Gegenwart,* ed. Othmar Hackel (Bonn: E. S. Mittler, 1985): 47–69.

Berlin—if not to the commander [of the First Army; Steinmetz] him-self, then at least to his chief of staff and the *Oberquartiermeister*[8]—the task of the First Army. This was, in addition to covering the Rhine Province, a decisive participation in the battle against the enemy's left flank. This obviously could not take place in isolation, but only in conjunction with the Second Army. The place where the First Army could be inserted depended not only on the Second Army, but also on the enemy's movement. If the latter should advance against the Second Army from the Saar, contact might occur on the line Homburg-Ottweiler. In that case, the proper place for the First Army was at Tholey. But if the enemy remained behind the Saar, an isolated attack by the First Army could lead only to defeat. The Second Army had first to approach the Saar before it would be time for the First Army to advance across the river for a possible attack on the hostile flank. His majesty the king expressly reserved to himself the right to give the order for such an operation because circumstances, such as those of the Third Army, were of importance both for the commencement and the direction of the attack. "Combined action of all these armies," added headquarters in the answer to General von Steinmetz, "can be arranged only by his majesty. In the execution of orders issued for this pur-pose, complete freedom of the army commanders to act according to circumstances will not be limited."

Just as in the 1866 case of Gen. [Carl Constantin] von Blumenthal, it also appeared appropriate to explain the royal headquarters' views of the Third Army's situation to that army's chief of staff. Third Army headquarters intended to await the arrival of all its columns and trains and not to take the offensive until August 7. Royal headquarters, however, was of the view that the army on the left wing ought to start the march on August 3 because of the need for subsequent cooperation of the entire German army. Therefore, Lieutenant Colonel von Verdy[9] was

8. In the Prussian army the *Oberquartiermeister* dealt with operations and tactics rather than with purely logistical matters, as might be implied by a literal rendering of the title.

9. This was Julius von Verdy du Vernois, a famous Prussian officer and Moltke's close confidant. Verdy later wrote widely read memoirs and a multivolume theoreti-cal work on war. See his *Im Hauptquartier der Zweiten Armee 1866* (Berlin: E. S.

sent from headquarters in Mainz to army headquarters in Speyer to explain the situation in person. As a result of this, the crown prince decided not to wait for his trains but to cross the frontier on August 4. In addition, the chief of the General Staff wrote on that day to General von Blumenthal that full freedom of action had been left to the Third Army in the execution of its task—which was to cover the left flank of the main army (the Second) with an immediate offensive to the south. Harmony in the two operations (of the Third and Second armies) could be achieved only by royal headquarters with due regard to the measures taken by the enemy. This was also the case for simultaneous participation of all three armies in the decisive battle. This would be the primary object and royal headquarters sought to regulate all movements to that end.

After the battles of Wörth and Spicheren, royal headquarters moved from Mainz to Homburg in the Palatinate on August 7 and to Saarbrücken on August 9 in order to assure unity of command (*einheitliche Leitung*), especially of the First and Second armies.

Information received up to August 9 allowed the presumption that the enemy had fallen back behind the Moselle or Seille. All three armies followed these movements on the roads assigned them by royal headquarters. As was written to General von Steinmetz on August 11 in reply to a renewed complaint, these instructions remained in force only until the cavalry had gained new information on the location of the main enemy strength. "In that case the armies will not only concentrate, but will also move closer together."

The First Army commander increased the difficulties of the advance on August 10 because he did not report the location of his headquarters or his corps. It was absolutely necessary for royal headquarters to know this so as to be able to make timely dispositions of the various corps. This became more and more necessary the closer the armies approached the enemy.

Mittler, 1900); *Im Grossen Hauptquartier 1870–71. Persönliche Erinnerungen* (Berlin: E. S. Mittler, 1895); and *Studien über den Krieg,* 3 vols. (Berlin: E. S. Mittler, 1892–1902). He also served as Prussian war minister.

Reports and information coming in up to the evening of August 11 indicated that a substantial portion of the enemy stood at Metz on the west bank of the French Nied.

It was necessary that the First and Second armies draw close together. The moment had arrived when it no longer sufficed for royal headquarters to lead the armies by [general directives].[10] The movements of the individual corps of the First and Second armies had to be definitely stipulated in advance to assure complete cooperation of all as the decision steadily approached. Royal headquarters therefore moved to Saint-Avold on August 11 and from then on followed the advance toward the Moselle along the road that formed the boundary between the First and Second armies—through Falckenberg-Herlingen—so as to be able to intervene on either side if necessary.

During the next few days royal headquarters supplemented its written orders to the army headquarters with verbal explanations by General Staff officers concerning its estimate of the situation and intentions. Thus, on the morning of August 14, Colonel von Brandenstein[11] clearly explained to the First Army commander that royal headquarters considered the task of the First Army, which stood on the French Nied only ten miles from the enemy at Metz, as anything but passive, even though it had a directive to remain in its positions on August 14. In vain did the representatives of royal headquarters urge General von Steinmetz to push his advance guards farther out. General von Steinmetz considered his task to be a purely defensive one; and, in fact, the enemy's position under cover of the guns of Metz precluded any direct exploitation of even the most decisive victory. Movements in the hostile camp on the afternoon of August 14 led to the battle of Colombey-Nouilly. This battle was fought without orders and against Steinmetz's will. His order to break off the battle was not obeyed.[12] If the movements in the French

10. Moltke's actual words were "wo es nicht mehr genügte, dem Grossen Hauptquartier die Armeen im allgemeinen zu leiten."

11. This was Col. Carl von Brandenstein, then a section chief in the General Staff. He later rose to the rank of lieutenant general (a two-star rank in the Prussian army) and served as chief of engineers and pioneers. He died on active duty in 1886.

12. Howard, *Franco-Prussian War*, 141–43, is less critical of the two corps commanders whose impetuosity exposed the army to a defeat, which was avoided only

camp were directed against the right wing of the Second Army south of Metz, an offensive from the direction of the Nied absolutely would have to be made. This was no less true if the French, retreating through Metz, attacked those German corps that were still crossing the Moselle above Metz.

This view was expressed in the directives issued by royal headquarters for August 16. These stated that the fruits of the victory of the fourteenth were to be gathered not in front of Metz, but on its other side with a forceful offensive by the Second Army along the road to Verdun.[13]

On the morning of August 15 the king, accompanied by his staff, proceeded from the headquarters at Herlingen to the battlefield. There he met General von Steinmetz.

The first reports of the opening of a fight west of Metz arrived at Herlingen at noon on August 16. Lieutenant Colonel von Bronsart of the General Staff, who had been sent from royal headquarters to observe the development of events on the west bank of the Moselle, had joined the III Corps.[14] He reported at 9:30 A.M. from Buxieres that an attack was about to be made on a hostile position at Rezonville.

Upon his arrival at Pont-à-Mousson, to which royal headquarters had moved in the afternoon, the chief of the General Staff found awaiting him a letter from Gen. [Friedrich] von Stiehle, Prince Friedrich Karl's chief of staff.[15] General von Stiehle had written to explain the estimate of the situation of his army at the time when it started for the battlefield. At that time, that headquarters had acted on the assumption that the question was one of contact merely with a large fraction of the French army. The Second Army intended to drive this French

---

by French inaction. Howard concludes that Generals Alexander von Zastrow (VII Corps) and Edwin von Manteuffel (I Corps) were unable to withdraw once the battle had begun, despite Steinmetz's order. Later on, Steinmetz arrived at the battlefield and again ordered a withdrawal. Zastrow simply ignored the order while Manteuffel "refused to receive" it unless Steinmetz delivered it in person.

13. Despite Moltke's choice of words, the battle was anything but a clear Prussian victory. Its real significance was the delay it imposed on Bazaine's escape from Metz. See Howard, *Franco-Prussian War*, 144.

14. This was Paul Bronsart von Schellendorff, later Prussian war minister.

15. Friedrich Karl then commanded the Prussian Second Army.

force off to the north with the nearest three available corps, while the army's left wing was to continue the march to the Meuse.

The high command attached even more far-reaching importance to the contents of the reports so far received and thought it recognized a new turn of events. It explained its concept of the situation in writing to General von Stiehle that evening.

Lieutenant Colonel von Bronsart submitted a verbal report in Pont-à-Mousson shortly after midnight. It was now known that two Prussian corps had been in a hard and bloody battle against a superior hostile force and that now the main thing was to send timely support to the corps in their positions. In the meantime, Second Army headquarters reached the same conclusion from the course of the battle of Vionville–Mars-la-Tour.

Because the gravity of the situation had become clear, his majesty the king decided to proceed to the battlefield with his entire staff early on August 17. There, on the hill near Flavigny, the royal headquarters and the command group of the Second Army had a lengthy exchange of views. From these discussions emerged the high command's orders for August 18.

After the battle of Gravelotte–Saint-Privat, one-half of the armies remained at Metz, the other half—the Third Army and the newly formed Army of the Meuse—continued the advance westward on a broad front against the Army of Chalons. All German armies received only general directives. The broad freedom of decision, which previously could be granted only to the Third Army and which had to be more or less curtailed in the cases of the First and Second armies after August 11, was restored.

On August 14, rumors of MacMahon's intentions to advance on Metz to relieve Bazaine caused royal headquarters, then on the road from Commercy to Bar-le-Duc, to discuss the situation with Third Army headquarters in Ligny.

From then on, the increasing probability of a French movement to Metz repeatedly forced royal headquarters not only to prescribe to the army headquarters the march routes to be taken by their individual corps and the manner of their use, but also to establish direct communications with the corps' headquarters to assure the successful completion of the gradually executed movement to the north. During these days, everything depended on the rapidity of transmission of orders.

On the other hand, royal headquarters, in all confidence on the evening of August 25, left it to the crown prince of Saxony (commanding the Army of the Meuse) whether and when he would march northward. This was because the Army of the Meuse, in Fleury, received complete information of the enemy situation far earlier than did royal headquarters at Bar-le-Duc. Also, Lieutenant Colonel von Verdy had been sent to Crown Prince Albert for a precise explanation of the views prevalent at the high command. The king met the crown prince of Saxony on the afternoon of August 26 in Clermont, after he had discussed the situation with his son [the crown prince of Prussia] and General von Blumenthal in Bar-le-Duc, to which point Third Army headquarters came on its route from Ligny to Revigny.

During the march to the north, royal headquarters also had to intervene occasionally with the Army of Metz, as two corps of the investing units were to participate against MacMahon. It was left to the discretion of Prince Friedrich Karl temporarily to abandon the investment on the east bank of the Moselle if necessary. But any French attempt to break out to the west was to be prevented under all circumstances. Finally, support of the army investing Metz was not necessary. That headquarters could therefore be given back its prior independence. Written exchanges of views between the chief of the General Staff and General von Stiehle until the fall of Metz kept army headquarters at Metz continuously informed of the general situation on the one hand and explained ahead of time the subsequent tasks of the Second Army. On the other hand, royal headquarters received valuable information about the situation at Metz and many other points.

On August 31, a short discussion of the general situation took place in Chemery (twelve kilometers southwest of Sedan) between the chief of the General Staff, Lt. Gen. [Theophile] von Podbielski, the quartermaster general, and General Blumenthal.

MacMahon's army was surrounded at Sedan the next day. It had not been necessary to issue an order for September 1. Royal headquarters and the army headquarters agreed on their estimates of the general situation.

The Army of the Meuse and the Third Army received only general directives for the march from Sedan to Paris. The manner of execution was left to them. Serious contact with the enemy was not to be feared. The armies of the Second Empire were either annihilated or invested.

Only general instructions were issued for the investment of the hostile capital. Nevertheless, personal discussion of the details took place with Generals von Blumenthal and von Schlotheim, the crown prince of Saxony's chief of staff.[16] This was on September 1 in Château-Thierry.

This latter means of communication was used repeatedly with success at Paris because of the permanent presence of the Third Army headquarters in Versailles and the proximity of that of the Army of the Meuse. The high command, of course, could not avoid issuing orders directly to German units in case of sorties by the Paris garrison. Such direct orders did not go through the army headquarters. Just as during the period from August 11 to 18 and during the march toward Sedan, in front of Paris everything depended on taking timely defensive measures.

After new armies had been formed in the unoccupied parts of France under the pressure of a powerful and unrelenting dictatorship, the surrounded army's attempts to break out of Paris stood in close conjunction with the efforts to relieve the capital. Defense against these armies was the principal task of royal headquarters. In this case, royal headquarters had no alternative but to send general directives from Versailles to the German commanders in the north, on the Loire, and in the southeast. Again, written exchanges of views with the chiefs of the general staff or the commanders themselves—with General von Stiehle on the Loire, General von Manteuffel and General von Goeben in the north, or General von Werder in the southeast—replaced verbal communications.[17] Whenever the latter communication was possible—for instance when General von Manteuffel took command in the southeast—the leaders were called to Versailles.

---

16. Karl Freiherr von Schlotheim, although serving with the crown prince of Saxony, was a Prussian general staff officer. He was a Saxon by birth but served his entire career in the Prussian army. He retired in 1889 after commanding an army corps following the Franco-Prussian war.

17. Edwin von Manteuffel, formerly chief of the military cabinet during the Prussian constitutional crisis of the 1860s, was one of King William I's most controversial generals. He commanded I Corps in the Franco-Prussian War and rose to the rank of field marshal. August von Goeben, also a legendary figure, commanded the VII Corps. Both received enormous financial awards after the campaign. Carl Wilhelm von Werder commanded XIV Corps. Goeben and Werder were both General Staff officers.

Direct orders from royal headquarters restricted the freedom of decision of the commanders only when the king's views were not carried out, or when reports of enemy activities made direct intervention unavoidable.

Thus, at the beginning of December, when the most serious attempt to relieve the capital was made from Paris, and when the Army of the Loire advanced for that purpose, his majesty considered it necessary to bring about a decision on the Loire by a direct attack on Orléans. The chief of the General Staff telegraphed this to Prince Friedrich Karl. After the battle, the chief of the General Staff also earnestly urged the prince's headquarters to begin a relentless pursuit.

Around the start of the new year, when the high command believed that the French intended to advance simultaneously from Le Mans and Bourges on Paris, the king telegraphed an order during the afternoon of January 1 to the Second Army to take up the offensive immediately from the line Vendôme-Illiers.

Because of a report that General von Goeben had occupied the capital of Normandy (Rouen) on the afternoon of December 5, General von Manteuffel (the commander in chief in the north) was repeatedly ordered by telegraph to begin immediate pursuit of the enemy to Le Havre while holding Rouen. Directives for the further action of the army followed.

When, in the middle of January 1871, General von Werder telegraphed to Versailles[18] a complete statement of his dangerous position at Belfort, the high command felt that further retreat by the XIV Corps would result in abandoning the siege of Belfort and the loss of the vast stores of material assembled there for siege operations. Moreover, it could not be foreseen where such a move might be halted. Then, too, the move would delay the intervention of General von Manteuffel's army, which was hastening there in forced marches. Therefore, at 3:00 P.M. on January 15, General von Werder received strict orders to accept battle at Belfort. As was no more than proper, he was thereby relieved from the moral responsibility for all consequences of any unfortunate outcome of the battle. However, the general had decided to adopt that course of action on his own initiative even before the orders were issued.

---

18. By that time the Prussian headquarters, along with a vast assembly of political officials, had moved to Versailles.

Because of the size of the headquarters, it was not always easy to keep the intentions of the army command secret. This campaign, like that of 1866, again showed how great are the difficulties when numerous princes (or high military persons who have no command) with their retinues and attendants increase the numbers at headquarters to approximately the strength of a cavalry division. Despite the presence of so many personalities who had to be treated with special considerations, the king was available at any hour, day or night, to the chief of the General Staff for pertinent decisions. Although as a rule the intended operations were kept secret, sometimes individuals sent home reports of what had happened or what they thought was supposed to happen. These reports frequently gained quite an importance because of their sources. The heavy demands already made on the telegraph by the most important orders were very substantial, and it is to the great credit of the quartermaster general, General von Podbielski, that he maintained strict control over this without regard to individuals.

No council of war was ever held, either in 1866 or 1870–71, as has so often been claimed. In the accounts of historical events, errors become legends, which are very hard to correct subsequently. To this category also belong the yarns which recount that the major decisions in our recent campaigns were due to prior councils of war. This allegedly was the case with the battle of Königgrätz. The actual process was as follows.

On hearing the report that the entire Austrian army was concentrated not behind but in front of the Elbe on the Bistritz, Prince Friedrich Karl, pursuant to directives previously received, ordered (on the evening of July 2) the First Army and the Army of the Elbe to concentrate very early the next morning opposite the enemy.

At 11:00 P.M., General von Voigts-Rhetz carried a report of this to the king at Gitschin.[19] The king sent him to the chief of the General

---

19. This was Lt. Gen. Konstantin Bernhard von Voigts-Rhetz, who was chief of the Second Army general staff (and thus overall chief of staff) in 1866. He was a jealous critic of Moltke but an extraordinary officer. He left a valuable set of letters, *Briefe des Generals der Infanterie Voigts-Rhetz aus den Kriegsjahren 1866 und 1870–71*, ed. A. von Voigts-Rhetz (Berlin: E. S. Mittler, 1906). He figures prominently in Craig's account of Königgrätz and Howard's of the Franco-Prussian War.

Staff. The latter immediately rushed to the king, who had his quarters on the opposite side of the market square. After the principal military counselor had explained the situation, the king declared himself fully in agreement that the following day all three armies were to be assembled to fight the battle. He directed that the necessary orders be sent to the crown prince, who would now have to cross the Elbe.

The entire discussion with the king lasted scarcely longer than ten minutes. No one was present but the chief of the General Staff. That was the "council of war" of Königgrätz.[20]

Another legend has crystallized in poetry, and even quite beautiful verses.

The theater is Versailles. The French make a sortie from Paris. The generals, instead of proceeding to the fighting units, assemble for consultation. They must determine whether one dared to keep royal headquarters in Versailles. Opinions differ. No one wants to speak out. The chief of the General Staff, whose business it is to speak, remains silent. Apprehensions are apparently enormous. Only the war minister[21] rises and energetically protests against such a militarily and politically disadvantageous measure as the evacuation of Versailles. He receives the warm thanks of the king for being the only one with the courage to speak out truthfully and without fear.

The truth is that, while the king and his entire suite rode to the V Corps, the marshal of the royal household, acting with excessive zeal, caused the court baggage to be hitched. This, of course, did not long remain hidden from the city and may have caused all kinds of hopes

---

20. Craig, *Königgrätz*, 83, describes the meeting as a "war council." He refers to Moltke's correspondence, but not to the above passage in which Moltke strongly denies that any "war council" took place. Kessel points out that for political reasons (his strained relations with Bismarck) Moltke was against using the term, which implied civilian participation. Nevertheless, this meeting, according to Kessel, was indeed a war council. See his *Moltke*, 472. Martin van Creveld, *Command in War*, 134, sides with Moltke on the grounds that the army commanders were not present.

21. Count Albrecht von Roon. As a perceptive young officer pointed out in 1910, Moltke sometimes regarded Roon as one of the pessimists (men of the negative) who were so difficult to work with. See Lieutenant Endres, "Wie bestrebte sich Napoleon sie Moltke die Einheitlichkeit der Heerführung zu gewährleisten?" *Jahrbücher für die deutsche Armee und Marine,* 1910, first half, 42–54, 162–78.

to arise in the minds of the sanguine populace. Four army corps guarded Versailles; no one dreamed of evacuating the place.

The daily routine in 1870 was as follows. Every day, except on days of engagements or marches, the king regularly held an audience at 10:30 A.M. Then the chief of the General Staff, accompanied by the quartermaster general, submitted the reports and messages that had come in and made new recommendations. The chief of the military cabinet, the war minister, and the crown prince (as long as headquarters of the Third Army was at Versailles) were present, but all only as spectators. The king occasionally asked them one thing or another. However, he never asked them for advice concerning operations or the recommendations submitted by the chief of the General Staff.

The king scrutinized these recommendations, each of which the chief had previously discussed with his assistants. The king's deliberations were marked by military judgment and an always-correct estimate of the objections against executing the proposals. However, since in war every step is bound up with danger, what had been recommended was approved without exception.

King William was in this case the actual commander in chief. The monarch, who has at his disposal the entire state with its means, has a proper place at the head of the field army only if he is capable of being the leader of his armies and of personally assuming the heavy responsibility for everything happening in the field. If these prerequisites are absent, his presence is bound to be injurious.

We see this on the French side in the middle of August 1870. On August 12, Emperor Napoleon relinquished command and appointed Marshal Bazaine commander in chief of the Army of the Rhine. The very dangerous vacillation on the part of the army's leadership came to an inevitable conclusion. Still, the emperor had not yet left the army and had only considered departing.

The emperor could not return to Paris without a victory. He therefore remained with the army for the present, where he had kept the Guard at his disposal as a sort of household unit. Suffering great bodily pain, the sorely tried emperor, whose dominion in France was already at an end and who no longer commanded the army, perceived that his fate not only depended on the battles in the field but also on those in parliament.

Marshal Bazaine therefore had to give more consideration to the emperor's security and to listen to the views of his suite, including the counsels of those who did not want to retreat to Chalons yet who did not bear the responsibility for the consequences of remaining at Metz. So that he could arrive at his decisions without interference, the marshal must have urgently desired that the emperor, and with him the numerous entourage of irresponsible counselors, would leave the army. Only *one* person may direct operations. Interference of different (even if well-intentioned) counselors deprives this will of much of its clarity and determination. Command depending on this will thus becomes uncertain. Correct execution of an idea, even if only partially corresponding to the existing situation, will sooner lead to the objective than a continual shifting to new plans. Countermanding orders inevitably undermine the confidence and energies of the units.

PLAN OF OPERATIONS: (1871–81)[22]

Even the first deployment (*Aufmarsch*) of the army—assembling the fighting means in readiness—cannot be planned without a previous plan of operations, at least in a very general sketch. One must consider in advance what one intends in the defense, just as for the attack. The first deployment of the army is inseparably connected with the operations themselves. In this matter, the most diverse geographical, governmental, and political factors have to be considered. Fortresses, favorable terrain sectors, railroad connections, the available fighting means, and the time for their assembly are given quantities. Politics, on the other hand, inserts itself as a changeable factor into our calculation of probability. This factor cannot be eliminated, since it is so important to the result. If the views shaping original deployment are incorrect, the work is completely without value. Even a *single* error in the original assembly (*Versammlung*) of the armies can hardly ever be made good again during the entire course of the campaign. However, all measures for the assembly can be thoroughly thought out long in advance, assuming that the units are ready for the field and that the transport service is well organized. Consequently, these measures must invariably lead to the desired result.

22. The German title is *Operationsplan—Kriegsobjekt und Operationsobjekt.*

In operations, the case is far different with the military employment of the means placed in readiness. Here, our will quickly encounters the independent will of the enemy. Thus operations depend not only on our own intentions but also on the enemy's. The former we know, the latter we can but surmise. What is most advantageous to the enemy may serve as a clue to what is probable. We can limit the will of the opponent only if we are ready and determined to take the initiative. But we cannot break it other than by the means of tactics—the engagement.

The material and moral consequences of every large engagement are so far-reaching that they will usually create a completely changed situation, a new basis for new measures. The principal point, then, is correctly to estimate the momentary situation and to arrange and execute the right thing for the foreseeable future.

The tactical result of an engagement forms the base for new strategic decisions because victory or defeat in a battle changes the situation to such a degree that no human acumen is able to see beyond the first battle.[23] In this sense one should understand Napoleon's saying: "I have never had a plan of operations."

Therefore no plan of operations extends with any certainty beyond the first contact with the main hostile force. Only the layman thinks that he can see in the course of the campaign the consequent execution of an original idea with all details thought out in advance and adhered to until the very end.

Of course the commander in chief will always keep his main objective in mind and will not be swayed by the changeability of events. Nevertheless, the way in which he hopes to attain that objective cannot be laid out long in advance with any degree of certainty. In the course of the campaign he must arrive at a series of decisions based on situations that cannot be foreseen. None of the successive acts of war are thus premeditated plans. Rather, all are spontaneous acts guided by military judgment. The main point in a series of genuinely special cases is to perceive the situation hidden in the fog of uncertainty, correctly

---

23. This emphasis on tactics (combat) over strategy was a common thread running through Prusso–German theory from Clausewitz to the Second World War.

to estimate what is known, to deduce what is unknown, to arrive at a quick decision, and to carry it out powerfully and consistently.

To the calculations of a known and an unknown quantity, one's own and the enemy's will, also come third factors that escape all foresight: weather,[24] sickness, railroad accidents, misunderstandings, and delusions, and all the effects which man may call luck, fate, or God's will, but which man neither creates nor rules.

Yet in spite of all this, the conduct of war has never degenerated into blind arbitrariness. A calculation of probability will show that all chance happenings ultimately affect, for better or worse, the one side as well as the other. Hence, the general who in each individual case orders what is the most reasonable, if not the very best, will always have a chance to attain his objective.

It is self-evident that mere theoretical knowledge does not suffice, but that, on the contrary, the attributes of spirit as well as character attain a free, practical, artistic development. Of course, this artistic sense must be honed by military education and guided by experience, either from military history or one's own life.

One must distinguish between the *object of the war* and the *object of the operation* of the attack. The former is not the army, but the land mass and the capital of the enemy, and within them the resources and the political power of the state. It comprises what we desire to hold or that for which we will subsequently trade. The object of an operation is the hostile army insofar as it defends the object of the war. This condition can cease if the defensive army is shaken by combat, if it is too weak, or if it stands too far away to be of effect or in terrain that precludes offensive action. In that case the country, a piece of terrain, or the capital may gain a greater importance than even the hostile army. This means that as far as the attack is concerned, war and operations objectives are one and the same thing.

A condition for a successful strategic surprise attack is that the decision for it is kept in absolute secrecy until the moment of execution. On the day the ultimatum is issued, not only mobilization orders but

---

24. After the campaign of 1864 Moltke wrote, "One can base no operations on weather, but one can base them on the season." This was added to the text in the *Militärische Werke*.

also march orders must be issued. Otherwise, special days have to be calculated for railway preparations. Finally, subsequent to that day, neither diplomatic negotiations nor political considerations must be allowed to interfere with the subsequent course of military events.[25]

HISTORICAL EXAMPLES

The Campaign of 1866

Three hostile groups stood opposed to Prussia in 1866: Hanover and Electoral Hesse, the South Germans, and Austria.

Hanover and Electoral Hesse could have become troublesome in the highest degree if left unobserved in the rear. In that case, they could have disrupted all communications with the Rhine and the duchies on the Elbe. Of course it was still questionable if they would subject themselves to the risk of actual hostilities, but in any case we were certain enough to separate these opponents before they could effect a junction. The only consideration in this matter was the resulting loss of time.

In spite of all the preparations for armament in Württemberg, Bavaria, and Hesse-Darmstadt, the South Germans were considered only nascent enemies. It was known how few preparations for war they had made in peacetime. The lack of united leadership and organization promised these units—excellent material in themselves—no large success. It was expected that they would come into action too late and in isolation. The best means, in this case, was an offensive that would engage them in their own lands.

The third group, however, had a strong and well-organized army that was already battle-ready.

---

25. Moltke's one-sided views on the dominance of military considerations even before an actual declaration of war became a firm tenet of most Prussian theory. For the Imperial army, this viewpoint reached its disastrous ultimate conclusion under the regime of Hindenburg and Ludendorff in 1917 and 1918. This passage also contains the germ of Schlieffen's ideas on the role of mobilization and military factors as autonomous factors in a crisis that might lead to war.

There lay the center of gravity (*Schwerpunkt*) of the entire question. A victory over the Austrian army, the operational object in the eastern theater of war, would inevitably have an injurious effect on all other enemies. However, the seven army corps in the eastern part of Prussia were insufficient to produce the requisite force for that purpose.[26] Should the two corps in the west also be used for the main decision, the Rhine Province would appear unprotected and only inferior forces could be sent against the South Germans.

Nevertheless, his majesty the king came to this difficult but momentous decision, which alone made it possible to generate sufficient numbers for the engagements the main army had to fight in the decisive battle, and finally at the hostile capital. The Rhine fortifications, although adequately garrisoned by Landwehr, could of course not prevent an invasion of the country. They probably could, however, prevent the enemy from gaining a lasting foothold there. If we succeeded in gaining the upper hand in the east, it would be an easy matter to regain what had been lost in the west.

To protect Prussia from hostile invasion, a special army was organized out of a portion of the units in Schleswig-Holstein and regiments designated for fortress garrisons (for which the 13th Infantry Division served as a firm nucleus). The fortress regiments could be assembled in the shortest time around Minden and in the immediate vicinity of the Hanoverian capital. One could thereby hope to disarm Hanover and the Electorate of Hesse, and then turn against Bavaria.

This improvised army had a threefold numerical superiority against it. It had to make good in energy and speed what it lacked in numbers. The first task was to ascertain where the fighting forces designated for the eastern theater of war were to be assembled and where their transport should be assembled.

The outposts of the Austrian I Corps stood at Tetschen, Reichenberg, and Tratenau. Under their protection, sixty thousand to eighty thousand men could be assembled at one of these three points in a very short time by utilizing available railroads. These forces certainly would

---

26. Here Moltke used the term "the monarchy," which has been changed to "Prussia" for clarity.

not have sufficed to carry on any real offensive war against Prussia. They were sufficient, however, to threaten Berlin or Breslau seriously if they chose to do so. In one direction stood the Saxon army as a ready advance guard. This army was only six to seven marches distant from the Prussian capital, which was unprotected by any large piece of terrain to the south. In the other direction, Breslau could be reached easily in five days of marching. An attack on Breslau was all the easier because Schweidnitz had long since been abandoned as a fortress due to our previous confidence in the confederation with Austria.

Nothing would have been more desirable than to find a position for the entire force that would have covered Berlin and Breslau simultaneously, even if it could not originally have protected the country on the west of the Elbe and on the upper Oder. The best point would have been Görlitz.

The difficulties in provisioning a quarter of a million men assembled at one point could have been overcome if there had been some chance that this mass would march soon. But these problems promised to become insurmountable if the assembly should last for an indefinite time, or if action should not result at all.

Concentration of the entire army at one point, be that at Görlitz or in Upper Silesia, required much time. If transportation were limited to a few railroads (and subsequently to only one), the deployment would be delayed for weeks. But the frontier provinces and Silesia required immediate protection. Thus, nothing remained but to establish two separate armies.

It is clear that in this case a concentrated Austrian army could have thrown itself with its entire force against one-half of the Prussian forces. But no matter what arrangements we made, none could change the geography of the theater of war or the fact that an enemy stood in Bohemia between the Lausitz and Silesia.

There was but one means to overcome this evil, and that was for us to invade Bohemia. In any case, the army corps first had to be transported by rail as close to the frontier as possible.[27]

---

27. Moltke does not say precisely to what frontier the armies must be moved. In this context, he must have meant close to the Bohemian frontier.

If we had not had to respect the Saxon domains, the lines from the Rhine, Westphalia, Pomerania, and Brandenburg would have sufficed rapidly to assemble a significant force at Dresden. As a matter of fact, however, the rail lines available to the Prussian transports ended at Zeitz, Halle, Herzberg, Görlitz, Schweidnitz, and Neisse. It was necessary to detrain the units at these points, which formed an arc some 270 miles in length, and to march from there. This of course was not the intended strategic deployment of the army, but only the unavoidable first stage of that deployment. Whether the further assembly of the yet separated parts should be done from these detraining points by marches on the periphery or by operations to the center remained absolutely dependent on the decision to conduct the war offensively or defensively.

Corresponding to the railroad terminals, the units detrained. On July 5, they stood thus: the Army of the Elbe (half of the VII and the VIII corps) at Zeitz; the First Army (IV, III, II, and Guard corps, from Berlin) at Torgau; the Second Army (V Corps and half of the VI Corps, with its other half in Upper Silesia) at Landeshut and I Corps at Görlitz; and the reserve corps in Berlin.

His majesty had directed that no field army was to function as a self-contained organization and reserved to himself the right to assign corps or divisions of one army to another according to the course of events.

During the entire month of May the Prussian frontier had been more or less in danger. Fortunately, a fighting force that was effectively superior to the enemy was soon assembled there.

Every military consideration made it imperative for Prussia to begin the campaign on June 6. Hope remained at the beginning of that month that the differences might be settled peacefully. At this stage, King William refused to take the first steps toward a war that would be so incalculable in its consequences for Germany. But when (on June 11) Austria demanded of the Confederation that all non-Prussian corps be mobilized, the Prussian government did not hesitate to take energetic steps. By this time, however, the Austrian movement was essentially complete.

While the larger part of the corps were still being transported, the necessary steps had been taken to bring the ones that had already arrived (the II, III, and IV corps) up closer to the Second Army in Silesia.

This could be done only by having them march along the frontier through a relatively poor forest area, during very hot weather, and along sandy country roads. The units went into cantonment but had to expect that concentration might become necessary at any moment. Any movement of units on such a scale always entails great difficulties in the matter of provisioning. The just-mentioned march to the east, directed by orders issued on May 30, had progressed so far by June 8 that III Corps was near I Corps at Görlitz, IV Corps was in the vicinity of Hoyerswerda, and II Corps around Senftenberg. Behind these three corps, the Guard Corps concentrated in cantonments around Cottbus.

IMPORTANCE OF FORTRESSES (1861–62)[28]

I hold the decided opinion that the military strength of our state would be diminished rather than increased by enlarging or increasing the number of our fortresses, not to mention the costs involved. The *army in the field* is the weight that is placed on the scales of political conflict. It, above all else, decides the outcome of war.

We must never expect of fortifications that which only active fighting forces can accomplish. The latter can act in any desired direction, the former in only one.

Fortresses gain their full significance only in conjunction with the army of operations. They alone cannot prevent an invasion; they gain importance only as supporting points for an army of operations in the open field. We want to defend the country with the army. Fortresses must support, not devour, that army.

The closer to the frontier we can place our defensive army under the protection of fortresses, the more advantageous such an arrangement naturally is. An assembly farther to the rear at the very start abandons a portion of the country. Nevertheless, one must consider if we are in a position to complete our concentration uninterrupted and before the enemy arrives at the chosen point. It is impossible to do so when opposed

---

28. The German title was *Bedeutung der Festungen für die Kriegführung.* This text omits a number of pages dealing with purely tactical aspects of fortresses.

by an enemy who is completely ready for war. In that case, all the fortresses at the extreme frontier of the country have the disadvantage of gaining their proper effectiveness only in a later stage of the war, when we take up the offensive. This assumes that an offensive can be conducted in the direction where they are located and that they—having been left to their own resources until then—have not succumbed.

If the enemy invades our territory, the strategic importance of fortresses increases with their proximity to the main line leading from the enemy's starting point to the nation's capital.

Nothing but the strategic value of a fortress for the defense of the country should decide whether substantial means are to be employed for its restoration or enlargement. The general condition of buildings and fortifications only then determines what has to be done according to the demands of the times, and even then only secondarily.

The course of a war cannot be foreseen. Therefore it would be impossible to determine the influence of fortresses on a war were it not for the fact that certain conditions are permanent or at least remain constant and decisive for a long period.

The political aspects of states change, but it takes a long period of time to change substantially the relationship between states. Probably no one will deny that Russia (which is engaged in domestic reconstruction), and Austria are presently (and will probably be for decades to come) far less dangerous neighbors for us than is France with its ready power. Probably no one, therefore, will deny that the fortresses along the Rhine will have a greater initial influence than those situated along the Vistula or the Silesian mountains.[29]

The armies of the neighboring states and the points where they can be concentrated to advantage are well known and rest on permanent foundations. The railroad net, following the main arteries of commerce, is absolutely permanent. It may be supplemented, but never substantially changed.

The large rivers traversing our country from south to north form a permanent bulwark of defense. The direction of transports and first

---

29. Here Moltke's predictive powers failed him, at least with respect to Austria. War with Austria came in 1866, with France in 1870, and not until 1914 with Russia.

assembly of the Prussian armies depend on all these permanent conditions. They can be foreseen and prepared in advance. Thus, the value of fortresses at the outbreak of war can be demonstrated.

The defense of the country must therefore cling to the large rivers and their fortresses and must keep in mind that the importance of river fortresses increases when they form continuous systems.

Of course, how actual operations develop becomes more uncertain the further we pursue their course. The most probable eventualities can be foreseen, however, because they depend on well-known and permanent conditions.

We must never lose sight of the experiences of former wars. Yet they give us no certain guide for present times. Decades and even centuries have passed since these wars took place and meanwhile the political and strategic situations have changed. What other significance had Schweidnitz, being situated in the then newly conquered Silesia,[30] and Graudenz, as the only fortress on the Vistula, for Frederick the Great than for us! Who would think that in a war with France, Stettin will for a second time have the same importance that it could have exercised in the special circumstances of 1806?

There remains only one way to gain the intended results. That is to investigate the military events of the future and to adapt as much as possible to present-day conditions. In this we have to reckon in part with unknown and mutable quantities, but also in many cases with known and permanent ones. We cannot attain an absolutely correct result, but we can discover the probable. In war that always remains the only foundation upon which one can base one's measures.

In case of war with Austria, we cannot concentrate our main force in Silesia. This would lay bare the shortest route from Bohemia to Berlin. Our defensive army would at once have to march down the Oder.

The Silesian fortresses therefore cannot be regarded as supporting points for the defense—at least not at the opening of the campaign, but they can play that important role in an offensive.

Such supporting points were absolutely necessary in the campaigns of Frederick the Great. It was necessary to assemble provisions for

30. Frederick the Great seized the Austrian province of Silesia in 1740, an act that touched off the War of the Austrian Succession. War was renewed in 1756, in the Seven Years' War, which pitted Prussia against the Austrian Empire, Russia, Saxony, and France.

the subsistence of the armies in advance. That had to be done in secure places—fortresses, naturally—which had to be as close to the frontier as possible because of the greater difficulty in transportation in those days. Since the Austrians had to take the same steps for their subsistence, they could not take the offensive into Silesia without investing or laying siege to these frontier fortresses.

Today, where the armies are so very much larger, where they are more independent in the matter of subsistence because of the requisition system, where the country is more passable and richer, such small fortified places have lost most of their importance.

We no longer need to secure our magazines with fortifications; we can secure them with distance. It is entirely immaterial if a few thousand hundredweights are transported by rail twenty or two hundred miles. An army that operates against Prague will receive its provisions more rapidly and more certainly from Berlin than from Schweidnitz.

UNTITLED (1866)

The recent campaign has again shown the advantages of the strategic offensive and undoubtedly we will do best in the future to conduct war not in our country but in the enemy's. In that case, of course, fortresses cannot offer direct support. On the contrary, the more numerous they are, the more they will absorb that fighting force which remains for offensive purposes. None of our fortresses was of any actual value during the recent campaign, but they nevertheless deprived the field army of the 150,000 men who were needed for garrisons.

By this we do not, of course, mean to deny the utility and necessity of fortified places, which arise at once if operations are pushed back into our own territory. Nevertheless, we will always endeavor to make our army in the field as strong as possible. Even the most recent experiences have shown how very useful a portion of the Landwehr is in maintaining the regular army at full strength during operations in the enemy's country. The reserve corps, organized from garrison units, held Saxony and portions of Bohemia and Bavaria in the rear of the army of operations. We would gladly have had more of them available to protect the lines of communications farther forward, and even to observe Olmütz and lay siege to Theresienstadt and Josefstadt without weakening the field army. This is because an attacking army does not like to give up units for such purposes. All these were tasks that the Landwehr could have performed easily.

It is very desirable, therefore, to limit the number of fortresses to the absolute minimum necessary. One can say that the stronger the field army is, the less will fortresses be necessary.[31]

UNTITLED (1871)

The fact that the fall of Paris decided the war was due less to the capitulation of the *fortresses* than to the subjugation of the *capital*. It was also due to the fact that the cessation of resistance at this important point happened simultaneously with the exhaustion of the entire country in the matter of credit and powers of resistance.

At Metz, we drove the French army into the fortress. At Paris, the hostile army completed its organization during the course of the investment of the fortress. The French army sought protection there of its own volition.

In both instances permanent links between the field army and the fortresses became fateful to the armies after they had failed to overcome the unnatural situation—in the former case forced, in the latter case created voluntarily—by successful sorties.

Metz and Paris became the turning points of operations because they had been sought out as the very last means of salvation and after lost battles. The French army would certainly not have held the open field for two months. It would have capitulated in the open field like the army at Sedan, for the Sedan fortress was insignificant.

UNTITLED (1871)

Modern wars will be carried on with armies of such strength that their provisioning can be accomplished only by means of railroads.

---

31. Here the editor has omitted a lengthy discussion of fortresses in the North German Confederation and resumes the narrative with text written in 1871, after the end of the Franco-Prussian War.

Having control of the railroads is of the utmost importance, but it seems to me to be entirely unjustifiable to erect fortresses, or even only forts, for that exclusive purpose.

The experiences of the most recent campaign have shown that the small French forts which kept us from exploiting French railroads were captured more quickly than we could repair blown bridges and tunnels. All those forts fell in a few days, as soon as we succeeded in bringing up siege material. For the latter purpose, the railroad line, which the fort was to protect, offered the very best means. It is true that the destruction of large structures blocks the railroad to us, while fortification blocks it to the enemy. Fortifications preserve for us the use of the railroad—but only at the point where it is destroyed. No fortification can prevent the enemy from destroying the railroad outside the range of its guns. Finally, the railroad net at the present day is so closely interwoven and under further development that it could be blocked only by a very large number of forts. The fall of each, presumably occurring very quickly, would be a material loss and a moral defeat.

One should not underestimate the advantage offered by defensible fortresses in dominating the main lines of communications, especially those situated at crossings of large rivers, which for self-evident reasons form the junctions of roads and railroads. The fortresses should not only be situated on railroads; the railroads should, wherever possible, run through the fortresses.

In contrast to the French fortresses, almost all of our large fortresses are located on important streams and, for that reason, have an increased importance as secure crossings. They allow us an extremely favorable freedom of maneuver and make all entrenched camps superfluous. The protection of fortified camps affords us in any case only a secure stream crossing. Investing a river fortress requires double the expenditure of investing a fort in the open. Finally, our main fortresses contain the capitals of our lands and the centers of commerce, which, with all possible means that can be used for provisioning and equipping an army, deprive the opponent of those means and preserve them for us. At the same time they form the well-driven nail that saves the invaded province for the state.

For that reason, however, the fortresses also attract hostile attack and oblige us to protect them as much as possible from destruction by bombardment. To accomplish this we must use detached fortifications located at great distance beyond the limit of artillery. The periphery increases with the radius and the number of works. This increases the expenditures for construction, maintenance, armament, and garrisoning. No state is rich enough to have many such fortresses.

We must take special care not to increase the requirements for garrison troops because, as experience has shown, our Landwehr has proven itself quite capable in the field in spite of the many difficulties in its organization and the great shortage of experienced officers and noncommissioned officers. If we, as is foreseeable, are compelled to establish fronts simultaneously to the east and west, we will absolutely need the formations of the mobile Landwehr divisions for the active support of the field army. We can achieve economy in fortress garrisons if we abandon not only newly acquired fortresses, but also a part of the older and less important ones.

UNTITLED (1872)

In the last war, the French fortresses indisputably had a substantial influence on the course of events. However, I can attribute actual usefulness to only the largest of them. Even places like Verdun, Toul, Soissons, and all the smaller ones never delayed the advance of our armies for a single day. It is true that they deprived us of the railroads in a very burdensome manner, but fourteen days' preparations sufficed to open these rail lines, whereas the destruction of bridges and tunnels interrupted traffic on them far longer.

Along its northern railroad route, after Metz had fallen, the 14th Division took Diedenhofen, Montmédy, and Mézières between November 13 and January 1. Three places were thus taken in 48 days, whereas the destroyed tunnel at Montmédy alone delayed traffic for 32 days. Repairing the tunnel at Nanteuil required 44 days, whereas the viaducts at Xertigny and Dannemarie cost 127 and 100 days respectively. Had we found the large tunnel at Zabern destroyed, we could not have repaired it during the entire campaign. Fortresses not located on large rivers have little importance as barrier points.

In spite of substantial problems with terrain and weather, the railroad circumventing Metz, more than twenty-two miles long, was completed in twenty-nine days.

One must further acknowledge that a few of the smaller forts served as supporting points for arming the populace. But such achievements are dearly paid for. We must remember that with relatively very small means we captured (in addition to trophies and military supplies) 1,200 officers, 40,000 men, and 2,018 guns in nineteen of the smaller forts. The moral effect of this is increased by the fact that a province whose fortresses fall into the hands of the enemy will, when peace is restored, be considered a conquest more certainly than if no fortresses had been located there.

Fortresses are useful only if they can be held or at least if their capture will consume substantial time and effort. I can therefore attach but little value to the statement that our smaller fortresses are justified as barriers along railroads.

Our large fortresses are designated as "maneuver places" and as "army fortresses." It is not at all superfluous to explain the two terms.[32] Our large fortresses deserve the first designation because they are all situated on main rivers throughout the country, because they form bridgeheads on both sides of the streams, and because they therefore afford complete freedom of maneuver and force the enemy to resort to double exertions. In addition, they enclose the country's most important cities. The latter's ample supplies are very important to the conduct of war.

If one of our armies is forced by reverses to evacuate the field, it needs protection against the enemy's direct pursuit. It also needs rest and replenishment of material and provisions. All these may be found in a retreat through a fortress. The fortress will thus separate the retreating army from the enemy and will gain hours or days for recuperation. Provision of this service to the army requires no large fortress; a smaller one will suffice—one whose outer works are incomplete. There is no need to make a great fortress out of it. If the enemy is so strong that he can invest the side nearest him, cross the stream in the face of the defender, and then advance in superior numbers, the question arises if we should enter the fortress or continue the retreat. I would never advise the first procedure. In a retreat we still have a chance to succeed. If there is no such chance, it is better to succumb in the open

32. Moltke's terms were, respectively, *Manövrier-Plätze* and *Armee-Festungen.*

field than to capitulate in a fortress. The latter has been the fate of all armies, as far as I can recollect, which have locked themselves up in fortresses.

The designation "army fortress" would be an erroneous one, I believe, if we were to suppose that all such large fortresses have to be prepared to receive armies within their walls.

Bazaine did not voluntarily close himself up in Metz. Originally he had to cover Metz because the general of engineers, [Gen. Gregoire] Coffinières, declared that he could not hold the fortress fourteen days without that protection. The marshal decided on his fateful step only when attacked from the west with every escape blocked. It was then not the fortress, but the French army within its walls, that tied down two hundred thousand of our men.

If we assume that there had been no Metz at all, the marshal in all probability would have reached Paris after costly battles and engagements. If we had encountered only a hundred thousand real soldiers at Paris, we could hardly have conducted the kind of investment that we did.

The great importance of the fortified capital to the defense of France cannot be denied. Fortresses of colossal size are able to receive within their walls entire armies, as Antwerp could hold the Belgian army, until a shift in political conditions.

One must further acknowledge that with very few exceptions there is scarcely a single fortress whose collapse could not be a disadvantage in some circumstances.

But this is not the decisive point. More important is the question, "How strong must we be in fortresses to be able to take the offensive?"

Not the fortress, but the army that we send into the field secures our position of power in the world. The advantage of conducting the war in the enemy's country is so obvious, and our own experiences speak so plainly on this point, that nothing further need be said about that. If a high degree of preparedness allows one to take the initiative, then railroads will protect the country better than fortresses.

The above question cannot be answered directly. One cannot maintain that so and so many hundred thousand men will guarantee success or that success could not be attained with fewer.

However, it is certain that for an offensive in force we need our entire field army and that all detachments made for the defense of fortresses must be replaced by the Landwehr. In addition, a few mobile Landwehr divisions are indispensable for rear area duties.[33]

The following seems to me beyond doubt:

1. The offensive remains the basic form of our conduct of war. Passive *holding* of the country therefore takes second place behind active *protection* of the country.

2. We need the entire field army and a portion of the Landwehr for the offensive; only the surplus may be used for the fortresses.

3. Money at the disposition of the state for military purposes must be expended on the field army and only secondarily on fortresses.

4. A substantial reduction in the number of fortresses is therefore absolutely necessary.

RAILROADS (1861)

Importance of Railroads[34]

Basically, each and every addition to the communications, especially to the railroads, must be considered a military advantage.[35] All railroads in the rear of an army are useful while it is stationary, as well as during a retreat. During an advance the railroad must first be captured. This means that the railroad, sure to be destroyed by the enemy, has to be repaired. The country on both sides must be under control before one can use it.

If we were assured that we could concentrate our fighting forces at the farthest frontier of the country and that we could remain there without any doubt, then all military objections to railroad construction in the interior of the country would collapse.

However, if we must effect our first deployment (*Aufmarsch*) in a

---

33. After War Minister von Roon's reforms in the early 1860s, the Landwehr became a second-line reserve force consisting primarily of older men and intended for duty along lines of communications and in quiet areas.

34. The German title of this essay was "*Bedeutung der Eisenbahnen für die Kriegführung.*"

35. For a study of the impact of railroads on Moltke's military methods, see Showalter, *Railroads and Rifles.*

sector farther to the rear, and if the country from there to the frontier is not secured, then all railroads have to be secured by fortifications at or near the points where they cross the frontier, or must be prepared for destruction by explosives.

Railroads acquire special importance where they cross large rivers. There, not only the railroads but also the bridges are of great importance. The defense of Prussia to the east and west is based on the four large rivers flowing through the country from south to north, along which our main fortresses are situated. We have no mountain ranges that form principal sectors.

The defense may never remain passive; it must be active. This means that we must prevent the enemy from crossing and must ourselves be able to move to the front at some other point.

Destruction of a railroad interrupts traffic; destruction of river crossings interrupts operations. If we destroy bridges to prevent the enemy from using them, we rob ourselves of the possibility of advancing across the rivers.

Railroads must cross the larger rivers only at fortresses because we must preserve the bridges for our use. Thus, it is necessary to enlarge almost all our fortresses, such as those at Cologne, Coblenz, and Mainz, and to construct new ones at Marienburg and Breslau. Since these are limited by financial means and garrisons, new railroads must cross rivers at existing fortresses.

A railroad bridge across a large river outside a fortress is a bridge built without regard to military advantages. The ensuing military disadvantages can be overcome only by immediate destruction of the bridge and loss of a portion of the national wealth.

A conflict between military interests and political/economic/commercial interests can therefore exist only at the frontiers and at large rivers. At all other points, full freedom of construction should not be denied. In case of competing lines, military interests will be decisive; but even the less favorable line, the means for whose construction has been raised, is better than none.

Addition of January 1870

The enormous influence of railroads on the conduct of war has unmistakably emerged in the campaigns of the last decade. They enormously increase mobility, one of the most important elements in war, and cause distances to disappear.

The continual and rapid growth of rail lines is bound to increase their importance and to make the railroads an independent factor in the conduct of war that will affect even the organic and tactical arrangements of armies.

Railroads increase the value of all transportable means of war, in contrast to the passive means. Among the different arms of the service, they give the infantry an increased value because it is the branch best suited for the rapid shifting of large masses from one point of activity to another. Rapid and continuous dispatch of transports allows the first concentration of the army directly at the threatened frontier. This, however, presupposes the increased efficiency of the units. Between the time of mobilization and battle, many units will hardly have time for target practice at regimental level and far fewer will have time to drill in large formations. All this speaks against shortening the length of service and for an increase in training time. It speaks for making as few changes as possible in command positions of all grades at mobilization, and, in general, for the greatest possible degree of readiness for war in time of peace. Furthermore, railroads demand and allow a decrease of all noncombat parts of the army and decreases in the loads carried by the soldiers, by columns and trains, and by medical organizations.

During the ten years ending in 1867, the Prussian railroads have increased about 64 percent in mileage but about 200 percent in their capacity to handle traffic. At the present time (January 1870), 1,620 miles of track are under construction. The neighboring states are by no means behind us in this regard. Because of this, we can easily calculate what can be done in the matter of railroad construction in the next ten years. It is in our interest to encourage railroad expansion, caused by the requirements of commerce in times of peace, but at the same time serving military interests, and not place any difficulties in its way.

The political situation plainly indicates that in the near future, and probably also for a long time to come, we will have either no war or one against neighbors on two sides. In the latter case, we would stand on interior lines of operations between a completely ready and a slowly arming opponent.[36] Everything will depend on a correct and timely decision that we use a substantial majority of our active fighting forces first

36. Moltke no doubt meant France and Austria, respectively. In later years Russia was the eastern power that raised the specter of a two-front war.

against the one and then against the other opponent. By this we put them to double use.

However, we need a highly developed railroad net for that purpose, and we may say that each and every new construction of railroads is a military advantage.

Considering the enormous development of railroads, the thought of blocking our own railroad net by fortifications has to be abandoned.

A line as strong as the Rhine cannot completely isolate our rail system from the west even in connection with the destruction of the bridges. In the matter of railroad transport, distances count for nothing and the railroad lines will gain connection along roundabout ways through neutral territory. The question in international law of whether or not material carried on railroads is war contraband has not yet been decided. However, neutrality can be violated. Until very recently, all the permanent Rhine bridges were protected by the works of fortresses and there was grave doubt whether others should be constructed. At the present time, and in consideration of the concentration of large armies, we must desire that the number be increased. The necessity for more bridges across the larger interior rivers of the monarchy is clearly evident if we consider that at the present time more than twenty thousand axles are in daily movement west of the Rhine and more than 110,000 west of the Elbe. Together these would form a train 245 miles in length. This entire amount of rolling stock can be brought across the Rhine, if a retreat becomes necessary, on only four bridges. This could be done on seven bridges over the Elbe, unless it falls into the hands of the opponent, as was the case with a thousand rail cars in Prague in 1866.

For a concentration (*Konzentration*) in the west, an extraordinarily large number of transports would use Mainz. Therefore a new bridge there, below the mouth of the Main, is in the interest of the fortress itself, as well as in the interest of the easier handling of the trains there. The bridge would be dominated by the works of the fortress. There should therefore be no military objections to its construction. It will also be to the advantage of commerce, as is shown by the fact that one railroad company is now willing to construct such a bridge at its own expense. We urgently recommend that authority be granted for this.[37]

---

37. The editors of the German edition noted that such a bridge was completed in 1908.

The growth of railroads has compelled a change of opinion in regard to their destruction. The destruction of even one of the most important structures now means only a temporary interruption of service. Modern construction techniques think nothing either of laying a provisional track around a fortress or of constructing a viaduct a hundred feet long or high. Moreover, larger demolitions only create larger obstacles for us to overcome when we eventually resume the offensive.

We have to become convinced that only *active fighting forces can prevent the opponent from using our railroads*. It is more advantageous, especially in the case of advanced detachments falling back on a dispersed main body, to create a series of smaller breaks that become more numerous as we fall back. We can easily repair these breaks in our subsequent advance.

Taking up rails and carrying them back on the railroad, together with the line and signal men, deprives the enemy of use of the railroad. Even lines already in his possession can be repeatedly interrupted by the population or by raiding detachments. In the latter regard, an unusually large field of activity is offered to commandants of fortresses located off the railroads.

If an expansion of our railroad net is therefore to be viewed as entirely advantageous in a military sense, then a more favorable view should be accorded the military estimate of new railroad projects. The construction companies should not be compelled to build in directions not in consonance with commercial interests. It will always remain desirable that the lines pass by our fortresses wherever practicable. If, however, we burden the entrepreneurs with costly structures (including construction of armored towers) we impel them to avoid those desirable directions (approaching a fortress), even if the fortresses should be in their direct route.

It is impossible to regulate such vital elements of nations as commerce and communications according to military requirements. Nevertheless, the most unencumbered development of these elements at the same time furthers military objectives.

In granting concessions for the construction of new railroads in any desired direction we must therefore insist that the arrangements for demolition, costing so little, not be confined only to the large structures, but should be planned at many consecutive points suitable for that purpose. If a double track cannot be laid down at the very start, we probably ought to demand that switches be created for the passage of military trains every seven miles.

There is a great difference between the arrangements of a railroad struggling in the first stages of covering its initial costs and one that already runs perhaps twenty to thirty trains daily in different directions. In new construction we should therefore make arrangements for provisional platforms and switches at the stations.

Not every engineer detachment should be considered capable of constructing these improvised facilities nor capable of interrupting as well as reconstructing the railroads. It is already well known that we need a technical organization for that purpose, trained in time of peace and properly equipped with all necessary material. Because we will require them simultaneously on different lines and on many points of one line, their strength should not be too small. More than twenty thousand men were finally employed in that manner in the American Civil War.

It must not be forgotten that the railroads, above all, are the inland roads serving the conduct of war. Their complexity and the vulnerability of their mechanisms require order and tranquility for operation.

In the enemy's country, even after repairs of interruptions that presumably will be found there, only the few lines lying directly behind the front of our advance (and which we can secure by complete garrisons) need be secured. Still, use of these lines will present substantial difficulties. Most of the personnel will have departed. Communications with the few remaining men in a foreign language, with foreign designations, signals, and so forth, will require officials from the home country to exercise the greatest caution and strictest oversight.

Conditions are different when based on well-arranged organizations in familiar conditions in one's own country. We have seen that Austria understood how to transfer an army from the Isonzo to the Danube in the very short time of our advance from Sadowa to Vienna, despite being limited to a few serviceable rail lines. In contrast to lines in foreign countries, railroads in our interior allow not only movements to the front and rear but also to one side or the other. Without requiring special great efforts, one division of thirteen battalions, twelve squadrons, and thirty guns can be transferred by rail within twenty-four hours to any point up to 180 miles away.

It need not be pointed out how easily threatened fortresses can thereby be relieved, how the difficulties of a formal siege can be increased, how the enemy's communications can be threatened, and how important it is for coastal defense and for measures against the enemy's flank and rear. All this assumes that railroads run in all those directions.

This shows that the railroads serve the defense better than the offense. With respect to materials, the defensive is the stronger form. In every state a portion of the defensive forces remains tied down locally and only the surplus portion becomes active externally. Both portions participate in the defense. However, the offensive will always remain the more desirable form.

If the sum of all fighting means is known and an increase is not foreseen, the main point will then be to strengthen the offense with the means of the defense. This is preferably done by the new element—the railroads.

TELEGRAPHS (1871–81)

Significance of Telegraphs[38]

The telegraph substantially assists the high command in making estimates of the military situation.

The ability to send reports quickly to even the most distant points and by circuitous routes offers the means to direct separated parts of the army according to a single will toward a common goal.

It is therefore imperative to establish telegraphic communications in every possible place. All independently operating parts of the army must always take care quickly to establish and maintain connections with the telegraph networks in their rear so that they can send reports and receive orders in a timely manner. Telegraphic or telephonic communications between detachments of the corps and field armies must be established during lengthy halts and even during engagements.

It has become increasingly important to maintain the secrecy of one's intentions and to restrict communications concerning operations to only

---

38. In the interest of saving space, the editor has omitted some minor passages in this section. The German title of this essay was *"Bedeutung der Telegraphen für die Kriegführung."*

what is most essential. Anything that is known in the army and that is reported home in letters or telegrams will quickly come to the attention of the enemy, who frequently has access to the telegraphic traffic of neutral states.

Private telegrams from a headquarters must be censored by authorities knowledgeable of the military situation. Telegraphic and written reports by newspaper reporters must especially be subjected to strict control, assuming that they are allowed access to the headquarters, which is entirely contrary to military interests. Under certain conditions it may be necessary to discontinue all telegraphic communications and even letters to the homeland in order to protect important secrets for a few days. Secrecy of especially important communications must be secured by the use of codes.

Telegraph lines are more easily disrupted than are rail lines. They can be protected only by strict punishment for all unauthorized damage. As in the case of railroads, destruction, as a rule, requires orders from higher headquarters. Nevertheless, communications that undoubtedly serve the enemy—those which are behind the enemy front—are to be destroyed. Even the smallest cavalry patrol can perform this useful function. It is especially important to locate the constantly expanding underground telegraph lines, which usually run along large roads and sometimes along railroad lines. Special care should be devoted to foiling the enemy's efforts to interfere with our own telegraph lines.

ACCOMPLISHMENTS OF THE TELEGRAPH

The Campaign of 1866

The field telegraph units expended the greatest efforts to meet the high command's requirements. They succeeded in this to a very great extent. Nevertheless, the lines they constructed to the rear were frequently disrupted. Villages were threatened with strong measures if this occurred near them again. Frequently this disruption happened because our soldiers were ignorant of the value of the telegraph. These types of disruption were especially distressful during the exchange of views with Paris. Important telegrams arrived only after many days or not at all. Thus, in the middle of July, Mr. Benedetti preferred to relocate from royal headquarters to Vienna so that he could use the reliable telegraph lines between Vienna and Paris.[39]

The Campaign of 1870–71[40]

To the Encirclement of Metz and Paris

After the German advance into France, royal headquarters and both the First and Second armies at first had to use the telegraph line between Saarbrücken and Kreuznach, while the Third Army used the line Landau-Ludwigshafen. The field telegraph units joined their advancing lines as follows: for the royal headquarters and the Second Army, through Remilly to Pont-à-Mousson; the First Army through Buschborn to Waibelskirchen (Varize); and the Third Army through Hagenau, Ober-Modern, and Lunéville to Nancy. The following crossing lines provided communications between those lines: Saint-Avold–Buschborn, Lützelstein-Saargemünd-Beningen and, later, Nancy–Pont-à-Mousson. In addition, individual short lines were established along the stretch Hagenau-Bendenheim-Steinburg for the Baden Division at Strassburg.

During the fighting around Metz the telegraph was extended close to the battlefields, to Courcelles, Gorze, and Thiaucourt. After we surrounded the fortress, telegraph lines connected the headquarters of the corps and individual divisions. Shortages of material prevented establishment of wire communications between the outposts and their headquarters. Relays and visual signaling had to take the place of the telegraph. A line was established between Mézières and Ueckingen for communication with the siege units at Diedenhofen. In August the state telegraph authority established a line from Pont-à-Mousson for the units surrounding Metz and from there, going around Verdun, to Clermont in the Argonne.

39. This reference is to Count Vincent Benedetti, the French ambassador to Prussia. On his role in the origins of the war, see Howard, *Franco-Prussian War,* 52–55. A more complete account is in Willard Allen Fletcher's *The Mission of Count Benedetti to Berlin, 1864–1870* (The Hague: Mouton, 1965).

40. For full citations of the German and English editions of the larger work, see notes 44 and 46 in the introduction.

During the advance on Chalons, the royal headquarters used the line from Bar-le-Duc to Commercy, which branched out from Commercy via Thiaucourt to the Third Army, going around the fortress of Toul. Because rapid communications were then particularly necessary among the individual parts of the operating armies, all available strength had to be employed from August 21 to August 25 to connect the corps headquarters of the Third Army with the army command and the royal headquarters. Telegraph lines then immediately followed the army as it marched to the right to Varennes and Cernay en Dormois. Cavalry relays met the requirements of telegraphic communications from the latter point because of the exhaustion of all telegraphic materials. Immediately after the battle of Sedan, the city was connected through Montmédy and Consenvoye with the line between Clermont and Metz.

During the subsequent march on Paris, royal headquarters and the Army of the Meuse constructed telegraphic communications on the line Nancy-Paris, which later was extended from Lagny to Ferrieres and Versailles. In this manner royal headquarters remained in continuous communication with the units investing Metz and Strassburg and with the advancing parts of the army. In the meantime, the Army of the Meuse had connected Laon (after its surrender) with Riems and by the time of its arrival at Paris had placed in operation the line Lagny–Roissy–Saint-Brice. This was done by September 20. The Third Army extended its communications from Épernay through Montmirail to Coulmiers during its advance. This line from Coulmiers connected with the main line at La Ferté sous Jouarre and extended as far as Palaiseau through Villeneuve–Saint-Georges and Longjumeau.

During the events described above, it had become clear that the means available for field telegraphy were not sufficient for the goals at hand. From the outset, the army headquarters were unable to remain in contact with their corps. On the other hand, the field and rear telegraph services performed all that was necessary to ensure linkage between the army headquarters and the permanent telegraph net in the rear.

The field telegraph detachments usually worked in the front lines, and their materials were brought forward by the rear-area telegraph detachments. The latter in turn disassembled their temporary lines gradually as the state telegraph service extended its permanent lines.

At the beginning of the war it was not always possible to prevent our own units from thoroughly destroying the superficially constructed French telegraph lines. This made their rapid restoration difficult. The

German field lines were also damaged through carelessness. To this were added the facts that the engineers attached to the field telegraph sections originally had no practice in repairing the French lines and that they lacked the necessary materials. Although all these difficulties were overcome with time, at the end of August the pressing need for expanded field telegraphic services was evident. Prussia fielded five field and three rear-area telegraph detachments. In addition, Bavaria had a rear-area detachment and one field telegraph detachment for each of its two corps. Württemberg had one field telegraph detachment.

As a result, in September two field and two rear-area telegraph detachments were formed. They entered the theater of war at the beginning of October.

In order to ease the work of the state telegraph agency, which had taken over the telegraph service between the field army and the homeland, and which was able to perform this task only with great difficulty, telegraph directorates were formed in Nancy, Épernay, and Lagny.

In this manner the telegraph service gradually succeeded in fully mastering the wide field of its activity, although the vast extension of the theater of war and the rapid movement of the units frequently caused very great difficulties. It frequently happened that lines constructed with great effort had to be dismantled when a headquarters abandoned its march objective because of a change in the situation or the order countermanding the one for the construction of the line arrived too late. Construction of lines was accomplished most rapidly when the telegraph detachments were attached to the advance guard and kept pace with it. Often they rushed ahead of the advance guard under a special guard. In such cases the telegraph stations sometimes came under enemy fire or had to withdraw in the face of a sudden enemy advance.

The unfavorable weather was not without influence. It slowed construction or destroyed lines already completed. Finally, the repeated intentional damage inflicted by local inhabitants and guerrillas was disruptive. This could not be prevented because of the length of the lines and the weaknesses of the occupation units, in spite of their great alertness.

To the End of the Campaign

During the siege of Paris, Versailles became the permanent center of the constantly expanding telegraph system. After the lines constructed at the outset of the blockade had been gradually expanded to a complete circle around the city, two parallel lines surrounded the capital. Starting at Versailles, these lines traversed the following places: Longjumeau, Villeneuve–Saint-Georges, Lagny, Gonesse, Margency, and Saint-Germain en Laye. One of these lines, into which flowed the lines from the outside, provided the primary communications of the royal headquarters with the army commands and the rear-area services. The other one, with its numerous branches, provided communications between the individual parts of the army investing Paris. It connected not only all the corps headquarters and the outlying divisions and brigades, but also important points of the outpost lines and observation points and, later, the groups of siege batteries in their areas. Two main lines provided communications with Germany. They stretched from Lagny through Bar-le-Duc and Nancy to Landau, and from Riems and Metz to Saarbrücken. After the armistice went into effect, the forts were connected with the encircling line and with each other. In addition, during the occupation of Paris, three stations were established within the capital.

For communications with the armies entrusted with protecting the encirclement of Paris, during the course of the campaign lines were established to Amiens, Rouen, Dreux, Chartres, Orléans, and Montargis through Melun and Montbard to Dijon and through Troyes to Chaumont-en-Bassigny. The lines of the armies and detached forces fighting in the provinces joined the main lines at those points.

When the First Army advanced toward the Oise after the fall of Metz, the field telegraph followed it by using the existing lines through Riems and Soissons. Before the battle of Amiens, lines were laid from the previous terminal station at Montdidier to Breteuil and Moreuil in order to ease communications with the army's flanks. As soon as the line continued to Amiens after its fall, direct communications with Versailles, through Creil, were established. With the further march of the army to Rouen, two lines were established leading from Amiens through Poix and Buchy and through Poix and Gournay to Rouen.

After the victory on the Hallue,[41] we made efforts to link the sepa-

---

41. This reference is to a minor engagement near Amiens in December 1870. Each side lost about a thousand men, the French another thousand as prisoners during their retreat. See Howard, *Franco-Prussian War*, 394–95.

rately operating parts of the army as much as possible. Thus lines were erected from Amiens through Corbie and Albert and in the area near Peronne, which continued from there to Combles and Ham. After the battle at Bapaume and the fall of Peronne, these lines were improved. Amiens was connected with La Fère through Ham. Thus the forces united in the Somme position gained all the advantages of expeditious reports and orders. This was of value during the operations before the battle of Saint-Quentin. During the pursuit a line was established from Ham to Saint-Quentin and Bantouzelle.

When the Bavarian I Corps and the 22d Infantry Division were sent to Orléans and Chartres at the beginning of October, both locations were joined to the lines encircling Paris. The former line had to be partially abandoned after the engagement at Coulmiers, so that Toury formed the final station for the Grand Duke of Mecklenburg's newly formed army detachment. As soon as the Second Army approached and the detachment took up a position between Chartres and Rambouillet, Épernon was connected with Nogent-le-Roi. The lines followed the grand duke's advance toward Le Mans in early November and passed through Nogent-le-Rotrou. At the same time, the rear telegraph net was expanded by lines from Versailles through Dreux, Chartres, and Bonneval to Arpajon. During the further movements of the army detachment to Beaugency and later to Toury, the line to Chartres was maintained, as was the direct union with the Second Army's lines from Bonneval through Biabon to Toury.

The Second Army constructed two lines—from Blesme through Montierender and Chaumont-en-Bassigny to Troyes—as it moved from Metz toward the middle Loire. During the army's accelerated marches from the area around Troyes-Chaumont to the west, telegraphic communications were extended from Troyes through Sens to Nemours, and later from Pithiviers. Subsequent lines were joined from Versailles through Corbeil, by repairing French lines, and also through Angerville.

The lines in the Second Army's area could be improved right up to the struggle at Orléans. During the battle the lines were extended forward and into the city itself on December 5. Thereafter, lines were extended to the advanced corps from Orléans to Châteauneuf, Beaugency, and La Ferté Saint-Aubin.

During the advance of III and X corps toward Tours, the line from Orléans to Beaugency was extended through Blois to Vendôme. In the second half of December the Second Army concentrated in the area around Orléans and the army detachment took up a position near Chartres. The telegraph net was expanded by the line Vendôme-Châteaudun-Bonneval, Châteaudun-Orléans, Chartres-Courville, and Châteauneuf-Montargis-Gien. The latter line was extended to Briare on December 31.

During the movement of units toward Le Mans at the beginning of January, telegraph lines were extended in that direction from Chartres through Rogent-le-Rotrou and from Vendôme through Saint-Calais. After the occupation of Le Mans, connections were immediately established between that city and Alençon, Conlie, Château Courville, La Fontaine, and through Tours to Châteaudun and Blois. As the XII Corps fell back from Alençon to Rouen, it established a line from Chartres through Evreux to Rouen. An additional line went from there through Buchy to Dieppe.

In the southeastern theater of war, the headquarters (at Mundolsheim) of the force laying siege to Strassburg were connected with Bendenheim, near the battlefield of Kronenburg, with the Baden Division at Oberschäffolsheim, and through Rastatt to the detachment in Kehl.

After the fall of the fortress [Strassburg], the XIV Corps advanced to the south. The line from Blainville-la-Grande to Épinal was joined to the large line Landau-Nancy-Paris. The shortage of material precluded the establishment of additional telegraph links. Only after Dijon was taken could the stretch of line from Épinal to Vesoul be placed in operation.

The wide extension of the XIV Corps's deployment early in November made the requirement for rapid communications especially evident. Although one rear-area telegraph detachment and a small amount of material was available, Vesoul was successfully connected with La Chapelle (through Lure) and with Dijon (through Gray). This contributed substantially to the corps' concentration in Vesoul, which was accomplished in only two days after receipt of the order on December 26. The stations at Dijon, Mirebeau sur Beze, and Gray were abandoned and a new line for the 4th Reserve Division was established from Vesoul to Villersexel.

When the corps again marched northward at the beginning of January, the lines constructed south of the stretch between Vesoul and La Chapelle had to be abandoned, as were the stations west of Lure during the final concentration behind the Lisaine. Communication with royal headquarters was possible only through Mühlhausen. Within twenty-four hours, the most important points of the Lisaine position were connected with royal headquarters. Thus it was possible telegraphically to send reports and orders during the ensuing battle. This was of substantial importance for the conduct of the engagement. During the further movements after the battle, and for the common operations with the other parts of the newly formed South Army, lines were established from Lure through Villersexel to Rougemont, and, gradually, from Lure through Vesoul, Gray, and La Barre to Byans.

After the French East Army crossed into Swiss territory, lines were constructed from La Barre through Dôle to Lons-le-Saunier and Dijon, as well as from Gray to Fontaine Française and Auxonne, and through Dijon to Beaune and Montbard.

In spite of their early lack of practice, the increasing capabilities of the new telegraph formations were up to the demands placed on them. They proved themselves as an effective and indispensable means for facilitating political and military activities.

By the end of the war the field telegraph service reached a length of 10,830 kilometers, of which 8,252 were reconstructed French lines, 798 kilometers provisional, and 1,780 field lines. It had 408 stations. The state telegraph service maintained 12,500 kilometers of wire and 118 stations.

CHAPTER THREE
THE BATTLE

In the essays printed in this chapter, Moltke discusses basic features of the most important aspect of the Prussian army's theory of war: the battle. From Clausewitz to the end of the Second World War, German theorists, not to mention field commanders, emphasized the destruction of the main enemy army as the basis of operations and as the determining feature of military strategy. The reader should pay particular attention to Moltke's definition of strategy and tactics, to the absence of any idea of "levels of war," and to the absence of an "operational level" between tactics and strategy.

In their consideration of the conduct of the battle, these essays employ the two fundamental principles of the initiative of the subordinate commander and cooperation of the three basic arms. Although this volume concentrates on Moltke's theories on the art of war at the expense of many of his tactical concepts and essays, the reader will find much in these pages about tactical issues during Moltke's days as chief of the General Staff.

The editor has selected these essays from volume four, part three of Moltke's *Military Works.*[1] When printing them in that original volume, the General Staff relied primarily on previously unpublished or little-known essays, documents from its archives, and, for historical examples, on its official histories.

---

1. *Moltkes Militärische Werke*, 4, part 3: *Moltkes Kriegslehren: Die Schlacht* (1912).

STRATEGY

Strategy is a system of expedients; it is more than a mere scholarly discipline.[2] It is the translation of knowledge to practical life, the improvement of the original leading thought in accordance with continually changing situations. It is the art of acting under the pressure of the most difficult conditions.

Strategy is the application of sound human sense to the conduct of war; its teachings (*Lehren*) go little beyond the first requirements of common sense. Its value lies entirely in concrete application. The main point is correctly to estimate at each moment the changing situation and then to do the simplest and most natural things with firmness and caution. Thus war becomes an art—an art, of course, which is served by many sciences.[3]

In war, as in art, we find no universal forms; in neither can a rule (*Regel*) take the place of talent.

General theories, and the resulting rules and systems, therefore cannot possibly have practical value in strategy. Strategy is not constituted like abstract scholarly disciplines. The latter have their firm and definite truths upon which one can build and from which one can go farther. The square of the hypotenuse is always the sum of the square of the other two sides, no matter whether the right triangle is large or small, or whether its apex is pointed east or west.

Archduke Charles maintained that strategy was a scholarly discipline (*Wissenschaft*), tactics an art. He held that this "scholarly discipline of the commander in chief" (*Feldherr*) should "determine the course of military undertakings" and that the "art" had only to execute the strategic projects.

General von Clausewitz, on the other hand, says: "Strategy is the employment of battle to gain the ends of war"[4] and, as a matter of

2. Moltke used *Wissenschaft,* here translated as scholarly discipline rather than the English term "science."

3. Moltke's words on this point left a lasting impression on Prusso-German military theory. The German army's classic manual of the Second World War began with the statement: "The conduct of war is an art, a free creative activity based on a disciplined (*wissenschaftliche*) foundation." See Germany, Chef der Heeresleitung, *Truppenführung,* 2 vols. (Berlin: E. S. Mittler & Son, 1933), 1, 1.

4. Clausewitz, *On War,* 177, contains this citation from book 3, chapter 1. The reader consulting the passage cited here should be aware that the frequent use of "op-

fact, strategy furnishes tactics with the means for battle and assures probability of victory by directing the movements of the armies and bringing them together on the battlefield. On the other hand, strategy reaps the fruits of success of each battle and makes new arrangements based thereon. In the face of a tactical victory the demands of strategy become silent. These demands attach themselves to the new situation. Strategy must keep the means that tactics require in readiness at the proper time and place.[5]

The strategic object governs the premeditated decision (*Entschluss*) to engage in battle. A resulting accidental encounter, which happens often, is purely an act of tactics. Strategy governs the movements of the army for the planned battle; the manner of execution is the province of tactics. The former issues directives, the latter orders.[6]

VICTORY AND SUPERIORITY (c. 1875–80)

Rapid Decision[7]

The character of the present-day conduct of war is marked by the attempt to obtain a great and rapid decision. Calling into service all

---

erational" in the English translation lacks a true German equivalent. The word "operational" appears well over two hundred times in the English version, but only about six times in the German, and then in a much narrower context linked to lines or bases of operations. The translation renders more than thirty German words as "operation."

5. In this discussion, as did Clausewitz and virtually all other German theorists, Moltke upholds the traditional division of war into the two spheres of tactics and strategy. German theory, unlike modern American doctrine, did not interpose a third level (operational) between tactics and strategy. Moltke frequently used the term *operativ*, but not as an equivalent to the modern terms "operational" or "operational level of war."

6. Directives (*Weisungen*), in the German usage, were general instructions used by higher commanders. Orders (*Befehle*) were more specific and usually related to tactical situations. Moltke frequently issued restrictive orders, just as lower commanders could issue directives to their subordinates if that were appropriate. Everything depended on the situation, and it would be a mistake to draw firm lines either between directives or orders or between which levels of command should issue them.

7. The German title was: *Sieg und Ueberlegenheit. Schnelle Entscheidung.*

those capable of bearing arms; the strength of armies; the difficulties of sustaining them; the enormous cost of being under arms; the disruption of commerce, manufacture, and agriculture; the battle-ready organization of the armies and the ease with which they are assembled, all press for early termination of the war.

Smaller battles have little effect on this early termination of the conflict; still, they make possible and open the way to the main decision by battle.

HISTORICAL EXAMPLES

The Campaign of 1866

"Such a rapidly concluded campaign is unbelievable. After exactly five weeks we returned to Berlin." Very few marches sufficed to concentrate the main armies—the First and Second armies—in the eastern theater of war along the line Bautzen-Glatz on the Bohemian frontier. Nonetheless, the final concentration could be accomplished only through driving the enemy back, through engagements. We required only ten days to force the Austrians to accept decisive battle. On the morning of the day of Königgrätz, July 3, our forces occupied an eighteen-mile front. With such an extension the enemy dared not allow themselves to be attacked. On the other hand, the offensive advance concentrated all the corps on the battlefield itself and thus changed the strategic disadvantage of separation into the tactical advantage of completely enveloping the enemy.

The Prussian army detachments that had started at Dresden (the Army of the Elbe), Görlitz, and Frankenstein, on June 22 were before Vienna and Pressburg on July 22. Within thirty days they had covered 225 miles in the direction of the main operation.

In the eight days of the main engagements, two hundred guns, eleven colors and standards, and 39,800 prisoners were captured. Deducting all losses, including all detachments guarding hostile fortresses and securing rear communications, 184,000 combatants, three-quarters of the original effective strength (254,000), as against 271,000 Austrians, arrived at the Danube.

This number could have been very quickly brought back to more than two hundred thousand by calling up the echelons still in the rear.

Sufficient siege guns and bridging materials were available and, considering the spirit of the troops after their unbroken successes, the intention was to carry operations to the farther bank of the Danube when French mediation succeeded in finding a basis for peace.[8]

The objective in the western theater of war was reached without a great decisive battle and only through smaller engagements. This objective was to terminate the war with Prussia occupying the entirety of, or at least the larger part of, the territory of all her enemies so that she could dictate the conditions of peace. Unity of leadership and unceasing activity offset the enemy's numerical superiority.

The Prussian forces at Wetzlar, Minden, and Hamburg—separated by some 220 miles—could be concentrated only in the course of operations against the enemy. Here, however, in contrast to the unity of Austrian leadership, we saw contingents of eight different states from the Leine to the Danube. They were more or less unprepared and were united only in their hostility to Prussia. None of them was in a position to stand alone against Prussia. Their particularist concerns could be overcome by the direst emergency only to the extent that six of them were finally concentrated at the end of the campaign.[9] It thus became possible to take the offensive with 47,000 Prussians against 100,000 allies and to advance, in forty-seven days, 335 miles from the Elbe to the Jaxt.

The Campaign of 1870–71

The war, carried on with enormous forces (pitting in August 1870 approximately 500,000 Germans against 300,000 French) was finished in the short space of seven months.

8. Prussian troops were well outside Vienna when the armistice was concluded. The final treaty called for the Prussian army to withdraw from Austrian territory. Bismarck thus prevented the army from making its desired victory parade through Vienna.

9. "Particularist concerns" refers to the seemingly endless small-state rivalries (political, cultural, economic) among the many smaller German states. This phenomenon persisted even within the army until the First World War. See the editor's *The King's Finest*. For the larger context of particularism, the reader might consult some of the standard surveys of German history. Hajo Holborn's *History of Modern Germany* incorporates a discussion of this problem, especially in volume 3.

Eight battles were fought within the first four weeks (Wörth, Spicheren, Colombey-Nouilly, Vionville–Mars-la-Tour, Gravelotte–Saint-Privat, Beaumont, Sedan, Noisseville), causing the French army to abandon the field.

After the Fall of Metz, more than 300,000 men, 10,000 officers, 4 marshals, and an emperor were in captivity. Nothing like this had happened since the Babylonian captivity of the Jews. Nevertheless, the government in Paris and Tours persisted in its resistance and forced the unfortunate country deeper into ruin. The people were armed in all provinces.

Enormous but inferior new formations offset our original numerical superiority. It thus became necessary to fight twelve new battles (Amiens, Beaune-la-Rolande, Villiers-Champigny, Loigny-Poupry, Orléans, Beaugency-Cravant, Hallue, Bapaume, Le Mans, Lisaine, Saint-Quentin, Valérien) to secure the decisive siege of the hostile capital.

Twenty fortified places were taken, and there was hardly a day on which no large or small engagements took place.

The war required great sacrifices of the Germans, who lost 6,247 officers, 123,453 men, one flag, and four guns. The total loss to France cannot be stated; however, there were the following French prisoners: in Germany, 11,680 officers and 371,881 men; in Paris, 7,456 officers and 241,686 men; disarmed in Switzerland, 2,192 officers and 88,381 men. This was a total of 21,328 officers and 701,948 men. The Germans captured 107 flags, 1,915 field guns, and 5,526 siege or fortress guns.

Strassburg and Metz, taken from the fatherland in times of weakness, were won back and the German Empire rose again.[10]

VICTORY THE MAIN POINT—SUPERIORITY (c. 1875–80)

Rallying Positions

Victory in the decisions of arms is the most important moment in war. It alone breaks the enemy's will and forces him to submit to our will. Neither the occupation of a certain piece of terrain nor the cap-

---

10. In 1919 the Treaty of Versailles returned both Strassburg and Metz to France. Born in victory, the Second Reich expired in a military defeat.

ture of a fortified place, but only the destruction of the hostile fighting force will be decisive as a rule. It is therefore the most important object of all operations.

Everything available must be thrown into battle in all circumstances, for one can never have too much strength or too many chances for victory. The very last remaining battalion should therefore be brought to the battlefield. Many battles have been decided by units (*Truppenkörper*) arriving on the battlefield only in the evening of the day of battle.

It would be wrong to leave a part of the units in rallying positions to protect a retreat. By doing so we weaken the forces whose victory in any case makes a retreat unnecessary, and whose retreat is seldom brought to a halt by a rallying position, which is all too easily swept along by the pursuit.

Tactical victory secures all strategic connections. For that reason all available forces must be brought up. It is unnecessary to emphasize the fact that a numerical superiority of between thirty thousand and forty thousand men makes itself felt in every situation, provided only that this superiority is at the correct place on the day of decision. There is absolutely no way to assure one's success against an enemy possessing a twofold numerical superiority. Consequently, one should not lightly seek a decision with a smaller army if one can become superior within a few days.

If the concentrated strength of a still-separated enemy is greater than ours, we dare not await completion of our concentration. On the contrary, we must attack with what is available if there is any chance at all of a partial victory.

THE BATTLE (c. 1866–80)

War has the object (*Zweck*) of executing government policy by force of arms. Battle is the means to break the opponent's will to resist. These same intentions are the basis of all large and small actions. They are the means to bring about the situation that finds its solution in a decisive battle. But they are not the only means. Many important objects of the war can be attained without fighting: by marches or by choice of positions—in short, by operations.

An enveloping movement that causes the enemy to retreat; a rear guard, which by its action and position induces the enemy to desist from attack; a reconnaissance that has seen what it desired to see, all have reached their objectives without combat.

We must never forget that a battle cannot be fought without sacrifices and that its outcome can seldom be foreseen with certainty. The main objectives of the war can be attained only by destruction of the hostile army in the open field, that is, through battle.

We must not lose sight of the fact that there are essential differences in the goals and in the manner of command of large and small units. What is necessary for the former is not right for the latter. Space and time have for each a different meaning. The agility of the units and the personal influence of the commanders are greater and the peculiarities of the terrain are of decisive influence [for smaller units].

The handling of large formations (*Heereskörper*) cannot be learned in time of peace. One is limited to the study of particular conditions (for instance the terrain), and to the study of experiences of prior campaigns. But the progress of technology and new armaments, in short, entirely different conditions, suggest that neither the means previously employed to gain victory nor the rules established by even the greatest commanders may apply in the present.

Peacetime maneuvers, even those on the largest scale, allow only a very incomplete picture of actual war. In maneuvers, units arrange for their provisions far in advance and their movement does not depend on their burdensome though necessary trains. But above all, in peacetime maneuvers the decision of arms lacks the realistic effect of the moral element, and decisions (*Entschlüsse*) are not made under the pressure of the heavy responsibility of real war.

Leadership in Battle

As a rule, battle is the normal consequence of the deployment. The last march orders usually take the place of previous battle dispositions. Given the current extended battlefield,[11] a unified command of an army on the day of battle is possible only in a very general way.

---

11. Here Moltke used the term *"ausgedehnte Verhältnisse,"* by which he clearly meant the expanded battlefields of his time, as compared with experience in earlier wars of the eighteenth and nineteenth centuries.

Commanders of army corps and even of divisions must judge the situation for themselves and must know how to act independently in consonance with the general intention. Undue haste or an attack by columns meeting the enemy before support can be given by neighboring columns is dangerous when opposed by a strong enemy, and can lead to defeats. But when the enemy is not yet deployed, taking the initiative is of the utmost value. In that case one must not hesitate to commence the battle, but one should always keep the battle objective consistent with available forces.

When the enemy is encountered, or when the advance units report his approach, the higher commanders should proceed to their leading detachments to orient themselves personally as to the strength, position, and movements of the enemy and the terrain on which the battle probably will be fought. But they should take care that during their absence the units do not become engaged without their knowledge and consent.

A calm examination of the situation must precede the decision to commence a battle. Very seldom will it be possible to break off combat without serious losses and without endangering the morale of the units, especially once the infantry has become seriously engaged.

It is further important to find the correct moment for commencing a serious engagement. The orderly tactical deployment (*Entwicklung*) of at least a part of the forces must, as a rule, take place first—unless the main objective is to contain a retreating opponent.

It is not easy to discern the correct moment for the tactical deployment of the march columns, but it is of great importance. The units should remain in march formation as long as security allows, because a premature deployment delays their arrival and consumes their strength to a very great extent. If the enemy is in a defensive position, the heads of the columns should not be allowed to approach too closely before deploying. This is to avoid premature, costly, and perhaps decisive combat.

In addition to the chief of the General Staff, who remains at the side of the commanding general during the entire action, the following should receive the necessary information of the decision: the commanders of the cavalry and artillery, and the senior engineer officer. Thereafter, these officers must keep themselves continuously informed as to the further intentions [of the commanding general].

At the commencement of an engagement all high commanders should proceed to more rearward positions that allow a sufficient overview and which make them visible to their units. There they will remain so that reports will reach them without delay and with certainty. With the exception of those few cases where their personal intervention may be necessary, it is of far greater importance that they keep a clear overview than that they assist in a few minor details.

In large battles it will usually be irrelevant whether the supreme commander views any single part of the battlefield or not. He must act on the basis of reports and will often have a clearer conception of the situation if he receives his information from all parts of the battlefield in the same manner. He can then calmly reach his decisions far from the confusing effects of the fighting.

The decision (*Entscheidung*) of a battle begins when one side gives up the battle as lost. Many times battles have been won because the enemy believed himself beaten before the victor did, even though he was no less shaken. In case of doubt, one must therefore persist.

Near the end of the battle—when the units have perhaps become intermingled after leaving their original positions, and when impressions of all sorts make their effects felt on the supreme commander in rapid succession—it will be of great importance (though very difficult) for him to develop a clear picture of the condition of his and the hostile units, and of the entire situation. Far-reaching orders, possibly the most important of the entire campaign, may now be demanded of the commander in chief.

The supreme commander accomplishes the most when the decision (*Entschluss*) approaches, if he has a clear view of the operations necessitated by the result of the battle. These may be exploitation of the victory or compensation for a defeat. The correct starting point for a new phase of operations lies on the battlefield itself.

Independence of Subordinate Commanders

Because of the diversity and the rapid changes in the situations in war, it is impossible to lay down binding rules. Only principles and general points of view can furnish a guide.

Prearranged designs (*Schema*) collapse, and only a proper estimate of the situation can show the commander the correct way. The advantage of the situation will never be fully utilized if subordinate commanders wait for orders. Only if leaders of all ranks are competent for and accustomed to independent action will the possibility exist of moving large masses with ease. The absence of these characteristics inevitably leads to loss of time.

In time of peace, the habit of acting in accordance with correct principles can be learned only if every officer is allowed the greatest possible independence. In that case, the practical intelligence of subordinate commanders will understand how to act in war according to the wishes of the superior commander, even when the latter cannot expressly state his will because of time and conditions.

In doubtful cases and in unclear conditions (which occur so often in war), it will generally be more advisable to proceed actively and keep the initiative than to await the law of the opponent.[12] The opponent frequently can see our situation just as incompletely as we can see his, and will occasionally give way where the actual situation itself would not have required it.

Leaders of individual parts of the army must remember the old rule always to march in the direction of the cannon thunder. Tasks (*Aufträge*) prescribing another direction must be reexamined to ascertain whether they were issued under conditions that did not foresee the ensuing engagement. In most cases, support rendered on the battlefield is of more value than execution of a special task. In the face of a tactical victory all other considerations recede into the background.

HISTORICAL EXAMPLES

The Campaign of 1864

On February 2, 1864, the Prussian I Corps under Prince Friedrich Karl was to advance from the country between the Eider and the Eckernförde Inlet to the line Eckernförde-Kochendorf-Holm. It reached

---

12. Here Moltke used the phrase *"als das Gesetz vom Gegner zu erwarten,"* another variation of the "law of the battlefield" as used in modern Western armies. Here, as always, Moltke emphasizes the will and activity of the enemy rather than abstract and impersonal concepts such as dominate some modern armies. In this view, the battlefield has no law in itself. Such laws are the product of either friendly or enemy action.

that line by 9:00 A.M. The corps could have accomplished its assignment (*Aufgabe*) early in the morning, but it would have been forced to take up a front on two sides, toward Fleckeby as well as toward Missunde. The prince therefore independently decided to continue the march to Missunde that day to take possession of the forward land or even of the bridgehead itself. Underlying this decision was the consideration that the Danes probably would not hold, but would abandon their trenches at Missunde if effectively fired on by the artillery. In any case, the prince acted entirely in the sense of his broader task: to arrive at Flensburg ahead of the enemy after the other two corps had taken the trenches.

As is well known, the undertaking against Missunde on that day failed; the crossing at Arnis was not accomplished until February 6. Nevertheless, the decision arrived at independently demonstrates a correct appreciation of conditions and the enterprising spirit of the commanding general.

The Campaign of 1866

Information on the decision by royal headquarters to attack on July 3 had been brought to the I Corps of the Second Army early in the morning by the adjutant, Count Finckenstein, who had to pass through the I Corps district on his trip to the crown prince.[13] Count Finckenstein handed the letter to the outpost commander for immediate transmittal to the commanding general, Gen. [Adolf Karl] von Bonin. This letter contained orders for the immediate assembly of the units and left it to the general to advance independently even before arrival of orders from Königinhof.

General von Bonin believed that he had to wait for these orders. They arrived at 7:45 A.M., or, as has been stated by the orderly officer carrying them, at 7:15 in Ober-Praussnitz. Corps headquarters issued its orders one hour later.

For a long time detachments of the advance guard at Chroustow had

---

13. Count Reinhold Finck von Finckenstein was an adjutant to Wilhelm I. He was killed at the battle of Vionville in 1870 while commanding the 2d Guard Dragoon Regiment.

heard cannon thunder coming from the area of Sadowa, but had sent no special report of it to corps headquarters. At 9:20 the advance guard received orders to start. Its vanguard started at 9:30.

Before corps headquarters started the march, it heard the heavy artillery fire. The march was then expedited as much as possible. The corps sent a general staff officer ahead to obtain information on the engagement.

At eleven o'clock the advance guard had not yet reached Gross-Bürglitz and the rear of the corps was still at the Elbe. At 3:00 P.M. the corps was still back between Wrchownitz and Benatek, where parts of the Guard and the VII corps had, at that time, already defeated the Austrian right wing (II and IV corps) and had advanced as far as Rosberitz-Lochenitz. Only after 3:00 P.M. did the I Corps advance guard successfully enter the battle at Rosberitz.

Informed of the situation at 3:00 P.M., and thus fully aware that his corps had to make a lengthy march, the I Corps commander could have used his own discretion to alert his corps at once and to place it in readiness at Gross-Bürglitz. There he would have been opposite the First Army's left wing (7th Division at Cerekwitz) and, as the battle turned out later, his support in the fight for possession of the Swiep Forest would have been extremely valuable.[14]

The case stood differently with the division commanders of the Guard Corps and VI Corps. The 1st Guard Division was in and around Königinhof, its advance guard at Daubrawitz. The thunder of cannon coming from Daubrawitz induced Gen. [Constantin] von Alvensleben to start

14. The Swiep Forest was a key area northwest of Königgrätz at the far left wing of the Prussian First Army. That army's 7th Division, under the command of General von Fransecky, fought a costly battle there against superior Austrian forces until elements of the Second Army arrived from the north to assist by attacking the Austrian right flank. Here the account implies that the corps commander, General von Bonin, should have exercised his initiative by moving rapidly to the developing battle in the Swiep Forest. Instead, Bonin refused to move until the Second Army commander, Crown Prince Frederick, had given him a direct order to do so. On this somewhat complicated action, see Craig, *Königgrätz*, 113–14. More complete accounts may be found in Oscar von Lettow-Vorbeck, *Geschichte des Krieges von 1866 in Deutschland*, 2 vols. (Berlin: E. S. Mittler, 1896–99), 2, 437ff. The official Prussian account, translated here, is less critical but leaves no doubt that Moltke was not satisfied with Bonin's performance.

with his advance guard at 8:00 A.M., without waiting for orders, and march toward Jeritschek. There he expected, on the basis of information previously received, to encounter the enemy's right flank.

A message was left behind for the main body, and Lt. Gen. [Eduard] von Fransecky was given the assurance that the advance guard would be at Jeritschek by 11:30 A.M. It reached that place at eleven in the morning. At noon its artillery opened fire from a position at Wrchownitz on the heights of Horenowes.

Similarly, the divisions of the VI Corps, which had originally been designated for an action against Josefstadt and which had started in the direction of Welchow, independently marched to the sound of cannon. In spite of the almost bottomless roads, they reached the battlefield at Welchow and Hradina by 11:00 A.M. In this case the independent action of the subordinate commanders facilitated the orders of the superior headquarters.

Similarly, the Austrian subordinate commanders reacted to the Prussian success in a remarkable manner. The commanders of the Austrian II and IV corps had deployed their units on the line Horenowes-Maslowed-Cistowes instead of marching into position between the Elbe, Nedelist, and Chlum as Benedek's orders had directed.[15] They became engaged in the fights around the Swiep Forest. Repeated counterorders from Benedek remained fruitless.

Fransecky's division was unable to hold the Swiep Forest.[16] It was thrown back by the two and one-half corps opposed to it and held the edge of the forest only with the greatest difficulty. Nevertheless, the two Austrian corps pursued so energetically that their flank and rear remained as good as unprotected, for only forty guns were left by the II Corps in position at Horenowes. There the German crown prince appeared and decided the battle.

---

15. Generalfeldzeugmeister Ludwig Ritter von Benedek commanded the Austrian forces in 1866.

16. Fransecky, commander of the 7th Division of the First Army, was one of the most distinguished of the Prussian commanders of his day, but is virtually unknown today. His memoirs, *Denkwürdigkeiten des preussischen Generals der Infanterie Eduard von Fransecky*, 2 vols. (Berlin: Bol und Dickart Verlagsbuchhandlung, 1913), are a valuable source for the Prussian army in the middle years of the nineteenth century. He entered the army in 1825 and was nearly fifty-nine in 1866.

Although Benedek cannot be blamed for the independent action of these two generals, their conduct is easily explained. They had all the advantages; they had thrown Fransecky out of the forest and exploited their victory. Now, victory is a serious matter. It carries everything along. They believed themselves able to bring the matter to a decision there—and then the crown prince attacked them in their flank. They had to pull their units out of the forest to lead them against the crown prince, and they collapsed during these difficult movements. Such an assembly after a forest fight cannot be accomplished very rapidly, and thus the crown prince, on reaching Chlum, found the heights almost without defenders. Even Benedek himself was almost captured when riding toward Chlum.

Concerning now the dilatory obedience of these generals, I must say: Obedience is the principle, but man stands above the principle. In most cases, success alone decides who is right in war. Of course it is easy to pass judgment later on, so one must always be very careful when condemning a general.

The Campaign of 1870–71

None of the battles on the frontier had been planned by royal headquarters. Of the battles around Metz, Colombey-Nouilly and Vionville–Mars-la-Tour arose out of the initiative of subordinate commanders. Saint-Privat was the first planned battle.

Wörth

On the morning of August 6 the Germans undertook a strong reconnaissance, which, however, they discontinued at 8:30. The Bavarian II Corps had received orders to attack the hostile left flank with one division via Langensulzbach in case cannon fire should be heard at Wörth. For this purpose the 4th Division under Count Bothmer had advanced from Pfaffenbronn, where it had bivouacked at Matstall. When cannon thunder was heard on the left, the Bavarians advanced via Langensulzbach on Fröschweiler. They reached the opposite forest edge, but were unable to advance beyond it without effective artillery support.

The noise of the engagement heard at Wörth in its turn caused the

V Corps commander, General von Kirchbach, to resume the fight with his units at Wörth, especially as an engagement appeared to be ensuing in the direction of Gunstett. By this decision he intended to prevent the opponent from turning with his entire force against one wing of the German army. At 9:30 A.M. the V Corps artillery commenced firing on both sides of the Wörth-Diefenbach road. The XI Corps's artillery went into action farther on the left, and by noon 108 guns fought with those of the enemy, successfully as it seemed. The infantry crossed the Sauer at Wörth and made some progress by occupying a ridge, but could not hold it for any length of time against the enemy's superior attacks. The Germans held their defensive position on the west bank of the stream only with the greatest effort.

In the meantime, General von Kirchbach had already informed the neighboring two corps that he was attacking the enemy opposite him and that he was counting on their support on both wings. This request reached General von Hartmann (Bavarian II Corps) at 11:15 A.M., when he had already started to carry out an order from army headquarters intended for the V Corps but erroneously also sent to him, to break off the engagement. The general replied [to von Hartmann] that he would resume the attack as soon as possible. In the I Corps area, the advance guard had been forced back across the Sauer after a violent fight.

Thus, at noon on August 6, the three corps in the first line of the Third Army had become engaged in action with more or less strong parts of their corps, in which the advantages gained in the course of the action had to be given up in part, or were held only with greatest effort against strong attacks by the French.

General von Kirchbach faced the necessity of independently arriving at a decision that would be far-reaching in its effect. It was known to him that army headquarters did not contemplate a battle that day, but merely a change of front. The thunder of cannon heard very early in the morning at army headquarters in Sulz had caused the crown prince to send Major von Hahnke of the General Staff to the battlefield at Wörth for information. At 9:00 A.M., this officer reported the advance of the Bavarians, the entry into the battle of the V Corps's advance guard, and the fact that the entire V Corps had been alerted and had sent ahead its artillery. He also reported that heavy artillery firing was heard at Gunstett. Since the crown prince wished to fight only when he had all of his army together, he sent orders to General von Kirchbach "not to accept battle and to avoid everything that might lead to a new one." As just stated, these orders also arrived, erroneously, at the Bavarian II Corps and caused that corps to break off the engagement. A part of the corps was then falling back on Lembach, while the remainder assembled at Langensulzbach. Although General von Hartmann had promised his support, it could not become effective for some time.

Conditions were just as difficult on the left wing, where, as stated, the I Corps's advance guard had been driven back, greatly shaken, to the Sauer—and parts of it even across that stream.

The V Corps finally succeeded in temporarily silencing the hostile batteries and in gaining a firm foothold on the other bank of the Sauer. The difficulty of a frontal attack against the strong and well-defended position of the opponent on the opposite heights had become obvious during the course of the engagement. Therefore, a renewed advance by the V Corps had to lead to a decisive battle in which timely support of the corps advancing in second line could not be counted on.

On the other hand, it was recognized that breaking off the engagement without heavy losses to the advance guard was impossible in the present situation, and that the retreat of detachments from the west to the east bank of the Sauer, in connection with retrograde movements of the neighboring two corps, would give the opponent the undisputed right to claim a victory. This would be materially unimportant, it is true, but was not to be underestimated in its moral effect. Added to this was the noise of moving railroad trains heard throughout the night and in the morning, which seemed to indicate the continuous arrival of enemy reinforcements. Thus a delayed attack might encounter still greater difficulties.

Finally, General von Kirchbach had every justification for hoping for success from an immediate frontal attack, even if attacks from Langensulzbach and Gunstett were made only later. After mature consideration of all these factors, General von Kirchbach issued orders to his corps to resume the advance, reported his decision to army headquarters, and called on the neighboring corps for support. This decision brought about the battle of Wörth.

When, contrary to all expectations, the thunder of cannon at Wörth became still heavier at noon, the crown prince started off for that point with his staff. En route he received General von Kirchbach's report that he was unable to break off the engagement and that he had called for assistance from the two neighboring corps.

The crown prince arrived on the heights near Wörth at 1:00 P.M. and took personal command of the battle.

Spicheren

On the evening of August 5, royal headquarters in Mainz telegraphed to First Army headquarters: "As the enemy appears to be retreating from the Saar, you are left discretion whether to cross the frontier, but, if you do so, the Saar must be crossed below Saarbrücken because the road from there to Saint-Avold has been assigned to the Second Army." This telegram, however, did not arrive at First Army headquarters until the night of August 7.

In the meantime, Prince Friedrich Karl and General von Steinmetz had issued orders to their armies for the advance. As a result, the III Corps advance guard moved eastward on the morning of August 7. The advance guards of the VII and VIII corps moved west of the Rhine-Nahe railroad[17] toward the roads leading to Saint-Johann, so that a continuation of the marches of the right wing of the Second Army and the left wing of the First Army had to come together at the crossing of that frontier river [the Saar]. From the VII Corps, which advanced from the vicinity of Lebach, the 13th Division marched on Püttlingen.

The 14th Division had the task of proceeding to Guichenbach. During this march the division commander, General von Kameke, learned through messages that the hostile positions south of Saarbrücken had been evacuated and that only weak detachments had been observed between Drahtzug and the Stift Forest.[18] He reported this to VII Corps headquarters, which was then marching to Dilsburg, and asked if he could cross the Saar under these conditions to take possession of the heights

17. The Nahe is a small river running east and north into the Rhine about twenty-five kilometers west of Mainz. The railroad ran along the curve of the Rhine from Mainz to Ringen and crossed the Nahe as it flowed into the Rhine. A branch of the railroad ran southwest and south to Neunkirchen and Saint-Johann. It is to this branch line that Moltke probably refers.

18. Georg Arnold von Kameke rose to the rank of general and served as war minister after the Franco-Prussian War.

south of Saarbrücken before the enemy would have an opportunity to occupy them again. The answer was that he should act according to his own judgment.

In the meantime his advance guard, under General von François, had arrived at Guichenbach at 9:30 A.M.[19] Since the weather was cool and the units still fresh, the division commander ordered the advance guard to start again, to take possession of Saarbrücken, and to send outposts to the heights. The main body continued the march.

When the division approached the city, it met the commanding general of the VIII Corps, General von Goeben, who was returning from a reconnaissance ride to the Saar. He stated that he contemplated bringing his advance guard, which was then marching to Fischbach, up to occupy Saarbrücken. He changed his mind for the present in that regard when he found that the 14th Division had the same object in view, and offered his support in case the enemy should advance again.

The 14 Division's advance guard then crossed the northern of the two bridges between Saint-Johann and Saarbrücken. But as soon as the 3d Battalion, 39th Regiment had reached the drill ground (at 11:30 A.M.) the enemy opened up a heavy artillery fire from the northern projecting point of the Spicheren heights—Red Hill. This fire increased when the 1st Light Battery went into position west of the road on the southern slope of the hill and replied to the fire of the hostile artillery (apparently eight pieces) with visibly good effect.

In the meantime, the other two battalions of the 39th Regiment had deployed farther left on the northern slope of Reppert Hill. In addition, General von Kameke sent the 2d Battalion, 74th Regiment from the main body to cross the railroad bridge between Malstatt and Burbach to secure the crossing there by occupying the railroad cut at Deutsch-Mühle. The battalion was directed to maintain contact with the 39th Fusilier Regiment on the left. The other two battalions of the 74th Regiment were also sent to the west bank of the Saar to reinforce the advance guard, so that General von François then had both regiments of his brigade at his disposal.

19. Bruno von François commanded the 27th Infantry Brigade. He was killed at Spicheren on August 6, 1870.

Since the enemy did not show any infantry at any point and did not cross the line from Drahtzug to Red Hill at any point, it appeared that the engagement would not assume a serious character for some time to come. This proved the correctness of the original view that the French detachments were there to cover entraining at Forbach. Indeed, further reports of the forward cavalry stated the enemy's strength to be about three infantry regiments.

We now turn to the Second Army. From a report of the 6th Cavalry Division, army headquarters in Kaiserslautern learned early in the morning that the heights at Saint-Arnaul had been evacuated. Since this indicated a partial retreat by the enemy, and since it appeared that a complete withdrawal was probable, it seemed appropriate to occupy the Saar crossing, now free, and to remain close to the enemy's heels, without bringing about a premature offensive. In this sense Prince Friedrich Karl ordered by telegraph at 8:00 A.M. that both cavalry divisions (the 5th and 6th) would keep on the enemy's heels, that the 5th Division was to proceed to Saarbrücken and that the IV Corps was to send an advance unit to Neu-Hornbach on the same day. In accordance with these preliminary orders, all march objectives designated for the corps for the next day were correspondingly advanced farther to the front.

In the meantime, army headquarters had proceeded to Homburg, where at noon it received telegrams from General von Rheinbaben.[20] The messages revealed that part of the First Army was on the Second Army's march routes, so III Corps was directed to occupy Saarbrücken on that day. Prince Friedrich Karl authorized Gen. [Ferdinand] von Stülpnagel, the commander of the 5th Division, to order the 14th Division to evacuate the city and road.[21]

Even before the arrival of these orders, the III Corps commander, Alvensleben, on the basis of his own observation of the situation and

20. This was Carl Freiherr von Rheinbaben, commander of the 9th Division.
21. Thus Prince Friedrich Karl gave Stülpnagel plenipotentiary powers (*Vollmacht*) for this situation. In campaigns, the *Vollmacht* was a rarely used emergency measure conferring full authority in a limited context. The term also applied to a few officers sent on special assignments to foreign monarchs, particularly the czar of Russia. For an introduction to this special practice, see Lamar Cecil, *The German Diplomatic Service, 1871–1914* (Princeton, N.J.: Princeton University Press, 1976), 124–25.

after he had learned that the enemy had left Saarbrücken, ordered the 5th Division to occupy that place with its advance guard and to send the main body to within 2½ miles [of Saarbrücken].

The events on the west bank of the Saar had anticipated these measures. Before we follow the course of these events from the start of the 14th Infantry Division, it is of interest to examine the largely independent action of those leaders who were in the situation of being able to participate in fighting on the other side of the Saar.

The commander of the 9th Infantry Brigade, Gen. [Wilhelm] von Döring, having learned that the cavalry outposts had crossed the Saar, had ridden ahead beyond Saarbrücken early in the morning.[22] On the other side of the city he saw, between nine and ten o'clock, infantry columns marching from Forbach behind the French skirmish lines. The columns disappeared in the wooded terrain east of the road and behind the hills there.

This led him to believe that it would be safe for the 14th Division to advance by itself. He therefore sent orders to a brigade marching toward Dudweiler to continue the march without interruption to Saarbrücken.

On the morning of August 6, the 5th Division moved from the vicinity of Neunkirchen in two main columns toward the Saar in order to reach its designated march objectives on the heights of Dudweiler. The combined 9th Brigade marched on the main high road to Saarbrücken, the combined 10th Brigade toward Saint-Ingbert.

The units of the 9th Brigade had already entered their quarters, the advance guard in Sulzbach and Dudweiler, the main body in Friedrichsthal and Bildstock, when the previously mentioned order of General von Döring alerted them for the continuation of the march on Saarbrücken at noon. General von Stülpnagel, receiving information of this about noon, immediately rode ahead to Saint-Johann with a squadron and the light battery of the advance guard.

The 12th Regiment of the 10th Brigade was in Neunkirchen. The remainder of the brigade had gone into quarters at noon in Spiesen

---

22. Döring, one of the heroes of the Franco-Prussian War, was killed at Mars-la-Tour on August 16, 1870.

and Saint-Ingbert. Very shortly, a report from the 6th Cavalry Division announced that the division was about to concentrate between Ensheim and Ormesheim because hostile troops were said to be advancing from Habkirchen on the Blies toward Assweiler. General von Schwerin therefore directed his brigade to assemble at Saint-Ingbert; the part of the brigade headquarters in Spiesen reached there by 2:30 P.M. At the same time, the 12th Regiment reported that it had received other orders.

Meanwhile, when corps headquarters in Neunkirchen received the same report from the headquarters of the division commander, General von Döring, also in Neunkirchen, General von Alvensleben immediately issued orders to assemble as many units of his corps as possible in Saarbrücken during the course of the day. The 12th Regiment and the 6th Division's 20th Regiment were to be brought up by rail to Saint-Johann. Orders were sent to Saint-Ingbert to start the 52d Regiment and all artillery available in that vicinity to Saarbrücken. These latter orders could immediately be obeyed by General von Schwerin because his units had already been assembled. Only the 1st Company, 52d Regiment, was left behind to guard the railroad station. At 4:00 P.M. the brigade started to march in the direction ordered. The general himself hastened ahead to the battlefield with the squadrons and batteries.

As he arrived in Fischbach, General von Goeben found that the division commander, General von Barnekow,[23] hearing the sound of cannon, had on his own initiative started the advance guard (Colonel von Rex)[24] just when it was about to place outposts toward the Saar. At the same time, the main body of the division had been alerted in its quarters around Wemmetsweiler and Landsweiler. In order to have it at hand not too far away from the advance guard, Goeben ordered the 72d Regiment of the 32d Brigade (Colonel von Rex) and the two available batteries to follow to Fischbach. He also ordered the 31st Brigade to advance to Quierscheidt. General von Goeben was thus assured that

---

23. Albert Christoph Freiherr von Barnekow commanded the 16th Division throughout the campaign.

24. Rudolf von Rex, from an old Saxon noble family, became a brigadier general in January 1871. He was a relatively unusual Prussian general in that he declined to join the Evangelical Church and remained a member of that branch of the Lutheran Church which declined amalgamation early in the nineteenth century.

the 16th Division would participate in the struggle on the other side of the Saar. Under these circumstances, he did not deem it necessary to bring up the 15th Division, the leading elements of which stood at Holz. He himself rode back to Saarbrücken.

When the advance guard under Colonel von Rex left the forest in the Köller valley at 1:30 P.M., an officer who had been sent ahead to the 14th Division reported that support seemed not immediately necessary but that it would be desirable for the 16th Division to proceed south of Saarbrücken. At that point, General von Barnekow ordered the advance guard to continue its march toward Saint-Johann. The main body received orders to follow.

As stated above, the commander of VII Corps, General von Zastrow, had authorized the commanding general of the 14th Division to act according to his best judgment. However, he shortly thereafter thought it best to bring his entire corps up to the Saar. He sent Captain von Westernhagen of the General Staff to Einweiler to obtain the approval of army headquarters. General von Steinmetz had reached Einweiler around noon. The commander in chief approved General von Zastrow's estimate of the situation as follows:

> The enemy has to be punished for his carelessness. To prevent him from reoccupying his positions on the left [west] bank of the Saar, he approved occupying that position in the interest of the Second Army. We ought also to attempt to interfere with the entraining at Forbach of the weakly protected French units.

In the meantime, new reports had arrived at VII Corps headquarters in Dilsburg. These created doubt as to whether the enemy was actually continuing his retreat or if fresh French units were not advancing on Saarbrücken. When approval of his recommendations was received between noon and 1:00 P.M., General von Zastrow immediately took the following measures:

> The 13th Division received orders to advance toward Völklingen and Wehrden, to send its advance guard in the direction of Ludweiler and Forbach, and to inform itself by patrols of the strength and intentions of the enemy at Forbach. The 14th Division was to take position on the left [west] bank of the Saar at Saarbrücken with

a reinforced advance guard; the main body to draw up toward Rockershausen, to construct a crossing there, and also to send patrols toward Forbach. These instructions had already been exceeded in consequence of the prior authorization for independent action. The corps artillery received orders to march to Püttlingen (north of Völklingen).

After dispatch of these orders, General von Zastrow started with his headquarters toward Saarbrücken. At the same time, the commander of the First Army had directed his quartermaster general, Colonel Count Wartensleben, to hasten ahead to Saarbrücken for a closer examination of conditions there.[25] On the way, this officer read the reports coming from the battlefield to VII Corps headquarters, which showed without doubt that the engagement had increased in volume and importance, a fact that was confirmed by the steadily increasing thunder of cannon. The colonel sent information of this to General von Steinmetz at Einweiler.

The above account shows how, in consequence of messages from the west bank of the Saar since early on the morning of August 6, all measures on the German side aimed at a timely and extensive intervention and how the commanders in the forward line especially strove by their independent decisions to anticipate orders from higher authority. It was especially due to this latter circumstance that the 14th Division was supported, even at a late hour, by the neighboring corps. We shall see how decisively that support intervened in the difficult struggle that the 14th Division had started by itself.

The short distance between the low heights on the west bank of the Saar and the stream crossings made it desirable to gain a foothold farther in front. This was to secure the crossings and to force the apparently weak hostile forces away from their dominating positions, from which all Prussian movements could plainly be seen. An advance for that purpose seemed to be even less dangerous to General von Kameke because,

---

25. Hermann Ludwig Graf von Wartensleben was a General Staff officer and large landowner in Prussian Saxony. A famous figure in his time, he was known as "Wartensleben-Carow" because of his estate, Carow. He retired as a general of cavalry and served in the upper house of the Prussian legislature, the *Herrenhaus*.

as already stated, he could count on the support of the neighboring corps in case of need. Therefore, shortly before noon, he ordered General von François to drive the hostile artillery from Red Hill.

The division's main body received orders to cross the railroad bridge west of Saarbrücken with the 28th Brigade, with the batteries to advance through that town. This advance started the battle of Spicheren.

At the start, the 14th Division found itself confronted by a force twice as numerous. Nevertheless, it made progress, captured a part of the Gifert Forest from the enemy, enveloped Stiring-Wendel, and gained a firm hold on Red Hill. But, by 3:00 P.M., the insertion of fresh Prussian forces became absolutely necessary to support the division in its unequal battle. The division was then extended in a fighting line nearly three miles in length. The deep columns of the Brigade Doens [French] were plainly visible as they descended the slope of Pfaffen Hill toward Spicheren. It had to be expected at any moment that the greatly superior enemy would push back or pierce the weak front line.

When General von Goeben arrived at Saarbrücken, he assumed command of the engagement by virtue of being the senior officer present. This occurred at a time when the 28th Brigade had entered the wooded vicinity of Stiring, when General von François had taken the edge of Red Hill, and when the units in the Gifert Forest began to give way to the superior enemy. Direct support of the weak—and at that moment hard-pressed—left wing in the Gifert Forest was urgently necessary. General von Goeben therefore decided to use the newly arriving units against the steep, wooded northern slopes of the Spicheren heights in order to hold them permanently, and then to advance along the plateau, flanking the hostile position. Holding back a reserve appeared inadvisable in this momentary crisis, where everything had to be done to stabilize the wavering engagement. In case of need, the parts of the III and VIII corps expected later could serve in support.

At that time—between 3:00 and 4:00 P.M.—only the leading detachments of the 5th and 16th divisions were available. They arrived nearly simultaneously, the former on Winter Hill, the latter on Reppert Hill.

Later on, the III Corps commander, General von Alvensleben, arrived by railroad in Saint-Johann. He immediately hastened to the engagement and came to an agreement with General von Stülpnagel, who had been present with the light battery since 2:00 P.M., thus before his advance guard (5th Division) had come up. They agreed that the intended attack against the French right wing had to be made with as much force as possible. The measures taken, and to be taken, though stemming from high commanders of different corps and armies, were consistent with the measures taken by General von Goeben and were agreed upon by the various commanders consulting with each other. In general, Generals von Döring, von Stülpnagel, and von Alvensleben directed the movements from Winter Hill; Generals von Kameke, von Barnekow, and von Goeben those made via the Reppert and Galgen hills.

At about 4:30 P.M., General von Zastrow, the VII Corps commander, arrived on the battlefield and, as the ranking officer, assumed overall command.

A mighty struggle then ensued on Red Hill and in the Gifert and Pfaffen forests for possession of the heights. The struggle swayed back and forth as the continued arrival of fresh units on both sides shifted the advantage here and there.

A little before 6:00 P.M., the commanding generals of the III, VII, and VIII corps met on the top of Galgen Hill to agree upon further measures for carrying through the struggle. At that time, on the far right wing, the positions in front of Stiring-Wendel were still held. On the left wing, a gradual advance by Prussian units in the engagement on the heights had become visible. The success of the day seemed assured. General von Goeben made a telegraphic report in this sense to the king. General von Alvensleben, who had observed the course of the engagement from Winter Hill, considered it desirable to give more force to the advance on the Spicheren plateau. He utilized the arriving parts of his corps for this and took over command of that part of the line of battle.

While en route to the battlefield, General von Zastrow had sent an officer to Völklingen to inform the 13th Division of the change in the situation since the dispatch of the corps' orders from Dilsburg. He believed that the division was marching on Forbach. But then reports arrived of the unfavorable turn of the fight at Stiring-Wendel, and the hostile rounds exploding on Galgen Hill clearly indicated the enemy's progress. As a result, the general rode to Folster Hill personally to reconnoiter conditions on the right wing in preparation for a counterattack. He ordered the batteries to advance from Galgen Hill to Folster Hill. From the latter position they were able to intervene more effectively in the fighting on the plateau, which by that time extended toward

Forbach Hill. Before the commencement of this phase of the engagement, the high commanders had decided to bring cavalry and artillery onto the Spicheren plateau to exploit the success attained so far by the infantry. The commander of the 32d Brigade, Colonel von Rex, who had participated in the fighting of the 40th Regiment, had especially urged support by the artillery.

Returning from the meeting of the generals on the road to the left wing, General von Alvensleben issued special orders to the III Corps artillery commander, Gen. [Hans Adolf] von Bülow, on the employment of his guns. He directed General von Rheinbaben, on the other hand, to attempt to advance with his cavalry which, hastening to the sound of the cannon, had assembled on the battlefield during the afternoon. But the cavalry made no progress in that terrain, and only two batteries could be brought into positon on the plateau.

While the bloody struggle on the Spicheren heights continued after 6:00 P.M. with great stubbornness on both sides, the main endeavors of the attack turned against Forbach Hill and against Stiring-Wendel. When darkness came, the forest at Forbach had been taken. Its envelopment had been substantially eased by the enemy's commitment of his last forces in the continuing fight for Red Hill and the Gifert Forest. He then had no further reinforcements left for the fight around the Spicheren Forest. The French then commenced a retreat at all points along the plateau.

The First Army commander had received the reports of his quartermaster general, as well as a report of the advance of the 16th Division to Saarbrücken. As a result, General von Steinmetz proceeded at once to the battlefield, arriving there at about 7:00 P.M., and immediately rode to the Spicheren plateau. The thunder of the French guns on Pfaffen Hill, mixed with the weaker infantry fire, accompanied the last convulsions of the enormous struggle. Far off, near Forbach, artillery fire was heard, apparently indicating the intervention of the 13th Division.

In the execution of its orders, the advance guard of that division had arrived around noon at Völklingen and had joined the advance guard in occupying the nearest villages on the Saar. Since Hussar patrols on the west bank of the river reported the advance of hostile battalions from Gross-Rosseln, Maj. Gen. [Alexander] von der Goltz pushed the Jäger battalion and one Hussar squadron forward via Wehrden. The division commander, Gen. [Heinrich] von Glümer, received a report of this between noon and one o'clock when he and the main body reached the vicinity of Püttlingen, where he intended to go into quarters. He immediately rode with the 4th Squadron and the 6th Light Battery to join the advance guard at Wehrden.

At Wehrden, the thunder of cannon coming from the southwest had been heard for some time. Recent reports said that the enemy was engaged in combat between Stiring-Wendel and Forbach. Major General von der Goltz had therefore decided to accompany the entire advance guard against the enemy's left flank. The division commander agreed and sent an order to Püttlingen to alert the main body and have it follow the advance guard.

In conjunction with the reinforcements brought up by General von Glümer, the advance guard then started the march on Gross-Rosseln. One Jäger company and one platoon of Hussars had already gone ahead via Clarenthal to Schöneck. When the units approached the vicinity of Gross-Rosseln at 4:00 P.M., the corps orders issued three hours before in Dilsburg (to advance on Völklingen and Wehrden, with the advance guard moving on Dudweiler and Forbach) reached them. The measures directed in these orders had been basically executed. By not cooking en route, the units had marched about twenty-two miles since 5:00 A.M. without encountering the enemy. Far away, on Forbach Hill, was a large enemy encampment. But the thunder of cannon in the east, the sound of which was diminished by the forests, had ceased, and the engagement there appeared to have ended. The division commander, who was with the advance guard, had also received a report from First Army headquarters stating that the commanding general did not intend a more serious battle on the west bank of the Saar that day. Under these circumstances, General von Glümer halted his units north of Gross-Rosseln and placed outposts. The main body received orders to bivouac at Völklingen.

At 6:00 P.M. the thunder of cannon was again heard at Gross-Rosseln. At the same time, the Hussar patrol that had been sent out reported that the engagement continued south of Saarbrücken. The officer sent by General von Zastrow also arrived just then, bringing word that the 14th Division was engaged in hot combat on the Spicheren heights, as well as a request for the 13th Division to join in the battle.

As a result, Major General von der Goltz immediately started the march on both sides of the Rossel toward Forbach. A fight ensued with dismounted French dragoons. While these retreated, Forbach was not occupied by the advance guard of the 13th Division. The main body followed up in the meantime to Klein-Rosseln. While the 13th Division exerted no influence on the battle, its mere presence greatly influenced the French retreat. The latter did not dare fall back on Saint-Avold, but retreated south toward Oetingen-Saargemünd.

In complete contrast to the comradely assistance that the Prussian commanders gave each other at Spicheren, and in complete contrast to the pressing forward of the units to participate in the fight, stood the strange hither and thither movements of the divisions still in the rear of Gen. [Charles Auguste] Frossard's divisions. Three of the former had begun marching to his support, but only two arrived after the conclusion of the fight.

It is interesting to follow the conduct of these French detachments, which were in a position on August 6 to provide the expected battlefield support. In the morning, and at the time when the 14th Division moved on Saarbrücken, General Frossard had telegraphed his estimate of the situation to Marshal Bazaine in Saint-Avold and had recommended that he be supported by placing reinforcements in readiness to meet any contingency. The marshal had promised to do this and had issued orders to the three divisions that were at Saargemünd, Püttlingen, and Marienthal—not more than ten miles away. Marshal Bazaine apparently considered the units at Saint-Avold indispensable for holding the main road because he expected a German attack from Karlingen against Saint-Avold as a result of a communication from imperial headquarters. In the late afternoon, when the marshal became anxious about the result of the battle, he sent an infantry regiment by rail to Forbach. That regiment did not reach Forbach because the railroad was already taking fire from the 13th Division. The regiment returned unsuccessful.

The Division Metman in Marienthal, which had started in the forenoon via Beningen by order of the marshal, apparently moved forward—but very slowly and with interruptions. When the Cavalry Brigade Juniac, in the lead, approached the battlefield, General Frossard, who had plenty of cavalry, sent that brigade back to Beningen. He did this because he considered it necessary to keep the main road clear for the retreat, especially for the vehicles. The Division Metman arrived at Forbach late in the evening and occupied the heights east of the village, not yet held by the Germans, where it learned of the II Corps's retreat. Thereupon it also marched at once, and at daybreak on August 7 reached Püttlingen.

In consequence of the cannon thunder heard around noon, General Castagny in Püttlingen had arrived independently at the decision to set out with his division, but had taken a direction much too far to the right. After he had marched his men barely 4½ miles, the engagement appeared to have ceased in the north, and the division returned to Püttlingen. The unit had just arrived there when the thunder of cannon was heard again. Then, at 6:00 P.M., the division again started out, this time straight toward Forbach. During this march Marshal Bazaine ordered the division to join General Frossard. After it had reached Völklingen, around 9:00 P.M., and the advance elements were as far as Forbach, news arrived of the II Corps's retreat. The division then turned back toward Püttlingen a second time, and arrived there, like the Division Metman, at daybreak on August 7.

At Saargemünd, where the Division Montaudon had arrived on the morning of August 6 to relieve General Failly's units, the loud cannon fire also was heard. But only when orders arrived from Saint-Avold to advance on Gross-Blittersdorf did the division set out (at 4:00 P.M.). At 7:00 P.M. it reached the vicinity of Rühlingen. Since it was late in the evening, General Montaudon sent an officer ahead to inform the II Corps that he would support it the next day. But he learned the outcome of the battle at midnight, and then he joined the divisions Metman and Castagny in the vicinity of Püttlingen on the morning of August 7.

The French generals had forgotten that the successes attained in the campaign of 1859 for the most part rested on the independent decisions of subordinate commanders.

The battle at Spicheren was so entirely unexpected by German royal headquarters, that General von Stiehle, the Second Army chief of staff, reported from Homburg at 1:50 P.M. that the French were retreating from Forbach. Royal headquarters therefore issued orders to both armies to follow the enemy.

It has subsequently been said that the battle of Spicheren was fought at the wrong place and that it thwarted royal headquarters' plans. It is true that the battle had not been foreseen. However, there will be few cases where a tactical victory does not fit into the strategic plan.

Success of arms will always be thankfully accepted and fully utilized. Through the battle of Spicheren, the French II Corps was prevented from marching off undamaged. Contact had been gained with the main hostile force and royal headquarters had gained a basis for further decisions.

French Imperial headquarters had been placed in an exactly opposite situation. We know that the French army, in a state of unreadiness and divided into two poorly organized halves, had remained stationary and indecisive for fourteen days, during which time the German forces concentrated in a confined space. Thereafter, based on the First Army standing in readiness in the mountains, the Second and Third armies marched in divergent directions.

A victorious [Prussian] advance had of necessity to separate the enemy armies still more. Misfortune on a large scale could force only the German armies to concentrate again.

After the Germans seized the initiative, the French high command was forced to subordinate its decisions to those of the opponent.

In passing, we remark how well the opening of a campaign demonstrates the importance of a day lost either in mobilization or transportation. If we imagine, for instance, that our operations of August 6 or 7 had been delayed, then the crown prince would have found opposite him on the Sauer two instead of one French corps. The emperor could easily have concentrated his four corps around Saint-Avold on August 7. Even on August 8, provided the strong marches had continued without any interruption, we could have attacked with only four army corps, for five of our corps—I, X, Guard, IX, and XII—still required three days to close up.

By that time French Imperial headquarters had undoubtedly awoken from its fine dream of an easy march into Germany. By then it must have recognized the necessity of having to assemble both armies for the protection of its own territory. This could have been effected without danger in the vicinity of Nancy–Pont-à-Mousson, provided the very bitter decision had been taken to execute a retreat at the very start. In that case, Metz would have covered the left flank and the critically important railroad to the rear would have been fully protected.

If the French then intended to avoid a retreat of their main army and only to draw up the neighboring army, the former would have had to occupy a position at least of sufficient strength and concentration as to be fully capable of waiting for the arrival of the latter.[26]

COOPERATION OF ARMS (c. 1860–75)

During peacetime training, special care must be given to mutual support of the arms since their characteristics complement each other.

Only proper *cooperation* enables each individual arm to exploit its full effectiveness.

After the reconnoitering activity of the cavalry is finished, artillery and infantry have to bear the brunt of the action for the time being. The other arms act in support. After the decision, artillery and cavalry in turn play the main role.

Infantry

The combat power of infantry rests on the effect of its fire. Its success depends on attaining fire superiority and exploiting it decisively and rapidly.

For that reason, individual marksmanship training is of the utmost importance. Nevertheless, only correct and efficient fire control will fully exploit this training.

The more fire effect is concentrated in time and target, the greater will be its moral effect. Numbers of hits alone are not decisive, but rather the resulting effect produced upon the morale of the enemy.

The amount of ammunition carried along is limited. Senseless squandering of ammunition should be prevented by strict discipline. The infantry must husband its ammunition and should not fire at too great a range. But where a hostile unit is thoroughly shaken, or where its morale can be broken by enormous losses, every expenditure of ammunition is justified.

---

26. Here the editor has omitted a paragraph on subsequent events centering around Marshal MacMahon. This paragraph was not particularly relevant to the foregoing passage on Spicheren and contained some errors noted by the editors at the time of the essay's publication in 1912.

Timely replenishment of ammunition should never be neglected. It is frequently proper to issue cartridges from the ammunition wagons to the men prior to or at the opening of the engagement.

In order to husband our strength, and when the question is merely of relatively minor firing, it is frequently better to have a small number of riflemen fire the appropriate amount of ammunition than to oppose the enemy with a large number of men—possibly under unfavorable terrain conditions.

The effect of hostile fire demands measures for protection. The best measures are correct and efficient use of the terrain. Commanders and men must therefore be well practiced in this and must know how to utilize even unimportant objects for cover, both when moving and when halted. Commanders must be accustomed rapidly and independently to adopt those formations, according to terrain and kind of enemy fire, which can be counted on to diminish its effects. Where one intends to conduct a stationary engagement, the protection offered by the terrain can be increased by field works, especially by trenches. But the spirit of the advance must never be curbed by artificial works. Nor must trenches interfere with a subsequent movement that appears to be advantageous. All considerations of cover have to be subordinated to considerations of fire effects.

Infantry whose flanks are secured is unconquerable as long as it pays no attention to losses inflicted on it by long-range fire and as long as it preserves its equanimity. This conviction must be awakened and fostered in the infantry. The men should constantly be told that the enemy is at a disadvantage as long as they have him in their rifle sights and that losses will be suffered only when retreat commences, because the stationary side can fire without interference and with calmness.

Every man must be unshakably convinced that it is far more dangerous to retreat than to stand fast or to advance.

Infantry must be drilled to overwhelm a retreating enemy with its most effective fire. It is not sufficient to throw the enemy back. He must not be merely shaken, but must be annihilated. Hot pursuit should be avoided as long as the enemy is within effective rifle firing range.

Exhaustive application of such a pursuing fire at the proper moment, even if rapid forward movement has to be stopped, forms an important element of infantry combat and must become second nature to leaders, as well as to the men.

The long range of infantry fire compels great depth in formations and great distance between the firing line and closed-up detachments in the rear. On the other hand, the great fire effect of modern small arms exposes forward detachments to rapid annihilation. This causes leaders special difficulties that require great proficiency to overcome.

Proper measures can more easily be taken if the detachments standing or marching in each other's rear are under a single command. Then movement and supports[27] are regulated by the same hand and interspersing of different units on the fighting line will be felt less.

The stronger the front, the more justifiable is an attack against a flank. A deep formation and a command structure arranged in depth are appropriate both to meet and to execute such an attack.[28] It is therefore usually advisable to employ the regiments of one brigade alongside of each other and to assign each battalion a unified combat task.

Once committed, infantry units remain in combat until the decision. Relief of the foremost fighting line, which cannot be accomplished under fire without the greatest disadvantages, is therefore to be avoided even in practice drills. The fighting power of the forward line must be fully utilized; its dissolution must be prevented by timely support, not by relief.

As a rule, the victory is his who has the last reserve and uses it decisively.

The difficulties of command arising from the extension of the firing line and dividing the force into small units absolutely require that all subordinate commanders, especially company commanders, endeavor to rejoin their larger units (battalions, regiments) and that the higher commanders continually strive to keep their units well in hand.

High commanders must not commit the infantry earlier than is demanded by the conditions of the engagement.

Commanders of units to be committed must receive definite tasks (*Aufträge*) but not be limited in the choice of means to accomplish

27. Here Moltke means supporting units directly behind the forward line of combat units.

28. By "a command structure arranged in depth," Moltke meant units deployed in depth so that command channels ran from front to rear rather than laterally along the front line.

them by the fire and free use of their subordinate units. The smaller is the possibility of normal command in combat, the more certain is failure of the methods practiced in peacetime, the more important is an appropriate, clear, and definite order from above and compliant comprehension from below.

High commanders must avoid accompanying their originally committed units to the forward line so as to be close to the engagement. They must remain near the uncommitted units and watch with greatest strictness that these do not become engaged contrary to their intentions. High commanders will exercise greater influence on the engagement by correct employment of reserves than by useless interference with the independence of subordinate commanders in the forward line.

Before the decisive attack is commenced, infantry fire, supported by the artillery, must be brought to close range.

In consideration of the difficulties attending changes of direction and shifting units under effective enemy fire, it will be advisable to deploy the infantry in suitable breadth outside of that effective fire zone so that each unit can proceed directly to the front as much as possible.

In meeting engagements it is important to effect the tactical deployment with the least possible loss of time. The leading detachments may frequently have to commence the engagement before the end of the main body's deployment if one desires to retain freedom of action. The leading units must then be supported in a correct manner by the following units.

The more the defense has utilized its inherent advantages in regard to choice and preparation of its position, the more must the attack advance according to a well thought-out plan.

Premature charges by the leading detachments are ruinous in such a case and may endanger everything. It will be expedient to issue separate orders for deployment and subsequent attack by the infantry and have only a few advanced detachments take up positions at a suitable distance from the enemy during the deployment.

If the infantry has begun to attack, it must endeavor to bring its fire onto the enemy as quickly as possible at the most effective range. Covered ground is most favorable for that approach, especially if the attack leads to one of the enemy's flanks. Where one is exposed to hostile fire, splitting into smaller detachments at greater depth will decrease losses. In close terrain the commanders will have to pay special attention to keeping the units together.

Crossing the hostile fire zone until our own fire can begin will always constitute a crisis in the engagement.[29] We should do our very best to shorten such a crisis, that is, to keep on moving toward the enemy without stopping up to a range that allows superior or at least equally effective fire. If this is not possible, an advance by sections will be necessary and one must strive for cooperation between the firing and advancing sections.[30] If our artillery cannot furnish effective support in such a case, an expenditure of a very large amount of ammunition at long range can be justified, provided the commander exerts good fire control.

We must always remember, however, that any advancing movement temporarily stopped by a stationary firefight is difficult to start again and that we should therefore, as a rule, move at once up to the decisive range.

Having arrived at an effective range, the commanders of the leading units can best see where it is possible to take possession of a nearby sector of covered terrain. In doing so they will use their judgment in pushing as far forward as the enemy's fire and their own strength allow.

The highest commanders will be able to give appropriate energy to the engagement by sending in reserves where the advance promises the best success and where the skirmish lines are about to be overwhelmed by hostile fire, but especially where success is to be exploited.

The chances of success in the final assault will increase the more

29. This "*Krise im Gefecht*" was a staple phrase of the Prussian literature to and beyond the First World War. It was the subject of numerous articles in the army's literature and referred to what John English has termed the "problem of the last 300 yards." In a sense this was the supreme tactical question of the First World War, which the Germans regarded as never having been fully resolved. In any case, Moltke's phrase here is another example of his defining the terms of major tactical debates for decades.

30. Here Moltke suggests an early form of the now commonplace concept of "fire and movement," with one portion of a unit firing to suppress enemy defensive fire while another portion moves toward the enemy.

we succeed in creating unity of action between detachments having the same objective.

Infantry must know how to conduct enveloping attacks wherever they are possible without time-consuming flanking movements and disadvantageous extensions of the front.

Concentric fire multiplies rifle fire and permits a portion of the attacking line to fire while the rest advances to the assault.[31] In such an enveloping attack against a hostile flank, special protection should be arranged for security of the flank of the enveloping detachment against enemy reserves. For that reason we should always have a reserve on the extreme flank of the enveloping element.

The defense can select its position and reinforce it; but it leaves freedom of action to the attacker. He can bring up his forces under cover and attack some point of the position with superior numbers. The defender's infantry should therefore occupy its works only when the attacker's intentions have become clear. This does not preclude appropriate work in strengthening the position. Insofar as sufficient time is available, the defender should arrange for several contingencies. In addition to digging trenches, determination of distances is one of the most important preparations.

The foremost line of the infantry defense usually should be forward of that of the artillery. The terrain above all should govern the distances. In selecting the line, commanders should always keep an eye on the most effective mutual support possible between the different arms.

It should be remembered that the insertion of reserves into the forward line across open terrain and under hostile fire is possible only with great losses, which substantially decrease the value of the reinforcements. Where such reserves cannot be brought up under cover, it will be better to post them in or directly behind the firing line.

The defender needs strong detachments behind the front in order to drive the attacker out of the position should he have entered it at

---

31. By concentric fire, Prussian theory meant the entire line firing toward a single, narrow section of the enemy's line. The Prussians thus hoped to gain fire superiority at that point and sufficiently to suppress enemy fire so that a local assault was possible. It was one of several methods of dealing with the admitted superiority of modern defensive fires.

some point or to prevent a partial success from becoming a general success. Firm intervention by the commander will especially be required after a frontal attack has been defeated so as to prevent piecemeal frontal counterattacks. On the other hand, the threat of an attack or an attack against the flank of the attacker will frequently prove very effective.

In posting its units, the defense must remember that the attacker will in all probability direct his main efforts against a flank. The main reserves must be positioned to the rear of one or both flanks either to prevent a decision or, in a favorable case, to be able to move against the enemy's flank. The location of the reserves should be selected far enough to the rear that they do not become engaged in combat against the will of the commander in case of an enveloping movement by the attacker. Otherwise they would be able to intervene only by a frontal counterattack.

Far-reaching turning movements (*Umgehungen*) in which the attacker divides his forces give the defender a favorable opportunity for a quick offensive. He must never forget that fire effect by itself, no matter how much favored by the terrain, cannot bring about a victory. It is only the means to a sudden and unexpected attack against the enemy with concealed reserves at a favorable moment.

Unshaken infantry need not fear a cavalry charge as long as the infantry maintains its composure. This is of far more importance than the infantry's momentary formation, which is without value unless it increases the unit's feeling of security. The main thing is effective fire effect. Mass formations are of little value for any other purpose and produce great losses under fire. However, we must bear in mind to what extent the morale of our own units makes such precautionary measures unnecessary.

The infantry must furnish the greatest possible support to our own cavalry charges and must also endeavor to exploit fully the diversion of the hostile fire caused by the cavalry to gain some advantage in the engagement.

The artillery's effectiveness primarily depends on rapid range determination. For that reason, we can best reduce the effect of hostile artillery fire through movements that increase the difficulties of ranging. Where conditions and terrain permit, the infantry must try to push detachments, even weak ones, to within effective rifle range of the artillery. Even at long range, our modern rifles can become very annoying to the hostile artillery and can be used against it if our own artillery is not yet on the field in sufficient strength.

Cavalry

The effectiveness of cavalry in combat depends first on its speed (above all else on the rapidity with which the situation is clarified and understood), second on rapidity of decision (*Entschluss*), and finally on speed of execution.

Delay on the part of the command must be made good by swiftness of movement. The commander must never wait for orders where he can gain success by independent decision.

The cavalry commander must be capable of rapid estimation and conception of the combat situation and energetic action. He must know how properly to judge the situations of the other arms if he wishes fully to utilize his own.

No arm is as well suited to exploit success of the other arms as is the cavalry.

The principal fighting method of cavalry is the charge. Its main ingredients are striking the enemy at the proper point, with firm cohesion of the detachments, and force of the shock.

The most favorable point of attack is the enemy's flank. Care should always be given to overlapping and flanking attacks. The type of cavalry formation depends on conditions of strength and equipment, as well as on which combat arm the charge is directed.

Retaining both a supporting detachment in close proximity to the first line and a reserve to meet all changeable conditions of the engagement is of special value to the cavalry.

If cavalry is at all able to attack successfully, that success is in most cases very great and decisive. To gain such a success, the cavalry must not fear any loss.

Cavalry should everywhere live up to the glorious tradition that our cavalry never stands to await the attack of hostile cavalry but advances to meet it, even if outnumbered.

Cavalry will fight dismounted for the purpose of achieving some combat objectives, especially temporary holding or opening of defiles. But in such work cavalry lacks the means of carrying on a protracted firefight, especially when opposed by infantry. In the attack, cavalry will usually employ as much force as possible at the start and, avoiding a long firefight, advance quickly.

If the object of the engagement requires it, dismounted cavalry will have to carry the fight to a decision.

In general, combat activities of the cavalry are threefold. Prior to and during the opening phases of the engagement, the cavalry will usually be in front. It reconnoiters the terrain and the enemy situation or protects the tactical deployment of our forces against premature discovery and surprise by the enemy. To perform these tasks, engagements with hostile cavalry may be necessary. These, however, should never be extended or carried to a finish except insofar as is necessary for attaining the object of reconnaissance and security of the deployment of other units. It is always a mistake when cavalry, attached to other formations, separates from them entirely and arbitrarily acts as it pleases.

Cavalry commanders must always adhere to the authoritative viewpoint that their activity furnishes the higher commander a basis for his important decisions and that cavalry must save the other arms from premature tactical deployment and having to detach units as much as possible.

When retiring to the rear of the other arms, cavalry should always be careful not to interfere with the fire effect of those arms.

Cavalry divisions that are far in the rear because of temporary arrangements must advance far enough at the beginning of large engagements, without waiting for orders, so that they can be employed in case of need without loss of time.

During the course of an engagement, often lasting for hours, cavalry must be held in the rear out of the effective fire zone, except for those detachments attached to infantry units or those operating independently against the enemy's flanks, rear, or lines of communications. Cavalry units dismount during these periods and may even feed their horses under certain conditions. During the fighting, turning points can arise which demand ruthless employment of cavalry, in exceptional cases even against unshaken infantry and artillery. Success can be attained only by massing the cavalry and persevering in executing the attack.

The general task of cavalry during this part of the engagement, however, is to assemble its forces so that they can quickly be used to the utmost. At the close of an engagement the cavalry usually is called to an important activity. All assembled forces must be employed and even large losses must not be feared.

If the enemy's masses are not yet sufficiently disrupted to allow an immediate attack, the next task will be to cover our pursuing artillery, whose fire will then open a path for the cavalry.

A victorious outcome of the fight offers cavalry an opportunity to achieve the greatest success. Men and horses cannot have too much strength for that purpose.

In other cases, our own retreating units have to be protected by the cavalry, hostile cavalry prevented from pursuit, and hostile batteries prevented from advancing.

Divisional cavalry should never leave its infantry during an engagement. It carries out reconnaissance during the fighting and protects the other arms from surprise. Divisional cavalry cannot be spared from having to remain under fire with the other arms. It will find means to decrease the resulting unavoidable losses through frequent change of position and through skillful utilization of the ground, even though these losses purchase the opportunities for victorious action.

While intervening in the course of the engagement, small cavalry detachments must take care not to hinder the effective fire of the other arms.

The mere presence of cavalry compels the opponent's other arms to interrupt their movements and to adopt measures that restrict their activity, thus causing the enemy larger losses while relieving us of restricting considerations.

While the mass of the cavalry rests, the commander keeps himself fully informed of the course of the engagement. He personally observes and sends officers to the divisions in the forward line. He remains in permanent communication with his immediate superior and ready to execute his orders quickly. He has the probable routes of movement reconnoitered and shifts his main elements behind the battle line to the most favorable point for probable employment.

Where there is not time for higher headquarters to issue proper orders, the cavalry division commanders act independently and on their own responsibility.

It is the cavalry's duty, after a successful battle, to take up the pursuit immediately, without further orders, and to maintain contact with the fleeing enemy. When the firefight dies down, all cavalry detachments must at once hasten to the front on their own initiative to be ready and available for their next tasks.

In case of a reverse, cavalry commanders are responsible for protecting the other arms as far as possible.

The commander of any cavalry detachment, even one acting independently on a temporary basis, is personally responsible for ensuring that everything possible is done to ascertain the whereabouts of the withdrawing enemy and to keep in contact with him.

In all peacetime exercises of the combined arms, special attention should be paid to the quick and independent employment of the cavalry at the end of the firefight.

The enemy must never be allowed to rest or to reassemble. This must be prevented by the employment of every available man and horse. Every step the enemy has to take to the rear increases his disintegration and brings closer the moment when he falls victim to the cavalryman's saber.

Field Artillery

The artillery attached to any formation forms an integral part of that unit. It must not leave the latter's march or fighting areas and must rejoin that formation without special orders after an action.

Artillery that is in an infantry formation needs no special guard, either on the march or in combat. Horse artillery or an independent cavalry division also need special protection only under unusual circumstances. Measures taken by the other arms must protect the artillery against surprise and hostile small-arms fire as much as possible.

Every unit has to extend immediate assistance as soon as it learns or observes that a battery is in danger.

The commander must hasten to the front to reconnoiter every artillery position. The selection of positions includes considerations of effect and those of cover, with the former taking precedence. Positioning batteries in line, which facilitates ranging by the enemy and increases our difficulties of observation, should be avoided wherever possible because it leads to great losses. Positioning batteries in a single line creates a single target upon which the enemy has already fired.

The strength of the individual echelons depends on the amount of artillery to go into action, on the terrain, and on the position of the other artillery.

The best location for the artillery is behind a ridge so that the muzzles of the pieces just about extend over the ridge, with the caissons, limbers, and so forth under cover to the rear or to one side.

Special value should be placed on taking up a covered position and on sudden firing. The time lost in opening fire is very immaterial.

It is advisable to provide earthworks for pieces standing in the open, provided sufficient time is available.

The fire effect of the artillery should normally be fully utilized at ranges beyond the effective range of infantry fire. The maxim that the infantry should never lack artillery support must always be adhered to. For that reason, artillery must not be afraid of the heaviest infantry fire at the decisive moment.

Accordingly, batteries accompany the infantry advance up to the point of the final assault (*Einbruchskampf*).[32] There its effect, increased by the short range, gains in importance through its increased moral impression. This amply offsets the unavoidable losses.

There are combat situations where unshakable resistance to the last moment is necessary and even honorable in the highest degree, even if it leads to the loss of artillery pieces. The artillery position must never be evacuated without permission of the commander of the units to which the artillery is attached. If he has sent no orders to the artillery, his consent must be requested if an evacuation is necessary.

As a general rule, movements to the rear are commenced at the walk. If several batteries are together, advance and retreat is usually done by echelon. A battery that has exhausted its ammunition does not retreat. It remains under hostile fire until ammunition is brought up.

The highest value is to be placed on good fire discipline in training as well as in combat. On the one hand, husbanding ammunition is necessary, whereas on the other, firing may be commenced at the very longest ranges. The selection of targets is governed by their momentary importance based on the combat situation.

In the attack, one should first silence the hostile batteries and then disrupt (*erschüttern*) that portion of the position which one desires to attack.

While a portion of the artillery accompanies the infantry and is always ready to exploit its success, the remainder must continue to fire from

32. The term literally means "the breaking-in fight."

its rearward positions as long as possible and must especially fire on newly arriving hostile batteries and on the enemy's reserves.

In the defense, the advancing units, especially where they appear in large masses, will form the most important target.

After a victory, the first pursuit is by fire. The artillery must participate in that to the fullest extent.

As soon as the enemy withdraws from the effective fire zone, the main body of the artillery follows at a rapid pace, protected by cavalry or infantry, and rains a hail of fire on whatever masses of the enemy it can reach. It prevents the enemy from halting and assembling. In this the horse artillery may be able to perform particularly good service.

In this manner the pursuit must continue as long as terrain, horses, and other conditions permit.

To cover a withdrawal from an engagement and in many phases of a retreat, artillery can perform the most important services.

In open terrain it is able by itself to ward off the pursuing enemy's enormous firepower from the march columns that are often forming under very difficult conditions so that an orderly retreat is possible. Strong artillery should be left in the final fighting line as long as possible for that purpose. It then falls back by echelon to the greatest degree possible.

Combat Engineers (Pioneers)

Due to their training and armament, pioneers are able to fight just like other units.[33] However, their special and most important task is the execution of technical work in sight of the enemy, work that can be of the greatest importance to the other arms and the course of the engagement.

The commander of the engineers and pioneers will in general be informed of the situation and of the intentions of the corps commander. Based on this, he submits his recommendations for possible strengthening of the position, for creation of communications, and for possible

---

33. The German term was *Pioniere.*

bringing up of entrenching material and tools from depots in the rear. He takes the proper measures for these after approval by the commander.

He has full freedom of the engagement field, but returns as often as possible to his immediate superior. At all times, he has the right to take his recommendations to the commander, who decides everything. The engineer commander decides minor measures that have no great influence on the whole.

Captains of pioneers have, to a certain degree, the obligation to take independent action. Momentary, unforeseen conditions may make their activity desirable and necessary.

The pioneer officer has to determine (or guess)[34] the needs of the units and seek to meet them. In this he must not wait for orders, and will consequently have to act on his own responsibility. Continuous and exact observation of the movements of the units and of the terrain is absolutely required for such action. The commanders of pioneer companies attached to divisions therefore are not bound to their units. They move about freely and may use their officers for reconnaissance purposes, with the exception of one left in charge of the company.

Pioneer companies should never be split up without good reason. The wagons with pioneer field tools always remain with the companies. The division bridge train may be left behind if the terrain precludes its use.

Among the duties to be performed by pioneers on their own initiative—even when no orders have been issued—are: repair of damaged places in roads the utilization of which is important, removal of obstacles, construction of crossings and bridges over creeks and ditches with locally available material, strengthening of artillery and infantry positions, following the infantry into battle, opening approaches to the hostile position when necessary, and assisting in securing the possession of captured localities.

On the other hand, setting up the bridge train, taking down bridges, destruction of railroads and telegraph lines and other large works,

---

34. Moltke's word here is *erraten,* which may be either "guess" or "determine." The point is lack of certainty, but "guess" seems a little too strong in English.

especially those of permanent importance, must never be done without orders from or approval of the corps commander. The independent actions of pioneer officers must always be in harmony with the general intention and must strive to maintain links between pioneers and the formations to which they are attached. In this way the command will not be forced to do without their services where they are most urgently required.

FORTUNATE AND UNFORTUNATE GENERALS

Success principally decides the reputation of a general. How much of it is his actual due is very difficult to determine. Even the best of men fail against the irresistible force of circumstances, and the same force will carry along the mediocre man. A capable supreme commander (*Feldherr*) can easily be defeated by a less capable one; but only the capable will have luck in the long run.

Where armies have commanders as in 1870, and where one has to reckon only with victories, strategy has everything that it needs.

We have had only victories. Gneisenau, however, led a beaten army to victory. We have not yet stood this highest test.

In failed campaigns, selfishness always demands that someone bears the blame. Had it not been for that someone, we would have been successful in everything.[35]

A beaten supreme commander! If the layman only had the faintest idea what that means! That evening of Königgrätz—when I think back upon it! Such a capable, brave, cautious general like Benedek!

It is the privilege of the Romance peoples always to have been "betrayed" when things go badly. In 1806 we called all commanders who surrendered their fortresses "blockhead," or "old woman"—but never traitor. It takes great courage to surrender, for at the very moment when the final word has been spoken, the conviction at once springs up everywhere that the surrender was unnecessary. At least that view is held by those who risk nothing. In that case the army becomes a

35. Here Moltke is speaking ironically, as the following section indicates.

danger, not to the enemy, but to the commander. Napoleon III eluded that danger in 1870 by fleeing from Sedan during the night. Bazaine remained in Metz.

The law is most severe with surrender in the open field, because *there* the army is able either to fight or to give way.

Bazaine *possibly* had the freedom to strike out; he was not able to escape.

He stood and fell with Metz, within its works. He would have been in the open field only after he had broken through the hostile ring. There he would probably have been *annihilated,* but surely he would not have *capitulated.*

At Sedan the army surrendered in the open field, and yet Wimpffen kept his head.[36] The man who stood at the head of the French government (MacMahon) at the time Bazaine was court-martialled was spared the fate of having to surrender in the open field only by a fragment of shell. He thus owed it only to mere chance that he did not do exactly what Bazaine did, and he it was who had to pardon his comrade, the very man who offered the most resistance to us in three battles; the man whom a number of generals in Metz wanted to imprison, accusing him of treason and incapacity. But none of them dared to take the lead in that arrest, probably because none of them felt that he could do any better than the marshal.

It is my belief that Bazaine had no intention of leaving Metz, for the following reasons:

He assembled all his reserves on August 16 behind his left wing. He sent no support by the Guard to the left wing on that day. He intended to save one army for France. He had hopes of playing a great role!

All of this is far from being *treason.* In different circumstances he would have been acclaimed a patriot. Who knows but what Bazaine sought the throne, or at least the *Lieutenance de France!* Even that would not have been treason—except in the light of September 4, 1870, and, of course, also only in the opinion of the government at the time of his trial.

---

36. This was French Gen. Emmanuel Felix de Wimpffen, governor of Oran when the war began. By a quirk of circumstances he arrived at the battle after all was lost, yet had to be the one to surrender the French forces.

Let us place ourselves in Bazaine's entirely abnormal situation.

[There were] a captive emperor, to whom the general had sworn loyalty, and an illegal government, which had usurped power. There was only the fatherland, but in whom was it personified?

Had peace with Napoleon been possible, Bazaine would have been the hero of France.

CHAPTER FOUR
1869 INSTRUCTIONS FOR LARGE UNIT COMMANDERS

Following the victorious 1866 war against Austria, Moltke ordered the General Staff's historical section to prepare a study of the army's strengths and weaknesses and the lessons of the campaign. This study, which pointed out many shortcomings of the Prussian army, was ready for the king on July 25, 1868. It served as the basis for a new set of guidelines for the army's senior commanders. This document became one of the most influential and enduring operational instructions ever written. Its principles endured for more than seventy years. Moltke wrote large sections of this document and carefully supervised the writing and reviewing of the entire project. Several relatively junior General Staff officers assisted in the project. Among these were then-Maj. Julius von Verdy du Vernois, then-Lt. Col. Count Hermann von Wartensleben-Carow, and then-Maj. Carl von Brandenstein. Prince Kraft zu Hohenlohe-Ingelfingen, a famous artillery officer, also assisted in the original study of the 1866 campaign.[1]

The new document, titled *Verordnungen für die höheren Truppenführer vom 24 Juni 1869 (Instructions for Large Unit Commanders of 24 June 1869)*, provided the basis for German theory on large-unit operations for more than seventy years. It was revised slightly in 1885, survived intact through the years when Waldersee and Schlieffen served as chiefs of the General Staff, and was reprinted with minor changes in 1910. Its basic precepts dominated the German army's classic manual of

---

1. This section is based on the General Staff's editorial introduction to the instructions, published in *Moltkes Militärische Werke*, 2, part 2, 167–69.

1933, *Command of Units.* No single surviving official document is more important for understanding the practical basis of German military theory.[2]

In publishing the *Instructions,* the General Staff relied on the authors' hand-written drafts. The document had a very limited circulation prior to its publication in Moltke's *Military Works.* This version, however, is not complete. The General Staff's version of Moltke's writings omitted the following sections: II, "Railroads and Telegraphs"; III, "Provisioning"; and IV, "Medical Services." These sections apparently were not Moltke's personal work. Their absence is of little importance to the overall focus of this volume. This section of the *Military Works* contains only the draft's text, and thus lacks the usual historical examples.

I. GENERAL

1. The field of real activity for an army is war. Nevertheless, its development, its normal state, and the largest portion of its life fall in times of peace.

This contradiction (*Gegensatz*) renders goal-oriented training difficult and raises the danger of a sudden transition [to war].

In peace, the moral element seldom comes to be of value (*Geltung*); in war it forms the precondition of every victory, the true value of a unit. In war, the qualities of character weigh more heavily than those of reason (*Verstand*). Many step forth brilliantly on the battlefield who would be overlooked in garrison life. In the conduct of war (*beim kriegerischen Handeln*) what one does often matters less than how one does it. A firm decision (*Entschluss*)[3] and persistent execution of a simple concept lead most certainly to the goal.

---

2. On the manual's enduring impact, see Kessel, *Moltke,* 505–06. On the later manual of the Reichswehr and Wehrmacht periods, see Germany, Chef der Heeresleitung, *H. Dv. 300/1 and 300/2. Truppenführung,* 2 vols. (Berlin: E. S. Mittler & Son, 1933).

3. German theory from Clausewitz through the end of the Second World War used *Entschluss* (resolution; normally meaning the solution of a problem) to designate the commander's decision in a tactical or strategic situation. Throughout this text *Entschluss* is translated as decision. This is not to be confused with the German term *Entscheidung* (decision) meaning a decision in battle. Thus the German words allow much greater precision. The text will use the English word "decision" where the German term is *Entscheidung.* On this point see the editor's "Abuses of German Military History," *Military Review* 66, no. 12 (December 1986): 67–68.

2. War places increased demands upon the officer, who has to earn the trust of the soldier (*Soldat*)[4] through his personal conduct. It is expected that he will maintain calm and assurance (*Ruhe und Sicherheit*). One wishes to see the officer at the point where the danger is the greatest. The bravest join him and pull the others along. The strength of the army rests in the platoon leader at the front and in the captain, upon whom all eyes are directed.

3. But this strength must be guided by the intelligence of the commanders (*Führer*), who bear greater responsibility the higher they stand. They must make the most difficult decisions (*Entschlüsse*) under conditions of physical exertion, mental excitement, deprivation, and suffering. Their decisions must be clearly and exhaustively communicated. The highest authorities (*Behörden*) above all lack time for calm reflection, and, just as frequently, the certain evidence that alone allows full insight into the prevailing situation. The reports that should form the basis for such full insight are sometimes insufficient, perhaps contradictory, or even entirely absent. They exaggerate danger on the one side or overlook it on the other. They may intentionally or unintentionally be misrepresentative, and they will more or less always reflect an individual interpretation. From such surrounding darkness what is correct must be discovered (often will only be guessed at), in order to issue orders. In the path of the execution of these orders enter incalculable chance and unforeseeable hindrances.

But in this fog of uncertainty at least one thing must be certain: one's own decision.[5] One must adhere to it and not allow oneself to be dissuaded by the enemy's actions until this has become unavoidably necessary. Simple action consistently carried out will be the most certain way to reach the goal.[6]

---

4. The German terms normally used for enlisted personnel were *Soldat* or, in the collective plural, *Mannschaften*. The German word *Truppe* (plural, *Truppen*) almost always means "unit" rather than "troops," although it is frequently so rendered. Throughout this text *Truppe* is usually rendered as "unit."

5. Here again Moltke uses *Entschluss,* meaning the resolution of the problem, not the English word "resolution" in the sense meaning a firm resolve to do something.

6. This text does not follow the widely accepted but erroneous practice of translating *Handeln* as "operation." The latter term applies to virtually all military activities and levels in the American usage, from movements of army groups to actions of platoons.

4. The handling of large army units is not to be learned in peace-time. One is limited to the study of individual factors, particularly the terrain, and the experiences of earlier campaigns. But the advance of technology, especially improved communications and new weapons, in short, completely changed circumstances, causes the means through which victory was previously achieved—and even the rules laid down by the greatest commanders (*Feldherren*)—to appear to be inapplicable in the present.

Peacetime maneuvers, even the most extensive, give only a very incomplete picture of real war. In them, the provisioning of the units is arranged ahead of time and they are not hindered in their move-ments by the burdensome and especially indispensable trains. But above all, peacetime maneuvers exclude any decision of arms and therefore the moral element.[7] Moreover, their great utility (*Nutzen*) ends at the moment when the sections maneuvering against each other come to-gether for a general engagement. The practice rides (*Übungsreisen*) of the General Staff afford a valuable guide, but not for the mass of the army and not under the pressure of the heavy responsibility of reality.

The teachings (*Lehre*) of strategy go little beyond the first premises of sound reason; one may hardly call them a scholarly discipline (*Wissenschaft*).[8] Their worth lies almost entirely in practical applica-

---

In the German usage, however, *Operation* had a very specific and limited usage; it was not interchangeable with such words as *Handeln*. This text thus uses operation only when the German text uses *Operation* or the adjective. The German army used the term operation to describe the movements of large units.

7. Moltke's term here was *Entscheidung*.

8. Moltke's term for teachings is the often-used term *Lehren*, frequently translated as doctrine, most prominently, perhaps, in the translation of Clausewitz's *On War*. *Lehre*, however, does not mean doctrine in most German texts. The German word for doctrine, *Doktrin*, contains implications of dogma and rigidity, whereas *Lehre* is less formal and controlling. Private writers frequently used this term to describe their personal theories, as in Wilhelm von Scherff's *Die Lehre vom Kriege*. Not even the most authoritative American officer would describe his theories as doctrine. In fact, the old Prusso-German army had no concept of doctrine in the modern American and

tion.[9] What counts is to comprehend in good time the momentarily changing situation and after that to do the simplest and most natural things with steadiness and prudence. War thus becomes an art that many disciplines serve. Steadiness and prudence alone do not by a wide margin make the highest commander (*Feldherr*), but where they are lacking, they must be replaced by other qualities.

Very large assemblies of units (*Truppenversammlungen*) are in and of themselves a catastrophe. An army concentrated at a single point is difficult to provision and will never be billeted. It cannot be induced to march, nor to operate (*operieren*). It can absolutely not exist in the long run. It may only be induced to strike.

It is therefore an error to concentrate all one's strength without an entirely definite goal and for reasons other than for a decision of arms (*Entscheidung*). One can never be strong enough for this decision, and to that end the employment of the last battalion on the battlefield is absolutely desired. But whoever would move first toward the enemy dares not go forward concentrated on a single road or only a few.

The problem (*Aufgabe*) of the command of large masses is to keep them separated for operations as long as possible and to assemble them in good time for the decision (*Entscheidung*).

No calculation of space and time guarantees victory in this realm of chance, mistakes, and disappointments. Uncertainty and the danger of failure accompany every step toward the goal, which will not be attained if fate is completely unfavorable. In war, everything is uncertain; nothing is without danger, and only with difficulty will one attain great results by another route.

5. Victory (*Sieg*) in combat[10] is the most important factor in war.

Western sense. That army used the term *Lehre* rather than *Doktrin* to describe the concepts in its official manuals. The German term *Wissenschaft* may be translated as science, but only with the understanding that its real meaning relates to any subject with a disciplined body of knowledge. The modern term "science" has too many technical, mathematical, and empirical connotations to serve as a good translation for *Wissenschaft* as understood in nineteenth century Germany and in the old Prussian army in particular. This text thus usually uses "discipline" as the translation for *Wissenschaft*.

9. Moltke's term was *konkrete Anwendung*.

10. Moltke here uses the term *Waffentscheidung*, literally "decision of arms."

Victory alone breaks the will of the enemy and forces him to submit to our will. Neither the possession of a tract of land nor the conquest of a fortified position will suffice. On the contrary, only the destruction (*Zerstörung*) of the enemy's fighting power will, as a rule, be decisive. This [destruction of the enemy's fighting power] is therefore the foremost object of operations (*Operationsobjekt*).

In the battle itself, the losses of the victorious side can be just as great as those of the defeated, and exploitation is necessary to reap the fruits of victory. In a concentrically conducted attack the main harvest may, in exceptional cases, be on the battlefield itself; as a rule it will be on the other side of it. By exploiting victory, one prevents the enemy from reestablishing himself and accomplishes what usually is to be attained only through a second battle.

The modern conduct of war (*Kriegführung*) is marked by the striving for a great and rapid decision. Many factors press for a rapid termination of the war: the struggle of the armies; the difficulty of provisioning them; the cost of being mobilized; the interruption of commerce, trade, business, and agriculture; the battle-ready organization of the armies, and the ease with which they may be assembled. Minor engagements exercise only a small influence in this, but they make possible the main decision (*Hauptentscheidung*) and break the path to it.

Preparation for battle is therefore the main task (*Hauptaufgabe*) of military training.

6. Even in peacetime, the command structures[11] of the army, which are already organized in peacetime and which continue in war with only partial expansion, serve to bring to fulfillment the will of the highest commander. This is accomplished through the unified action of all the parts, both in operations and in engagements.

The orders of the highest commander proceed along the intended chain of command (*Instanzenwege*) with certainty to the last man of the army, as long as the order of battle is not disturbed. If nothing is

---

11. Here Moltke used the term *Kommandoverhältnisse,* literally command relationships. "Structure" seemed more appropriate for the modern reader in view of the subsequent discussion.

ordered, the order of battle, which assigns each to his prescribed position, is valid. If this chain of command is lost, it is everyone's duty to restore it; but especially such is the duty of the leaders of small detachments, which, particularly in an engagement, are dissuaded by their subordinate units. Such leaders should not allow themselves to be searched after, but should eagerly return to the struggle under the command[12] of their nearest superior.

Certainly the order of battle is not to be maintained unconditionally and under all circumstances. Special goals demand special formations, detachments, advance guards, or other commands. But even then, one should bring together what belongs together and build no new whole from parts that previously belonged to different commands. A brigade acting as an advance guard is furnished with its brigade staff and two regimental staffs.[13] A combined brigade of six individual battalions, on the contrary, lacks both [regimental staffs]. Each battalion in such a case must be led with special orders.

There are many situations in which the officer must act according to his own judgment (*Einsicht*). It would be indeed absurd if he waited for orders in moments where often no orders could be given. As a rule, however, his work is the most profitable for the whole when he carries out the will of his superior.

7. Finally, the discipline of the units gives assurance that the will of the superior will everywhere attain execution.

If, under the exertions in the field, much of the behavior appropriate for parade is abandoned, this takes place at the order of, or with the permission of, the superior. Willful deviations from the established arrangement (*Ordnung*)[14] may in no case be tolerated, for the disintegration of discipline spreads like a virus.

---

12. Here Moltke used *Befehl* (order), but "command" seems more correct as an English equivalent.

13. Moltke here means that merely combining battalions from different units will not suffice because such a specially formed brigade will lack the normal regimental headquarters.

14. German military literature distinguished carefully between *Ordnung* and *Befehl,* which meant order in the command sense. To avoid confusion here, *Ordnung* is rendered as arrangement. Here Moltke certainly means order in a general sense rather than as a specific military command, written or verbal.

Discipline is the foundation pillar of the army; its strict maintenance benefits everything.

V. STRUCTURE OF THE ARMY[15]

1. The order of battle, as set up with the mobilization of the army, establishes the continuing, normal unity of all command and administrative authorities and units. It applies everywhere and shows everyone his place and his area of responsibility if special orders do not specify otherwise. It may be modified only in such cases and to the extent necessary for the attainment of precise intentions (*Absichten*).

2. The War Ministry arranges the order of battle of the army corps. The order of battle determines which units of the corps' peacetime establishments will go forth in the coming mobilization for fortress occupation, coastal defense, detached corps, and so forth, or if other corps do these things. After that, the corps commanders design the order of battle of their corps and submit these for all-highest approval.[16]

For the arrangement of the order of battle, the following principles are valid in accordance with the mobilization plan:

a. The standing peacetime organization is to be maintained as much as possible;

b. The corps is composed of
- two infantry divisions,
- a cavalry division (brigade),
- the corps artillery,
- the trains, and
- the administration.

c. Each of the two infantry divisions is formed by
- (as a rule) four infantry regiments on a peacetime footing,

---

15. The German title was *Gliederung der Armee.*

16. In this sentence Moltke uses *Generalkommandos,* which meant the corps commanders. Later in the century, and up to the First World War, the title usually given to corps commanders was *kommandierende Generale.* "All-highest" approval meant royal approval, although in 1869 this might have come through the war minister. One should remember that, in peacetime, corps commanders in the Prussian army had no superior except the king and each had the right of direct access to the monarch.

- a light cavalry division (brigade),
- a foot artillery section,
- one or two pioneer companies with a light field bridge or entrenching equipment, and
- a medical detachment.

In addition, the corps's Jäger (light infantry) battalion is attached to one of the two infantry divisions.

As far as possible, infantry divisons within an army corps are to be formed in equal strength, although the regimental organization is not to be disrupted to accomplish this.

An infantry division may not have fewer than eight infantry battalions. If it is not possible to form two divisons of at least this strength, then a corps will establish only one infantry division.

An isolated infantry battalion will be placed under the command of another regiment. A regimental command will be established only when it has at least two battalions under its orders. A brigade command will be established only when at least two regimental commands are placed under it. The brigade may be three regiments or nine battalions in strength (inclusive of the Jäger battalion attached to the brigade). Accordingly, if the infantry of a division adds up to only three infantry regiments, it forms only one brigade.

d. The cavalry divison (brigade) consists of the cavalry of the corps, insofar as it is not apportioned to the infantry divisions, and of a mounted battery.

e. The corps artillery consists of

- a foot section,
- the mounted section (with two battalions),
- the supply section,
- the bridge column and its accompanying command, and
- a medical detachment.

f. The trains.

g. The administration. [Both the trains and the administration] are established according to articles eight and nine of the mobilization plan.

h. The commanders and staffs not hereby employed are listed as "available."

It is possible that a nondivisional cavalry regiment intended for transport or for marching to its deployment must be attached to an infantry division for the purpose of the most rapid possible concentration.[17] This arrangement may continue until the corps is assembled and the cavalry regiment can be detached.

3. The following establishes the line of succession for the appointed commander as confirmed in the order of battle:

- The commanding general is to be replaced by the most senior division commander of the army corps.
- The chief of the General Staff by the most senior General Staff officer of the staff of the corps command.
- A division commander by the most senior brigade commander within the army corps.
- A brigade commander by the most senior regimental commander of that arm within the corps.
- The artillery commander by the commander of the field artillery regiment.
- The engineer commander by the most senior engineer officer present in the corps.
- A staff officer by the most senior captain (*Rittmeister*)[18] of the regiment or independent battalion.
- A company, squadron, battery, or column commander by the most senior lieutenant of the regiment (or battalion).

4. It is neither possible nor appropriate under all circumstances to maintain the structure of the army corps and the resulting command relationships established in the order of battle. Special goals, be they the execution of march, the conduct of an engagement, or such, will make modifications necessary. In such cases a "march or engagement organization" is temporarily established, and the order of battle reestablished as soon as the situation allows.

5. It may be necessary to assemble the greatest possible mass of cavalry under the direct order (*Befehl*) of the highest war command. Massed cavalry may be needed either at the beginning of operations

---

17. Prussian cavalry consisted of two types, designated by function and assignment. "Divisional cavalry" consisted of small formations attached to infantry divisons for local reconnaissance and combat. "Army cavalry" consisted of divisions or groups of divisions for strategic reconnaissance or other missions for the high commands.

18. A *Rittmeister* was a captain of cavalry.

for reconnaissance of the enemy situation, in the course of a battle, or finally for an extended period for use in exploitation of a victory.

The cavalry divisions, especially of those corps that need them least for the moment, will be detached temporarily for the duration of such efforts. They will be placed under the designated "cavalry general" of the main headquarters or that of the army and will be reinforced by horse artillery and other detachments. This general thereafter operates independently according to directives received from the high command. For objects such as those mentioned, it may also be necessary to place the cavalry general under a large infantry formation (up to an infantry division).[19]

6. The formation of an advance or rear guard is an essential part of an annex to the order of battle and may vary from that only as little as possible. So-called combined advance guards are to be avoided on principle and are warranted only under entirely special circumstances.

The advance guard of an army usually will be composed of a unified infantry division strengthened by a cavalry division or a brigade,[20] or even an entire army corps. In the latter case, the corps must exercise its function through infantry reinforced by cavalry.

An independently operating army corps generally takes a unified infantry brigade including two to three batteries from the artillery formations of the same division in the advance guard. This is to be accompanied by a not-too-small cavalry element, according to the situation and the terrain. This cavalry can, in case of need, be taken from the cavalry division and strengthened by a mounted battery. One always takes a medical detachment and a pioneer company, which usually accompanies the light field brigade trains.

19. Moltke here used the term *Direktiven* for directives, although on many other occasions his term was *Weisung*. Thus the difference, both in Moltke's days and later, in forms of command was not (as is often erroneously assumed) between *Befehl* (order) and *Auftrag* (task), but between a specific *Befehl* and a general directive (*Weisung* or *Direktive*). Moltke's theory and practice recognized that either form could be appropriate, depending on local circumstances and personalities. Moltke had no dogmatic approach to leading by directives, as some have maintained. Nor did the Prussian army prior to the First World War have an overarching theory of command based on directives.

20. Moltke's term was *geschlossene,* a common term meaning a whole unit with its integrity intact, as opposed to a unit formed of parts of other units.

As a rule, a division forms its advance guard from a unified infantry regiment. According to the situation, the advance guard may consist of a few squadrons (but usually of the entire cavalry regiment with one platoon left with the main body) and at least a foot battery, a pioneer company with the light field bridge trains, and a section of the medical detachment.

With small detachments one must always take care that the tactical units[21] are disrupted as little as possible. It would be better that the advance guard be somewhat too weak or too strong in relationship to the entire force.

7. The separating out of a reserve is in general unconditionally necessary only for the engagement. A spacial separation of the same can have only the significance of avoiding congested columns because of the distances between the parts.

In a division or yet smaller body of units, congested columns are no longer a problem and there is therefore no reason to form a reserve.

But for the engagement a reserve may never be lacking. The disposition or the order at the beginning of the engagement specifies which units (*Truppenkörper*) should assume this function. At the same time it is made clear that the reserve unconditionally remains at the direct and exclusive disposition of the commander.

8. In general, therefore, care must be taken for the greatest possible retention of the original order of battle and to stick to it strictly. This is so that the units, as far as possible, remain in their usual formations (*Verbände*) and command relationships. If a unit must give up one of its elements for the formation of an advance guard or a reserve, even then the individual parts must remain as long as possible directly under the parent unit's next higher command authority. So, for example, the corps command gives orders directly to an infantry brigade remaining with the main body after the formation of an advance guard.

The units (*Truppentheile*) for their part are duty bound to maintain the integrity of their elements. When the changing situation of battle

---

21. Here Moltke uses the very common German term *taktische Einheit,* which means a unit, usually no smaller than a battalion, that could perform battlefield functions in its own right.

causes separations, this unit integrity is to be reestablished as soon as possible. It is therefore the responsibility of the companies to stay with their battalions, and the battalions with their regiments and brigades. The divisional cavalry remains unconditionally in communication with the mass of the division's infantry, even when this entails losses. If they are not taken under effective fire, the division's batteries follow the movements of the infantry and accompany its attack at a short distance. Variations from the normal structure can be allowed only very exceptionally, for example if one scrapes together all the detachments still fit for the last resistance in case of disaster or for exploitation after a victorious battle. Then certainly all other considerations step immediately into the background compared to the one goal. *Nevertheless, the strictest maintenance or the immediate restoration of the order of battle* remains the rule.

VI. COMMUNICATIONS BETWEEN COMMANDS AND UNITS[22]

1. Continuous communication between command authorities and units is for the cooperation of all toward a single goal. It is therefore of the greatest significance and is indispensable for the orderly direction of the army.

This communication is maintained through orders from above no less than through messages and reports from below, the latter of which form the essential foundation of the first.

2. The issuing of orders (*Befehlsertheilung*) must observe official channels as far as possible, not only in operations, but also in the battle. Bypassing an intermediate authority destroys its effectiveness and causes it to appear superfluous. Where, in isolated cases, the direct intervention of the high commander is unavoidable to avoid loss of time, the bypassed channels absolutely must be informed of the relevant orders. Such deviations from the official channels are more justified on the part of the high command (*Heeresleitung*) than by subordinate

---

22. The German title was *Verbindung der Kommandobehörden und Truppen untereinander.*

command authorities. Time and space are of a greater significance for the former, which possesses the means to inform the bypassed officials about the orders. *Never may it happen that a commander does not know where the units subordinate to him are or what orders they have.*

3. The advantage, moreover, which the commander believes to achieve through continuous personal intervention, is mostly only an apparent one. He thereby takes over functions for whose fulfillment other persons are designated. He more or less denigrates their ability and increases his own duties to such a degree that he can no longer fulfill them completely.

4. These demands on the abilities of the high commander are already in themselves not small. It is far more important that the high commander retain a clear perspective of the entire state of affairs than that any detail is carried out in any particular way or another.

In the first respect, he needs his full mental calm and physical strength and must preserve both under the strain of heavy responsibilities, danger, and exertions.

In order to make important judgments (*Beschlüsse*) he must carefully balance uncertain and unclear reports against one another. It happens only too easily that one will attach a greater significance to what one sees directly in front of oneself, where perhaps one has taken part, than to the often vastly more important matter which is communicated from afar.

5. In general, one does well to order no more than is absolutely necessary and to avoid planning beyond the situations one can foresee. These change very rapidly in war. Seldom will orders[23] that anticipate far in advance and in detail succeed completely to execution. This shakes the confidence of the subordinate commander and it gives the units a feeling of uncertainty when things develop differently than what the high command's order had presumed.

Moreover, it must be pointed out that if one orders much, then the important thing that needs to be carried out unconditionally will be carried out only incidentally or not at all because it is obscured by

---

23. Here Moltke used *Anordnungen* instead of *Befehle.*

the mass of secondary things and those which are valid only under the circumstances.

The higher the authority, the shorter and more general will the orders be. The next lower command adds what further precision appears necessary. The detail of the execution is left to the verbal order, to the command.[24] Each thereby retains freedom of action and decision within his authority.[25]

One will not wish to articulate motives, expectations, and intents in orders because of concerns for secrecy. On the other hand, it is indispensable that the subordinate authorities recognize the object of the one who gave the orders in order to strive for the goal when circumstances demand that they act other than as was ordered.

Every command position should communicate only as much of the high command's intention as is necessary for the attainment of the goal. Seldom will the arrangements of the higher be simply repeated to the lower authorities. Certainly in war, where the giving of orders entails such heavy responsibilities, no one presses for that, contrary to peacetime.

It is, however, the first duty of a commander that he command, that he not allow things to proceed as chance leads them. Obviously, he must see for himself if and how his orders are being carried out.

6. It is advisable to repeat every verbal order, as well as every message that is intended to be conveyed, and to note the time of the dispatch. Whenever possible, orders and messages are to be dispatched in writing, with information of the place and time of their departure noted. Officers sent with messages and orders are duty bound to return to their commander immediately after the fulfillment of their task (*Auftrag*) with information on the precise time of delivery, in order to be ready for new dispatches.

7. *The most precise possible knowledge of the situation* is an absolute prerequisite for giving correct and appropriate orders. The units

---

24. Here Moltke used *Befehl* for "order" and *Kommandowort* for "verbal order."

25. Here Moltke used *Entschliessung*, which can mean either resolution or decision. For consistency in limiting "resolution" to the rather more technical military term *Entschluss*, the editor has chosen "decision," which in any case seems more in keeping with the present context of the term.

and subordinate headquarters, the outposts, the advance guards, detached sections, and so forth are therefore *unconditionally duty bound* to orient their higher command on the situation insofar as possible. The more similar the picture that all parts of the whole (the higher and lower commanders) gain from the reports, the more easily are orders issued and the more correctly will they be understood and the more uniform will the cooperation be.

A careful examination of the contents and wording of every message is necessary in order to decide correctly what is certain, what is probable, or what is only possible. Fears and self-delusion must gain no influence on the estimate of the situation. A correct evaluation[26] must emphasize the essential over the non-essential. A subordinate commander might scarcely think it worthwhile to send a message that his post was undisturbed by the enemy during a certain time. Nevertheless, this circumstance can be very important for the conduct of the whole.

8. At the end of an engagement it is usually of the greatest value for the high command to learn quickly which of the enemy's regiments and corps one has opposed and in what condition the enemy finds himself. The units are usually best able to recognize this, just as they are able to recognize the regimental numerical designations of the dead and prisoners, to discover the name of the enemy corps commander, and to indicate the direction of the retreat.

9. It is greatly in the interest of every (especially of a combat) element to orient both the higher command and adjacent units on its situation. One must remember that in times demanding great activity, especially in the critical moments of an engagement, the acting persons are little inclined, and may easily fail, to send back messages and communications. At that time they believe they need support. In order to be certain of continuous orientation on the situation, it is therefore advisable for the higher command itself to ensure reception of reports. To this end it is advisable to place an officer from the higher staff (with his own orderlies) in the engaged subordinate element as a reporter.

---

26. Moltke used the word *Takt*, literally, "measure" or even "time." In this context he meant what the modern reader would regard as an estimate or evaluation of the situation.

Such an arrangement is important to a great degree, especially for advance and rear guards, and may never be lacking. But it is also advisable in many engagements and for maintaining communications and co-operation with neighboring corps and armies. General Staff officers are to be employed on such missions in important cases.

These General Staff officers remain at their assigned posts and send reports through messenger officers. They return only if a personal report appears necessary or if the general situation no longer requires their presence.

A few orderly officers from the cavalry are always to be placed at the disposition of the headquarters of infantry brigades and divisions, which otherwise would not be in a position to expedite the necessary messages.

10. Arrangements in this sense will make it possible to lead large armies as well-integrated organisms and to bring cohesion and unity into the activities[27] and engagements of small detachments, upon which military strength so essentially depends.

VII. ORDER OF MARCH[28]

1. One should realize that a Prussian army corps, with its entire trains formed in a single column, has a length of about eighteen miles.[29] Movement soon lengthens this normal extension, which doubles on poor roads, in unfavorable weather, or through partial impediments. Therefore the advance element of the column has already arrived in the new bivouac before the tail [*Queue*] has left the old one. Thus it is obvious that, at the most, only one corps can move forward in one day on a single road.

2. Certainly when it comes to an engagement, one will leave behind the dispensable trains. But even the actual combat portion of a

---

27. Here Moltke's term is *Handlungen,* again not to be confused with "operations," which had a much more specific meaning than is the case here.

28. The German title was *Marschordnung.*

29. A German mile was about 4½ English miles. The German text says four [meaning German] miles.

corps formed in a column takes up a length of 11¼ [English] miles, thus the length of a normal day's march. The forward element can be supported by the tail only after the course of many hours.

3. It is therefore a mistake to believe that one is concentrated if one moves everything, or much of it, on a single road. One loses in depth more than one gains at the front. Two divisions, which march next to each other at an interval of 4½ [English] miles to 6¾ [English] miles, will more easily and better support each other than they would if they directly followed one another. It is clear in and of itself how important it is for large army formations to march in more than a single column whenever possible. This will preserve the strength of the units and will ease their lodging and provisioning.

4. This procedure is obviously limited by the number of available roads and by the necessity of mutual support.

One will not find numerous roads everywhere. To some extent parallel roads lead to the same point. Also, the columns must not be completely prevented from cooperating because of terrain barriers when it is foreseeable that such can be necessary.

Naturally, the number of parallel roads decreases as the space through which the march is to move becomes more restricted. An army assembled at a single point can move only cross-country. In order to march, it must divide itself either in breadth or in depth, something that is dangerous in close proximity to the enemy. If one wishes therefore to operate, one must maintain the separation of the individual parts of the army.

5. Here it is important that every column be formed of an integrated and battle-ready combat unit (*Gefechtskörper*) under unified command. The corps will therefore always optimally march in divisions. The corps artillery and the trains follow on the good roads.

6. In all marches, especially in those which lead to the enemy, there are two considerations: the least possible depth and easy deployment to combat.

With regard to the first, order and alertness are to be strictly maintained.

Only the authorized wagons may be brought along and only corps commanders or the commanders of independent detached formations may order or give permission to bring along other supply vehicles or, exceptionally, for the transport of packs.

The type of front (platoon, sections, and so forth) in which the columns march is determined by the most narrow point of the road to be used. Also, it must remain possible to create enough room, by closing together the entire column on one side of the road, so that commanders and messenger riders can pass by.

Infantry at rest must, whenever possible, avoid stacking rifles in the road. If the vehicles cannot leave the road without great difficulty, they may halt on the road in a single line. Individual disabled vehicles must always be moved off the road in order not to bring all the following columns (often at a distance of miles) to a stop.

In the second case, what really matters is to bring those units quickly to deployment which have to intervene in the engagement first. That determines the place of individual units in the march column.[30]

7. Where one can advance toward the enemy, the calmness that grows when the infantry, cavalry, and artillery are left each to itself, must be subordinated to readiness for combat, which requires combining them. But here also simplicity of formation is to be sought insofar as circumstances allow.

These constant changes obviously preclude a single regulation that would always be valid for the order of march.

Despite what already has been said about formation of the advance guard, holding back reserves, and so forth, the following are general rules for the march order of a division:

a. The infantry regiment located at the head of the main body belongs to the same brigade as that of the advance guard. It can then come to the support of the advance guard within the brigade and under the command of the brigade commander. The necessary detaching or forming of a new advance guard in the case of a change of direction can be rapidly directed without having to tear apart the second brigade. This remains, on the contrary, intact and available and can be held back in its entirety as a reserve for an engagement, which may be necessary according to the state of things.

---

30. Here Moltke used *Waffen* (arms, or branches), meaning the placement of units of infantry, cavalry, artillery, and engineers in the marching columns.

b. The divisional cavalry is normally responsible for reconnaissance. It therefore, in most cases, marches at the head and leaves behind only a few horses for messenger duty. A part of the cavalry that is forward without employment is best relegated to the tail of the column of the advance guard or the entire division.

c. The artillery with the advance guard, as well as that with the main body, must march as close as possible to the head in order to enter an engagement as early as possible. In the main body, the artillery follows the first regiment or even the first battalion, according to circumstances.

d. An engineer company with the light field bridge trains optimally marches in the tail of the advance guard.

e. The medical detachment follows the last combat unit of the division, but a part of it is in the tail of the advance guard if an engagement is expected.

f. The packhorses (*Handpferde*) follow directly behind each unit (battalion, cavalry regiment, battery). The packhorses (pack carts of the fusilier battalion and the cavalry), the blacksmith, the regimental staff wagons, and the vehicles of the high staff as a rule follow in the tail of the division and close up directly only upon the detaching of their part of the unit.

The remaining unit vehicles, medical carts, wagons with ammunition, officer equipment, and uniforms, and the further specialty wagons, as well as the columns and field hospitals attached to the division, together form that part of the "division trains" which can follow assembled at a greater distance in order to avoid stoppages and in order to prevent confusion in case of necessary movements to the rear.[31] A division will specify a cavalry detachment commanded by an officer for the protection of these elements against contingencies and for police lookouts. Some infantrymen (possibly the sick stragglers) are also to be assigned for this purpose.

Assignment of infantry munitions wagons to the artillery section is not allowed.

If one expects to attack the enemy, then it is appropriate to have a field hospital directly follow the tail of the division.

---

31. Quotation marks were in the original German.

The security of the trains basically depends on judiciously chosen marches and division of columns. Leaving back an entire unit for this purpose is justified only under special circumstances.

8. If small or large sections must march on a single road, they make their march arrangements in a way analogous to that of the division.

In the corps, the remaining parts of the division from which units were taken for the formation of the advance guard belong at the head of the main body. The corps commander thereby gains a means to reinforce and support his advance guard with units of the same formation. He can thus also hold back a reserve suitable for all circumstances. In many cases, especially when reconnaissance succeeds as the result of cavalry that has advanced far forward, it is recommended to commission the lead division itself with execution of the functions of the advance guard, which it then has to undertake with a part of its units appropriate to the circumstances.

The place of a cavalry division in the corps march column will be determined according to local circumstances. In general it will be either far forward, approximately in the tail of the advance guard, insofar as one thinks it necessary to have it there for reconnaissance. In other cases, it is to be inserted near the rear of the column because it will usually come into play near the end of the engagement.

As a rule, the corps artillery takes its place behind the second brigade of the main body, in some circumstances behind the first. To have it follow in the tail of the entire corps is proper only under entirely special circumstances. Because the corps artillery has a purpose[32] other than that of a reserve, it finds its place in the main body sooner and has to follow its movement and to prepare the main attack.[33] It needs time for this and in any case must come into action before the reserve infantry enters the engagement.

As a rule, within the convoy the first echelon (in three columns) follows at a distance of at most 4½ [English] miles, the second echelon (six columns) at a distance of a short day's march. A smaller

---

32. Moltke's word here was *Bestimmung,* which ordinarily would not be rendered as "purpose." Such seemed to the editor to be appropriate in this case, however.

33. Here Moltke means that the artillery will join the main body in action sooner than will the reserve infantry.

separation becomes necessary only after a battle. On the march, such would contribute to great disadvantages in the case of a retreat.

The pontoon column with its accompanying headquarters can often properly march with one of the munitions columns because its employment can always be foreseen a little in advance and because its dispatch can proceed at the right time.

Of the entire body of vehicles there remain those which were sent to the units or to the tail of the division, or also to the corps formations.

On the other hand, the trains battalion (at whose disposal the trains escort squadron is assigned if it is not with the vehicle park) with the designation of "trains of the army corps" follows the tail of the last unit at a great distance (perhaps 4½ [English] miles or more). Then follow the administrative section of the corps headquarters and its vehicles, if they are not farther forward in the march column, then the trains of the division in the same order and, finally, if not otherwise disposed of,

- the horse depot,
- the unassigned field hospitals,
- the field bakeries, and
- the vehicle columns.

As a rule, the munitions columns march behind the trains. In some circumstances it may be appropriate to advance the first echelon before the trains.

9. It goes without saying that special circumstances would demand modification of these statements.

If one expects no contact with the enemy, the column dissolves out of consideration for the most rapid possible deployment and the least possible depth. Then the wagons should directly follow their regiments and brigades for the reason of sparing and relieving the units. It remains absolutely necessary to maintain the standing organization for the trains and the vehicles as long as it is not expressly ordered otherwise. This is all the more important when the movements are to the rear for a few days. The commanding officers are then especially obligated to step in with ruthless vigor and with all available means to maintain order.

10. In the application of a march order, the main body of a division with its combined combat parts, with a normal depth of 7,000–8,000 paces, can march in a time of about 1½ hours to the head, even if it is significantly strengthened. The corps will, if it marches on three nearby roads, stand deployed for an engagement in the same time.

If, on the other hand, the corps moves on a single road, then its combat sections take up a depth of perhaps ten [English] miles, even if an advance guard is subtracted. The completed deployment can then be accomplished in not less than four to five hours. But such is necessary only if one wishes to fight at the point that the head of the column has reached.

If, on the contrary, one wishes only to support the advance guard, a complete deployment is not desirable. A complete deployment is to be avoided as long as possible, because an advance in a deployed front can proceed only slowly, because it depends too much on the terrain, and because it exhausts the units. A premature deployment is therefore absolutely to be avoided.

11. Next to battle preparedness, preserving the units is the most essential consideration in marching.[34] The greatest benefit for everything is a rigorous maintenance of order and discipline. Shortcuts that units or individuals create for themselves through deviation from order and discipline almost always become important aggravations for the whole.

The correct setting of the departure time for the individual parts of a column requires careful attention. A march of 13½ [English] miles is no difficult accomplishment for a soldier if he can go forward smoothly. But it will be difficult if the individual must halt and stand around for hours or if he can move only slowly. It goes without saying that night marches are to be avoided whenever possible. The commanders of small detachments have the authority to order halts in the hot hours of midday and to march farther later on.

This is not always possible when large detachments march in a single column. For them, the day of rest comes into effect.[35] This is also necessary in order to regulate meals and to ensure inner order within the units. It can even be recommended, especially in bivouacs, to lengthen the individual marches rather than to cancel the day of rest.

---

34. Moltke's term was *die Schonung,* which means conserving the units' energy and fighting strength.

35. Prussian practice called for an entire day's rest for marching columns every few days.

VIII. THE UNITS' STATE OF REST[36]

1. Arrangements for resting the units are basically conditioned equally by contradictory considerations: conserving[37] and readiness for battle. The first is to be allowed insofar as the necessary measures of the latter allow. Every commander within his area of competence is responsible for the security of his units; but he is equally bound not to neglect what prevents their attrition and exhaustion. He must remain mindful that in war the wastage from fatigue and sickness usually far exceeds losses in combat. Readiness for combat in the bivouac is purchased by the consumption of the strength of everyone. Conserving the units in the cantonment must be made possible through redoubled security discipline.

2. Beyond the customary cantonment (which is usually entered only during a pause in the operations) and the pure bivouac (in battle array), in war there is frequently a mixture of the two. In this, one uses the large or even the small towns available in the area by keeping the forces closely together. One takes quarters as densely as possible and leaves in the open only those units that could not be brought to billets.

3. A determination of the nature of the lodging belongs to the commander of every independent formation because he bears responsibility that his unit will not be attacked unprepared.[38]

4. In the assignment of cantonments of large units (*Truppenkörper*), the high command limits the districts of the main subordinate units through simple lines on the map. It must still determine to whom the villages between the lines belong. In an analogous way the corps command limits the districts of the divisions, which do the same for brigades, and so forth.

---

36. The German title was *Zustand der Ruhe der Truppen.*
37. Here Moltke means avoiding driving the troops to exhaustion and loss of combat effectiveness.
38. By the "commander of an independent formation," Moltke means an officer who, because of the size of his unit or the special situation of his separated deployment, is not dependent upon a higher commander for the details of his activities.

The consideration of timely assembly remains decisive (*massgebend*) for how widely the cantonments are spread out.

The grouping of the units within the cantonments must be linked to the order of battle; yet the cavalry, for the most part, must be doubled up with the infantry.

Divisions, especially those located very near to the enemy, must be so positioned that they can assemble themselves in the shortest time. Finally, the headquarters of the army, the corps, and the divisions will be brought into such a position relative to each other so that messages and orders go through official channels directly and quickly without unnecessary loss of time.

5. In a complete bivouac, the maintenance of the order of battle is to be observed. It ensures the rapid transmission of commands and maintains order in case of an alarm. After that, concern for shelter and comfort for the units comes into consideration. This includes protection against wind and weather, and the availability of water, wood, and straw.

The bivouac must not be observed by the enemy and must absolutely not be within range of his artillery.

6. In "bivouacking with use of villages," the greatest possible conserving of the units enters more into the foreground. The commander, especially the division commander, will determine to what degree readiness for battle is necessary within his formation, and after that he will specify which and how many units may rest in the site and where the others are to bivouac.

IX. SECURITY AND RECONNAISSANCE DUTY[39]

1. The measures for reconnaissance of the enemy situation and for security of both resting and marching units frequently go hand in hand and must often be simultaneously carried out by the same detachments.

---

39. The German title was *Sicherheits- und Aufklärungsdienst. Dienst* really means service, but also may mean duty, which is no doubt the most appropriate English equivalent. The reader should be aware that the German term for duty in the sense of an obligation to perform certain functions is *Pflicht,* which has a strong connotation of obligation and, indeed, is sometimes quite properly rendered as exactly that.

The leading considerations for them, however, are entirely different. Considerations for the latter are in general more passive in nature; those for the former, more active.

Obviously, the necessity to provide for its own security is immediate for every unit located near the enemy. The need to obtain intelligence about the enemy makes itself felt to a lesser degree and at a later time.[40] These relationships must be watched carefully, lest reconnaissance, which is incumbent upon every unit in the front line, be neglected for security and so that the fundamental basis of the decisions of the high command is not lacking.

2. Reconnaissance is intrinsically and almost exclusively the business of the cavalry, which will find therein a broad field of important activity. The individual rider, as well as the commander up to general, finds opportunity for distinction. Cunning and ability, rapid judgment,[41] and resolute action will be of worth even here. Extraordinary exertions in this cannot be avoided. Highly active undertakings (*Handeln*) are necessary on the part of the cavalry. It will thereby perform important services for the army.

It will always be of value to take a few prisoners as soon as possible. The sight of them makes a good impression on the units and from the numerical designations of their regiments one can often gain important information about the deployment of the enemy's armed forces. In general, there are two ways to clarify the situation. One seeks quickly to gain insight into the enemy situation through individual riders or small detachments, which are either unnoticed by the enemy, or at least give the enemy no time to take countermeasures. In the second way, larger detachments use brute force or combat to seek this information.

3. The former way obviously offers many advantages. It requires little strength and does not attract the attention of the enemy. One therefore prefers to use it in all circumstances. This is true even when one takes

---

40. Here Moltke means that units themselves are more likely to emphasize their own security, the need for which is inherent in their local situation, rather than reconnaissance.

41. Moltke used *Blick,* literally, glance. German military literature frequently used this to mean the ability to make a quick estimate of the situation.

along strong cavalry. One leaves this aside and sends out officers laterally in order to see farther. In this it is necessary to use trained and well-mounted officers with sharp and ready eyes. It is a question of coming quickly to a point that allows a broad view, using rapid judgment, many times in flight, to survey the recognizable details of the enemy situation, the state of his bivouac, his strength, direction of march, and so forth, and then immediately sending clear, complete, and, above all, reliable reports. One cannot entrust this to the common man or to the noncommissioned officer. This will surpass his intellectual capabilities and one will do well to send an officer whenever possible personally to ascertain the correctness of his [common man or NCO] report. Often it will be necessary to select an older, experienced cavalry officer, or even a General Staff officer, to whose job such rides do not properly belong. These officers take along only a few well-mounted orderlies and, in some circumstances, a small covering force (*Bedeckung*) for protection against enemy patrols. They above all seek to remain undetected, to bypass the enemy's patrols and outposts, or to ride around his flanks and, as soon as they are detected, to bring back their acquired knowledge without an engagement, relying entirely on the speed of their horses.

In this way one will most easily receive good and correct intelligence (*Nachrichten*). It will sometimes be advisable, especially in one's own land, continually to keep intelligent officers with weak detachments on the enemy's flanks. These officers will occasionally succeed in obtaining knowledge of the inner movements of the enemy, of the numerical designations of the corps and regiments present, and so forth. They need not be fearful about their communications with their own units. They send their reports, if necessary in a roundabout way, and return after making their estimates as soon as their continued presence there loses its value.

4. Where such a procedure is not possible because of the attentiveness and density of the enemy's forward units, it may be necessary to force these back or to break through them. It is thereby necessary from the start to set so much strength in motion that one is certain of attaining the object. This is because a failed attempt obviously will cause the enemy to become attentive, to take countermeasures, and to strengthen his forward units.

Such enterprises[42] are justified only if one wishes and is in a position to exploit them immediately. This is because today's situation will be a different one by morning.

Reconnaissance engagements, which are often bloody and costly, are to be entirely avoided without direct objects.

Reconnoitering with large masses of cavalry, possibly supported by infantry, which precede the movement of the army by many days' marches, can be especially needed at the beginning of a campaign (*Feldzug*) in order to clarify the general situation of the war. They are directed exclusively by the highest command (*oberste Heeresleitung*).

5. During quiet periods the outposts produce security in the narrow sense. To them also falls the acquisition of intelligence, but only secondarily. Their strength, disposition, and grouping depends essentially on the general military situation, as well as the length of time that one remains in the same place, and must be different according to the prevailing circumstances.

The more time the covering unit needs to make itself ready for battle, the more must the outposts be pushed outward. As a result, they must be stronger and more independent.

The longer one remains in a compromised deployment, so much more careful must the security be. If one makes a halt at night in order to again depart the next morning, it is usually sufficient to occupy the roads leading toward the enemy. If one wishes to remain the next day, then one will extend oneself to the sides, establish more cohesion in the line, and look after security of the flanks. In order to remain days or even weeks in a deployment, one must close oneself up with a greatly extended line that is impenetrable to enemy patrols and detachments. The general state of the terrain, the condition of the currently opposing enemy units, and the spirit of enterprise of their commander will all be of influence on the arrangements.

---

42. Here Moltke used the term commonly used to describe various types of military activities, *Unternehmung*. Its frequent rendering as "operation" is understandable given the current American application of that term for virtually every type of military activity at any level. Such is not the case in old Prusso-German theory, which never described such reconnaissance activities as Moltke is discussing as an "operation," a term the Germans used in a much more limited context than do most modern armies.

In all circumstances, these arrangements are conditioned on one's own position and the terrain. But good patrolling makes some posting of permanent detachments dispensable.

In cases where the outpost line should close many main road systems and where these should be interrupted at length or by terrain obstacles in their intersections, it is recommended to deploy two or more independent detachments near one another. They receive their directives from a common chain of command to the rear, usually from the commander of the advance guard, but they remain in contact and in communication with each other.

6. If one is not yet in close contact with the enemy, one will often obtain security far more completely and with less expenditure of strength by sending detachments, especially cavalry, far forward. These give us the certainty that the enemy is yet at a considerable distance and therefore needs time to reach us. Even so, one may allow concern for preserving the units and their comfort to prevail as long as the forward detachments maintain themselves in defiles and roads that the enemy has to traverse.

The units standing farther to the rear have only to protect themselves with light outposts or, under some circumstances, only with camp guards.

7. The advance guard always assumes responsibility for frontal security of units on the march without specific instructions. It must therefore occupy a suitably broad area. In the meantime, if the situation necessitates flank security, then the leadership must direct this and expressly commission either the advance guard or the affected flank column to do this.

The assignment (*Aufgabe*) of the advance guard is to conceal, to make possible, and to prepare the march of the main body and particularly to generate intelligence. Its strength and composition must therefore be sufficient to strike offensively and defensively.

The distance of the advance guard from the main body varies. It must be enough to protect the march of the main body from interruption, but may not be so great as to prevent the advance guard from being supported by the main body. A strong advance guard can be pushed farther forward than a weak one. The commander will have to consider the situation, his own and the enemy's strength, and the features of the terrain to find the correct limit.

All security measures must be so taken and executed that the march of the entire army is not delayed. This must not be managed with timid pedantry; what really matters is to protect the units from serious surprise attack. The possible proximity of weak enemy detachments presents danger only for weak detachments. A strong column of marching units is sufficiently ready for combat to repel enemy scouts, which will themselves usually be quite satisfied if they emerge unmolested.

Using sound judgment and boldness, one will prevent the enemy from gaining influence on the movement as a whole through demonstrations or teasing (*Reckerei*). One must remember that he who flanks will be outflanked and that a turning movement (*Umgehung*)[43] is dangerous only for the weaker side.

8. One best attains security on the march through the widest possible breadth of cavalry patrols. Only in very difficult terrain will infantry be at home in this activity. The cavalry will either itself overcome the resistance that it encounters or will be able to report to the commander of the advance guard at an early enough time that necessary orders can be given. In many cases a deep forward advance of cavalry patrols, with which one can also send small infantry detachments on wagons as support, will be the simplest and the best way to preserve the strength of the units. This can be employed even in less open terrain. If one allows a suitably strong cavalry force a considerable head start before the advance guard at the very beginning of the march, it will be less fatigued in its advance and will produce more rest and symmetry for the whole than it would if it marched directly at the head and had to be sent forward, usually in great haste, in every case of need.

An infantry supporting force (*Soutien*),[44] which at an appropriate distance successively follows from one suitable point to the next, will secure the cavalry against sudden defeat and allow it to make a broader and deeper advance.

---

43. Prussian theory distinguished between turning movements (*Umgehung*, literally, going around) and flank attacks (*Umfassung*), which had an entirely tactical application.

44. This French term was used routinely in official and private German military literature.

In a war of movement (*Bewegungskrieg*)[45] it can sometimes be appropriate, especially to avoid loss of contact with the enemy, to detach entirely one or a few squadrons from the mass of the forward units and make them independent. They can then follow the enemy as closely as possible without combat and without regard to the movements of our own units.

9. An advance guard will seldom be in a position to select its own place of engagement.[46] It must accept combat where it encounters the enemy. The advance guard occupies defiles to hold them open for the passage of the main body and can risk much because it expects rapid support.

A rear guard, on the other hand, will always seek a strong frontal barrier for its resistance because it seeks no decision, only to gain time. It attains this if it forces the enemy to go around its position. It is left to its own strength but has the choice of where it wishes to assert itself. While the opponent must carry the attack through to completion, the rear guard can break off the engagement as soon as it develops and as soon as it has found a new support in terrain to the rear.

X. TACTICAL CONSIDERATIONS[47]

A. Infantry and Jäger

1. In the next war our needlegun will not again be opposed by a far inferior rifle but, on the contrary, an entirely equal weapon. Superiority is no longer to be sought in the weapon, but in the hand that

---

45. Here one encounters one of the most fundamental distinctions in all German theory from Moltke to 1945. This theory distinguished between two types of war between major powers: War of movement (*Bewegungskrieg*) and positional warfare (*Stellungskrieg*). The fundamental principles of both remained substantially unchanged in Prusso-German theory from the mid-nineteenth century to 1945.

46. Moltke used *Gefechtsfeld*, literally a field of engagement. "Battlefield" would be a more commonly used English substitute, but the German term for battle (*Schlacht*) had a much narrower application than the American term "battle." This text, therefore, uses the word "battle" only when *Schlacht* appears in the original.

47. The German title was *Taktische.*

wields it.[48] This essential change must be taken into consideration when translating the experiences of the last war to future circumstances.[49]

2. The significant improvements in firearms make themselves felt in the extension of their reach and in the accumulation of effects at decisive points. The former property (extension of weapons' ranges) necessitates alterations in tactical deployment and the way units fight. The latter property gives the effect of fire an offensive character that it did not previously have. It can in some circumstances be absolutely destructive and, consequently, independently decisive.

3. Infantry has the power to repel any frontal attack with its rapid fire, even that of the most audacious opponent. The opponent's losses are thereby so numerous that his inner steadiness (*Halt*) can be shaken to such a degree that the same unit can repeat the same attempt only with difficulty.

This conviction must be awakened and ingrained in the infantry. *The infantry may assure itself that it cannot be attacked from the front and only has to be slightly concerned if it turns its back.*

An infantry [unit] whose flank is covered, which does not have to pay attention to losses from long-range fire, and which delivers a cold-blooded volley fire against the enemy's sometimes traditional dare-devil attacks, is invincible.

The bayonets of the attacker may do nothing against such a defense and even an equally good rifle is at a decisive disadvantage as soon as movement precludes its steady functioning.

4. The ease and rapidity with which our rifle is loaded and fired, thus precisely its excellence, brings the danger of a great expenditure of ammunition.[50]

The expenditure of a certain quantity of ammunition is an outlay

---

48. The reader should remember that the *Verordnungen* was written in 1869.

49. The "last war" was the Austro-Prussian War of 1866.

50. This concern about excessive and hasty expenditure of rifle ammunition appeared frequently in Moltke's writings. Exaggerated as this may seem to the modern reader, this fear was real and justified in the nineteenth century. On this point see Showalter, *Railroads and Rifles,* 85. On the other hand, even at Königgrätz, the Prussian infantry rarely if ever expended all its ammunition.

of strength, which may only take place where it pays for itself and from which real advantages may thereby be attained. But this danger is contrary to the weapon's extraordinary precision. In many cases its accuracy will substitute for the number of shots, especially at great ranges. No other army is yet trained in this area to the level of skill of our riflemen, who are taught to regard every cartridge as a jewel that is not to be given away for nothing.

The number of cartridges carried by the troops is restricted and is limited in comparison with the possibilities of using them rapidly. It would therefore be incorrect to seek effects by massed fire everywhere. But where the decision (*Entscheidung*) is concerned, every expenditure of ammunition is justified. It must always be the business of the commander to designate this instant.

5. It has already been related that the broadened area of effectiveness of the infantry rifle must necessarily lead to increased distances between both the units in combat and the sections remaining behind them. Consequently, it must lead to a looser front and deeper deployment.

The attacker, who has the initiative, is able to concentrate his masses without cover in order to lead them in a surprise attack on our most forward detachments. Timely support of forward detachments must therefore in the future be more carefully provided, even though increased distances make it more difficult. In this sense it will be advantageous if the detachments placed behind each other are under unified command.

The same hand controls the engagement and its support, forward and rearward movement, or breaks off contact. One should avoid mixing supporting units and forward units that do not belong together in the battle line. Such a mixture will be inflexible.

6. The stronger our frontal position is because of the effects of its fire, the more will the attacker direct his attack against our flanks. Deep deployment is suitable to counter this danger. Detachments of the second or third echelons, which are drawn forth to the sides without themselves going to the battle line (*Gefechtslinie*), outflank the enemy's flanking attack.

7. For defensive as well as offensive goals it will therefore be more useful to have large units that are deployed behind each other under the same direct command, rather than those which are next to each other.

8. The combat strength[51] of the forward echelon engaged with the enemy must be exploited completely. It is absolutely not recommended to replace it with a second echelon or even to strengthen it prematurely. Many times in battle (*Schlacht*) the victor is the one who has a last reserve to employ.

Certainly there is a false economy in munitions, just as there is in combat strength (*Streitkräfte*). However, if the forward fighting units and those in the rear standing ready belong to the same commander, he will judge the right moment when the support of the latter is necessary to avoid the physical and moral exhaustion of the former.

9. Thus, in some circumstances, it can be advantageous to depart from an infantry brigade's normal combat formation in which the two regiments stand one behind the other. Then the regiments are with flanks beside each other, but with their battalions in echelon behind one another. Hereby the regimental commander will be in a position to achieve a strengthening of the front, the securing of a flank, and supporting the engagement with his own battalions, as long as the brigade commander does not hold them back as a reserve for his exclusive proposal.

In such arrangements, the brigade commander will have to direct his attention especially to the cooperation of the flanks of the respective lead battalions.

10. For the battalion, the column in the middle in company columns is the normal formation for combat. This is done so that when the battalion deploys on line the second and third rifle platoons remain behind the third and sixth platoons and the skirmishers are never separated from their companies. The riflemen are, as a matter of principle, always to be supported by the companies to which they belong. The mixing of troops (*Mannschaften*) from different companies is thereby to be avoided as much as possible. This eases the giving of orders and unity of command.

11. In very intense fire, such large tactical bodies as battalions are not suited to remain in close formation within the range of the enemy's artillery. Even half battalions do not offer significant advantages with respect to reduction of the target and greater agility (*Beweglichkeit*).

---

51. Here Moltke used *Gefechtskraft,* which seems best translated as "combat strength" rather than "engagement strength."

First and foremost, therefore, one should preferably use the company column, all the more so because [the units] can again be very simply assembled in half and whole battalions, the already mentioned normal formation.

Combat in company columns, moreover, frequently brings a number of younger men to independent activity. The best success is to be expected from the intelligence that is widespread in the officer corps. In war, where no two cases are entirely the same, simple practiced forms do not suffice. Many times the subordinate commander must be allowed to act according to his own judgment. However, this creates difficulty in coordinating the engagement. This can be overcome only if all subordinate commanders, especially the company commanders, constantly try to rejoin their battalions and if the higher commanders constantly keep an eye open so that they do not lose control of their units.

The order of battle (*Schlachtordnung*) must therefore on all sides remain flexible yet intact.

12. At the same time the company column favors the extensive and simple application of dispersed combat that is demanded by present circumstances, it avoids mixing the third rank of all four companies in the skirmishing line, as so easily happens in the battalion formation.

13. Therefore, in peacetime and on the parade ground, units are to practice the movements and combat described in paragraphs 9, 10, and 11.[52]

The artificial evolutions that the regulation allows are henceforth to be practiced only for the schooling of the units. On the other hand, the simple forms that war demands must be capable of execution under the most varied circumstances—in unfavorable terrain, in the dark and without arrangements, or with a reversed front.

The commanders of small detachments know how to lead them with hand and arm signals or yells (or a whistle). The use of horns or bugles (*Signale*), on the other hand, which has been the occasion of mistakes and misunderstandings in combat, must remain reserved to higher commanders. They are used, for example, to order a general advance

---

52. This section marked one of the first efforts of the chief of the General Staff to establish combat formations and training points of emphasis for the Prussian army's tactical units.

where the goal cannot be reached in a timely manner by the dispatch
of orderly officers.

14. The infantry will cling to its proven habit not to fire at too great
a distance. The effects are all too little; one weakens one's own confidence and increases that of the enemy. The enemy's long-range fire
is best answered by individual and, indeed, the best riflemen. Massed
fire remains reserved for short distances, where a calmly delivered volley
works in an annihilating manner and breaks the will of even the bravest
enemy. At long range, however, it is necessary that the commander
be completely the master of his unit and that he alone designates the
beginning of the firing.

15. For the constantly differing engagement there are no universally
binding regulations (*Vorschriften*), but only suggestions (*Andeutungen*).[53]

If a defensive position is to be held with an open formation, sometimes a few hours are available for preparation. The infantry must not
fail to use its own means, where the terrain offers the riflemen no cover,
to create it with light earthworks that are rapidly constructed and that
offer no important barrier to subsequent advances.

From the battalion designated for the occupation of a part of the
position, two or, if necessary, four platoons go forward and settle in
as much as possible.

The support elements of the two companies concerned seek cover
close behind or even in the firing line. When the enemy begins his
rush, they fire in volleys, which in some circumstances can be delivered in four ranks.

The other companies of the battalion remain farther back with the
flags, formed in half battalions, but not more than 150 paces away.
Where the terrain offers cover, they attain the best protection when,
formed on line, they lie down on the ground.

With the exception of the soldiers specifically designated for long-
distance firing, the firing line commences firing on command when
the enemy closes to three hundred paces.

---

53. This was a fundamental principle of the Prusso-German army's tactics throughout
its subsequent history.

If the enemy continues to press forward and threatens an assault, the two remaining companies should immediately form in column and go to meet him with fixed bayonets and shouts of "Urrah." The second battalion should advance at a run upon hearing this shout.

After repulsing an attack, the firing line and the support remain in their positions. They will attain much more by firing on the retreating enemy out to three hundred paces than they would by pursuing him with their bayonets. Beyond this distance the cavalry could achieve more if it is available.

The half battalion again seeks cover. The second battalion returns to its position. Everyone reestablishes himself and awaits the next attack.

16. In order to go over to the offensive, rifle fire supported by the artillery must engage the enemy at effective range.

The commanders of the most forward detachments can best observe where it is possible to seize a nearby covering section of terrain and to use it (if an advance is at all ordered) according to their own judgment. The forward units go as far forward as the enemy fire and their own spirit (*Elan*) will allow.

If the enemy infantry appears to have lost its cohesion in its position, then the firing line advances to this point with the supporting element (*Soutien*) in a rapid and concentrated run. They concentrate there in a united mass.

The half battalion follows directly in column at a rapid pace in order to decide the matter with massed fire or the bayonet. The second battalion follows as a reinforcement with drums beating.

The rapidly advancing riflemen are a target that is not very easily hit. Nevertheless, they pull up in order directly to threaten the enemy with their fire.

Just as an open front is most favorable for the defense, so is covered terrain the most favorable for the offense, especially if it leads to the enemy's flanks. One must always seek to envelop the flanks. Yet the high commander has to be concerned that the gaps that easily develop in a continuous line are always covered by forward-moving rear detachments.

17. Because of its increased firepower, organized infantry need not fear an attack by enemy cavalry as long as it maintains its composure. This is much more important than the infantry's position, which is really of value only if it increases the feeling of security.

The greatest possible use of fire along the deployed front is the most effective counter to a cavalry attack. Still, it is necessary to refuse the flanks, possibly in a battalion square.

Concentrated formations (*Massenformationen*), which are usually created when cavalry appears, are but little suited for other combat purposes and produce great losses from artillery fire. It remains to be well observed how far the attitude of one's own unit is free of such precautionary measures.

18. Infantry is very dangerous for enemy artillery if even weak detachments come to within six hundred to seven hundred paces by skillful use of the terrain. In this case, long-distance firing at great range is entirely appropriate.

19. The Jäger battalions must be in position to meet the same requirements that in combat are placed on the infantry, and what has been said about the latter is valid also for the Jäger battalions. Their especially trained marksmanship should be used where, because of the covered position of the infantry or moving targets, long-range firing is essential.

At the decisive moment, rapid fire is appropriate for the Jäger infantry.

B. Cavalry

1. The greatly increased power of infantry fire cannot remain without effect on the situation of the cavalry.

Cavalry in the future will not, as previously, sometimes decide the battle by assaulting the battalions of the enemy that have withstood the events of the engagement. A cavalry attack is much more in need of the preparation of the other arms. The cavalry's activity has shifted more to the beginning and the end of the action.

2. This does not mean that the significance of the cavalry for the operation and for the engagement has decreased. This arm will subsequently, as before, be of the greatest influence even under the more difficult conditions. Among these are the increased distances necessitated everywhere by the improved ranges of weapons and the resulting longer attacking movements. Peacetime training must be concerned with this. With the attack closed and the horses out of breath, it is always difficult to bring into immediate action the designated portion of the divisional cavalry. It cannot be kept out of the engagement and must remain with the infantry, under fire to the end.

As for the rest, the cavalry must seek means to decrease the unavoidable losses with which the opportunity for successful activities is purchased. These means are suitable formations, movement, and, above all, clever use of terrain.

3. The mere proximity of the cavalry forces the enemy to adopt measures and formations that restrict his activity and increase his losses. The enemy must be concerned with protecting his batteries, may not extend his riflemen, and may not arrange his columns. Just as this mere presence of our cavalry, before it really appears, has a paralyzing effect on the enemy, so an absence of enemy cavalry frees us from all these limiting considerations.

4. The mission (*Aufgabe*) of the divisional cavalry is a difficult one and demands self-denial. During operations, the divisional cavalry takes over security and messenger duty, and, at least in a small area, has to be concerned with reconnaissance of the position and measures taken by the enemy. It may not leave its division and may not remain behind the infantry during an engagement. Rather, it has to follow the infantry's advance, to cover its flanks and to support its attacks. The more the effects of fire compel dispersed fighting, the more frequently will the divisional cavalry find opportunities for partial successes. But this is conditional on direct pressure of the unit and the commander's clear judgment and resoluteness. Fleeting moments, for example a forward- or rearward-moving battery, a deploying or flanking cavalry, or an uncovered line of riflemen, often offer opportunities.

5. The situation of the reserve cavalry is somewhat different. It will almost always be able to avoid effective fire by the use of terrain or by maintaining an appropriate distance during most of the battle. The arm's unique speed of movement allows it to approach only when the time for its intervention has arrived. As a rule this will first be the case when the coherence of the enemy battle line loosens and when the enemy infantry is shaken by great losses—thus near the end of the action.

The reserve cavalry will therefore usually wait inactively for hours. But this time must not be wasted. It is of great importance that it conduct reconnaissance of obstacles through which it presumably will have to pass and discover available passages in advance.

The commander takes a position where he can view the general course of the engagement. He will be clear in his own mind ahead of time where, against whom, and when the assault[54] of his mass of riders can deliver the final decision. For this and for the pursuit he must conserve the strength of his regiments. But, above all, he must retain his overview of the general situation.

6. For every cavalry unit, both those detached and those of the reserve, the old and glorious tradition lives on: the *Prussian cavalry never awaits an imminent attack, but on the contrary goes forth to meet it, even when outnumbered.*

7. Just as valid remains the rule that the cavalry maneuvers in column and attacks on line.

For the former, the squadron column of platoons offers important advantages. This formation's agility allows the unit to go around obstacles and to use every fold of the terrain. It offers fewer targets to the enemy's artillery and favors rapid deployment without interrupting forward movement. It also facilitates the difficult task of adopting the correct front, namely such a one from which an immediate and well-directed attack strikes directly at the proper point. This usually is an enemy flank.

If one can strike the point where attacks from different areas converge, then the effects will be greater and usually the enemy's countermeasures will be frustrated.

Hand-to-hand combat is to be inculcated in all cavalrymen. Peacetime training must emphasize that the thrust is more effective than the slashing stroke. The former reaches farther and only a short penetration knocks the opponent from the saddle.

Premature deployment is disadvantageous because long lines are unwieldy in movement, easily miss the correct direction, and come apart. They find cover difficult to obtain in open terrain and cannot easily escape the enemy's view and fire.

A line formation surely brings the greatest possible number of thrusting and slashing weapons to immediate use, but it requires protection of its flanks, whose security the flanking units or following echelons must

---

54. The word here is *Hineinbrechen*, literally, "breaking-in."

provide. To place everything on line is therefore not advisable for small detachments. Besides this, larger masses will seldom have the required room. Success in a cavalry engagement will more often depend on covering one's own flanks and seizing the enemy's. In this one must above all consider these measures. The reserve cavalry usually attacks with large detachments, thus with unified brigades. There are indeed combat situations where one must attack with the small forces that are available; but such partial attacks of individual regiments and squadrons dissolve the cavalry's organization, which is hard to maintain. On the whole, such partial attacks cannot easily lead to lasting and decisive results.

C. Artillery

1. The artillery assigned to a large unit by the order of battle or temporary attachment forms an integral part of the unit and may not leave its march and combat movement. The artillery follows the unit, if the latter is not already under fire, without needing a special order to this effect. It closes back up immediately after it ceases firing. Isolated maneuvering of individual batteries on their own authority is not admissible. Such batteries often are missing when their units need them the most.

2. On the march in appropriate disposition, a special covering force for the artillery is usually not necessary. In combat one establishes the special assignment of a covering force only temporarily and only when a battery proceeds without close connections with other arms. A lengthy attachment of infantry elements to the batteries is to be avoided. On the other hand, it may be necessary to assign special detachments the task of protecting the flanks of forward lines of artillery that have to take covered positions beyond the enemy's fire. Moreover, a unit must immediately render assistance where it finds a battery in danger.

3. The commander must rush forward and conduct reconnaissance prior to the occupation of every artillery position. In the choice of a position, concern for effectiveness always comes before cover.

As a rule, the highest hilltops are more suited for observation, while on the other hand, slopes afford units both cover and good effect. A wide and free field of fire is always the main thing.

Moreover, the artillery may be positioned by batteries along the entire front in order to use favorable positions, to avoid presenting a large target, and in order to direct concentric fire on special points of the enemy position.

The digging in of otherwise unprotected artillery pieces is advisable whenever time is available.

4. In general, two thousand paces is the maximum distance at which one can expect decisive effects, especially against artillery. Beyond that, fire is justified only against strong columns or if one wishes to delay the engagement. This is always to be done with caution, however, especially in open terrain, in order not to hinder one's own detachments.

Other unit commanders must pay attention to this and must not force the artillery to attack at greater distances.

In general, the fire should begin slowly enough that every round can be observed before the next one is fired.

If it is apparent that one has no effect, one must advance even if the enemy continues his fire.

At the beginning of an engagement the artillery will usually have no target other than the enemy artillery, whether already emplaced or arriving.

Since the artillery has only a single type of effectiveness, that of good shooting, and since this depends entirely on knowledge of distances, the position and target are to be changed as little as possible.

As soon as the opponent reveals the mass of his other arms, and especially as soon as his infantry columns advance for the attack, the artillery must concentrate fire exclusively against the other arms without regard to enemy artillery fire.

5. A battery that has exhausted its ammunition does not fall back. It remains, even if under enemy fire, until its ammunition is replenished. This is because the moral impression a retreat makes on one's own units weighs more heavily than the resultant losses.

Once a battery has been under fire it is absolutely not to be relieved. On the contrary, it is supported by the insertion of a new one. Only damaged guns are to be hauled back, if possible. *The artillery position itself may be evacuated only on the order of the commander of the unit to which the artillery is attached.* Even a certain amount of losses may not be a motive for this.

In order to *continue firing, a battery needs no horses and only a few men.* It must, in some circumstances, endure infantry fire. But in this case the unit commander must render immediate assistance.

There are circumstances in which the artillery has the duty of sacrificing itself in order to gain time for the other arms and to relieve the enemy's pressure.

An unshakable endurance to the last moment can therefore be necessary, indeed in the highest degree favorable, even if it ultimately should lead to loss of the guns.[55]

On the other hand, if the batteries are ordered to withdraw, they should proceed by steps because of the impression this makes and in order to avoid confusion. Only in the case of evident danger or in order to unmask rearward artillery positions may a withdrawal take place at a rapid pace.

6. The command of large units (*Truppenführung*) must always take care that this arm [artillery], having established the range of the guns, is able to open the fight.

The time during which the opponent approaches between the distances of two thousand and eight hundred paces is the most favorable for its activity.

It is therefore important, even in the first part of the engagement, to have available more guns than the opponent. The artillery's place in the order of march is to be arranged accordingly.

In order to prepare for the eventual decision, the entire artillery may be brought up to the shortest possible distance from the enemy. No part of it may be held in reserve. This advance will ordinarily be made in echelons. As far as possible, the positions are to be so occupied that they are not masked by the infantry.

7. In general, action by individual batteries must be the exception, while massed employment is the rule.

8. Large unit commanders send their orders to the batteries through the commander of the artillery within their staffs. The artillery commander remains with the batteries at the beginning of the engagement. The higher commanders inform him in advance about their intentions and leave the details of execution to him.

---

55. This was a radical departure for the Prussian artillery's theory. Austrian doctrine, on the other hand, recognized that guns must occasionally be sacrificed in support of the infantry. See Showalter, *Railroads and Rifles,* 193–95.

In the course of the engagement, the artillery fight must never lack unified command. Thus the battalion[56] commander determines where to position more than one of his batteries; the regimental commander where the corps artillery takes up its fire; the artillery brigade commander where the corps and divisional artillery work together; the artillery general where the batteries of different corps fight together.

XI. CONDUCT OF THE PURSUIT [57]

1. War must attain the goal (*Zweck*) of the government's policy by force of arms. The battle (*Schlacht*) is the great means to break the will of the opponent. This intent is the basis of all large and small engagements. These are the means to bring about the situation that ultimately finds its solution in the decisive struggle. But they are not the only means. Many important goals of war may also be attained without combat, through marches and through the choice of positions— in short, through operations.

A turning movement (*Umgehung*) that causes the enemy to retreat; a rear guard, which by its behavior and position causes the enemy to abstain from attacking; a reconnaissance that has seen what it wishes to see; all have attained their goals without combat. These are not to be accomplished without losses. Their conclusion[58] is seldom to be foreseen with any certainty.

2. One should therefore never strike a blow without a definite goal. This must constantly be kept in mind during the course of the struggle.

So, for example, an engagement should fix the opponent for only a certain amount of time, and should not be continued to the point of one's own defeat. Small detachments whose combat goals are often many-faceted and do not consist of the attainment of a victory must espe-

---

56. Here Moltke used *Abteilung,* which for infantry could mean any detachment of a larger unit. In the artillery, an *Abteilung* frequently meant a battalion.

57. The German title was *Gefechtsführung—Verfolgung.* "Pursuit" could also be rendered as "exploitation."

58. This may also be translated as "result." In older usages "conclusion" predominates over "result."

cially consider this. Their commanders must never forget that a fight involving the main body of their units is very difficult to break off. They must remember that the transition from combat to a march formation, which is necessary for a retreat, produces a crisis; and that a second, rearward, position may be occupied in the face of pursuit only under the protection of a strong and intact cavalry and favorable terrain.

3. Certainly it does not always fall within the power of the commander to avoid combat, and it can often be more advisable to complete the fight than to break it off.

In any case, the goal in war can never be more completely reached than through combat, and its main object[59] only through destruction (*Niederwerfung*) of the enemy's main power in open country—therefore through battle.

It is good to consider that, just as in the goals, so also there are basic differences in the ways of commanding large and small units. What is necessary for the former is not always correct for the latter. Space and time have a different significance for smaller units. The agility of the unit's detachments and the personal influence of the commander are greater. The peculiarities of the terrain are of decisive influence for smaller units.

4. In the doubtful cases and in the unclear circumstances that so often exist in war, it is usually more advisable to proceed actively and to retain the initiative than to await the law of the enemy.[60] He can often view our situation only a little, and will sometimes yield in cases where the actual state of affairs would not have made this necessary.

5. The commander of the individual parts of the army must remain mindful of the old rule always to march in the direction of the cannon thunder.

Tasks (*Aufträge*) that have ordered another direction be taken are then to be subjected to one's own consideration. These tasks were perhaps ordered under circumstances that did not foresee the battle now

---

59. *Hauptziel* in German.

60. This is a variant of the well-known phrase "the law of the transaction" (*Das Gesetz des Handelns*). Modern Western military theory frequently states this as "the law of the battlefield."

under way. In the majority of cases the assistance rendered on the battle-field is of more worth than the fulfillment of special tasks, because all other considerations fade into the background compared to a tactical victory.[61]

6. The much-discussed question of whether the battle should be conducted offensively or defensively cannot be answered in a universally valid way.

The closest and most evident sign of victory is that at the end of the battle we possess an area that the enemy held at the beginning and which he would not have given up without more or less being defeated.[62] Every victorious battle must therefore end with an offensive advance. The question is, however, if the battle should begin that way.

The advantages of the offensive are sufficiently recognized. We thereby dictate the law of the transaction [or action] to the enemy. He must accommodate his measures to ours and must seek means to resist them. But he can find these means.

The offensive knows what it wishes to do in advance. The defense is suspended in uncertainty, but can guess at the intentions of the opponent.

Going forward to attack electrifies the spirit, but experience has shown that these high spirits can change to the complete opposite with extremely high losses.

It cannot be denied that a man firing while stationary has the advantage over the advancing firer, that the former finds support in the terrain and the latter a hindrance, and that if calm steadfastness opposes zealous élan, the effects of fire that have become so much greater in our time decide the issue. If we are able to occupy a position that the opponent will presumably attack because of military or political reasons, or because of national pride, then it appears advisable in the beginning to take advantage of the defensive before we take the offensive.

With the impulse to advance that by experience inspires our units and their officers, what is needed from above is scarcely urging on, but, rather, restraint. The unit itself feels best when the possibility arises

---

61. Compare with Clausewitz's views in *On War*. This is a common theme throughout nineteenth- and twentieth-century Prusso-German literature.
62. Clausewitz used almost this precise definition of victory.

to go forward to seize a section of the battlefield. The higher command has merely to support these successive advances with its available reserves and to parry counterstrokes. Thus, the battle consists of a string of short offensive thrusts, which usually follow unsuccessful attacks on the opponent until the main reserves can exert decisive pressure.

7. In this sense, proper positions are important, but their character is essentially changed from previously.

We will often want the enemy to attack us. In that case, we will not select an unassailable position. We will want to go over to the offensive in good time and therefore *could, in such a case, not use a frontal barrier that would hinder this.* The prevailing element of the effects of fire reaches its highest development on the open field. A previously scarcely noticed gentle swell in the terrain becomes a strong position if it has a wide open field of fire in its front and if our reserves have a view of the enemy. It assures all three arms of the highest degree of effectiveness.

But if the frontal barrier is dispensable, indeed for decisive battle has become disadvantageous, a flank support is still always desirable. In the absence of a firm piece of terrain, it may be provided by a battery whose wide-ranging fire halts the enemy's turning movement at a great distance.

Excessive extension of a position's front is to be avoided. In order to conduct the engagement at length and to be able to keep its course under control to some extent, today one will still need about five to ten men per pace of the front line, according to the nature of the terrain.

It will likewise be possible to place the main reserve of an army marching to battle so that it cannot be reached by enemy projectiles. But the echelons held back to support the forward combat line (*Gefechts- linie*) cannot be secure from this fire because of their location. In the meantime, very much is already accomplished if they at least stand out of sight of the opponent, if he only suspects their position, and if one can withdraw from the direction of his fire by a sideward movement.

Villages and patches of forest will frequently change hands repeatedly in lengthy combat. This is because the range of modern weapons allows the attacker to concentrate an overpowering fire. Terrain elevations, on the other hand, offer more cover and usually a wider field of fire. They will therefore henceforth add to the strength of a position more than any village or forested locale. If time allows, the battlefield may be further strengthened by the work of the pioneers. From narrow and unconnected trenches one may hardly expect a lengthy resistance. Often it will be more advisable to dig in only the batteries, to strengthen villages, to repair passages, and so forth.

8. One will not always succeed in occupying positions that the enemy must attack and in which we will have the advantages described above. In many cases, on the contrary, one will be forced immediately to take the offensive.

From what has been said, one is to infer that a frontal attack will produce little success and great losses. One will therefore have to turn against the flanks of the enemy position.

Should this happen with undivided strength, smaller detachments may suffice with a small change in the direction of march. A division, for example, even with favorable terrain, occupies a front scarcely 1⅛ miles in width.[63] An army of more than a hundred thousand men, on the contrary, occupies more than 4½ miles. Going around its front will take a day's march. The decision of arms is thus postponed to the following day. This allows the opponent time to escape and usually endangers one's own communications while the movement attempts to threaten the enemy's.

Another means consists of fixing the enemy's front with a part of our own strength and enveloping his flank with another part. But then it is necessary that we remain strong enough opposite the enemy front not to be overpowered before the flank attack becomes effective. We must also be active enough along the front to prevent the enemy from throwing himself with superiority against our flank attack. In all circumstances we must divide our strength.

The moral effect of a flank attack will, merely through fire alone, be more important against small detachments than against armies. On the other hand, the latter will not so easily escape the results of a successful flank attack because of the greater difficulty of its movement.

If the army approaches the enemy while concentrated before the battle, then any new division of forces for a flanking attack or a turning movement against the enemy requires a flanking march within his tactical sphere of action.

---

63. Moltke used the figure of a quarter of a German mile, which was the equivalent of 1⅛ English miles.

If one does not wish to engage in such a dubious enterprise, there remains only a strengthening of that flank from which the opposite-standing enemy flank should be overpowered. But this is of use only in a frontal attack. This can nevertheless succeed if one is able to spare parts of the reserves in the center and on the opposite flank.

The circumstances are by far more favorable if the forces coming from separated points can be concentrated on the battlefield itself, and if the operations are so conducted that a final short march from different sides simultaneously leads to the enemy's front and flank. Strategy has thus accomplished the best that is to be attained, and great results must be the result. No foresight, obviously, can guarantee that operations with separated armies will in reality lead to this final result. This is, rather, dependent not merely on the calculable size, space, and time, but in many cases also on the result of preceding partial engagements, on the weather, on false reports—in short, on those things that in the human sense are called chance and luck. *Great successes in war are not to be attained without great danger.*

9. In all battles and under all circumstances, one must use everything that is available. One can never have too much strength available nor too great a chance for victory. It is not advisable to leave behind a part of the units in a rallying position for protection of a retreat. One thereby weakens the forces whose victory makes a retreat absolutely unnecessary, but whose retreat seldom will come to a halt at a rallying position, which will easily be brushed aside by the pursuit.

On the other hand, a reserve may never be lacking in an engagement.

Such a reserve is to be explicitly designated by the disposition for the battle or by an order at the beginning of the engagement. It remains exclusively at the direct disposal of the highest commander, who holds it out as long as possible and takes care that it is not engaged against his will. He therefore should hold it directly under his own eyes.

Many battles are decided by units that occasionally arrive by chance only on the evening of the day of battle.

10. If one attacks the enemy, or if the advance units report his approach, even the higher unit commanders do best to move to their most forward detachments in order personally to familiarize themselves about the strength, position, or movement of the opponent and the terrain on which the fighting will probably occur. The commander must then in all calmness consider if he will conduct the engagement at all and how in general he will do it.

The following must be informed about the decision (*Entschluss*) in addition to the chief of the General Staff (who during the entire course of the action remains at the commander's side): cavalry and artillery commanders and the senior engineer officer. They must be informed as far as necessary about the commander's broad intentions.

The commander of the artillery then has to ascertain the most advantageous position for the main body of his batteries and to bring them into the engagement as much as possible, after receiving the commanding general's permission, so that they come up to the enemy soon and in superior numbers at an effective range.

The senior engineer officer familiarizes himself with the terrain. He then makes his proposals for possible strengthening of the position, as well as for establishment of communications. He implements his plan after receiving [the commander's] approval.

Both the senior engineer and the artillery commander may move freely along the entire battle line, but they return as often as possible to the highest commander. They have the duty to pay attention to everything that makes their arms effective and have the right on their own initiative to take their proposals to the commanding general. The commanding general decides. Naturally they themselves arrange all minor measures having no substantial influence on the general situation. The cavalry general is not bound to his arm, which usually first comes to action late. He has to ascertain in advance the conditions under which he probably will be called to act. He does this through his officers, through his own contemplation of the terrain, and through his continuing observation of the course of the engagement.

11. At the beginning of the engagement, all high commanders return to a more rearward point that allows a sufficient overview and which is visible to their own units. They remain there permanently so that reports and inquiries can find them with certainty and ease. With the exception of a few cases in which their personal intervention may be necessary, it is infinitely more important that they maintain a broad and clear overview than that they assist in the improvement of a few details. *They need their full mental calm and physical strength until after the final decision and therefore have every reason to move around sparingly.*

12. Even during the artillery's opening deployment (*Aufmarsch*), the other units are to be directed to the points that they should take in the engagement. As long as security allows they remain in their march formation, because a premature deployment delays their arrival and would consume their strength to a very great degree.

In the meantime, reports and information are to be sent, measures for observation of the flanks are taken, the trains and columns are to continue their advance, the medical preparations are made ready, and the forward dressing stations are to be established.

The chief of the general staff[64] completes, through the staff, the orders of the commanding general to the unit commanders and effects their dispatch by officers specially tasked with this and then notes the time of the main moments of the engagement.

13. As a rule, every change of position of corps and divisions in the battle line results from an order of the highest commander or at least with his permission.

In cases where it is certain, even without such an order, that the attack or withdrawal of any large unit is immediately necessary, and therefore may be ordered by its commander, a message will always be sent immediately [to the highest commander].

14. During the course of the fighting, the commanders of all ranks continually have to think and to consider that *the general shape of their units' distribution and battle array are maintained.* After the conclusion of every fight in which their units were seriously engaged, the commanders will attempt to reassemble them quickly and to reestablish their inner order. They thereby gain the capability for new activity. This is always necessary because in war, and especially in combat, one can never know with certainty what the next moment will demand.

15. If one wishes to attack, then one must do so with resoluteness. Half measures are out of place. Only strength and confidence carry the units with them and produce success.

16. In the defense, units will remain covered and intact as long as possible in order to preserve their composure. This is the essential precondition for an effective fire.

---

64. Here Moltke means the general staff of the corps, not the chief of the General Staff of the entire army, who after 1864 became the field commander of the deployed armies.

17. During an engagement, the commander of the artillery must observe the artillery fight to achieve proper cooperation of the batteries. At the proper time, near the end of the battle, he gives the order to bring up the munitions columns. He will consider where the artillery should take a position in case of the necessity of a retreat. This is in order to afford the retreating units a respite and to stop the pursuing enemy. Such tasks now fall to the artillery more than previously because of its present wide sphere of effectiveness. In some circumstances, one must not hesitate to sacrifice guns.

At the conclusion of a victorious engagement the artillery frequently has the job of breaking the last remnant of the enemy's powers of resistance. The enemy's security batteries are to be overcome quickly, even at the shortest range. The artillery uses its long-range fire to create terror in the retreating and shaken enemy units.

In this, the artillery must work in masses. The cavalry will cover the artillery and will be prepared to begin the pursuit as soon as possible.

18. Near the end of the battle, the commander and his unit will often have fallen into confusion after leaving their original positions. Then all kinds of impressions influence the high commander quickly and intensely. It will be especially important to the commander, but certainly difficult, to have a clear picture of the condition of his own units and those of the enemy, and in general of the entire present situation. *Far-reaching orders, perhaps the most important of the entire campaign, may now be required of the high commander in the shortest time.*

For this it is necessary that the general staff officers of the commander's staff and the subordinate corps and divisions be completely knowledgeable about the distribution and condition of the enemy strength, as well as on the positions of their own forces. It is also necessary that the headquarters staff rush to the high command to give reports. They have to declare which units have participated the least or not at all in the engagement and are most available for pursuit, security, or covering for a retreat. At the same time, these units are to receive orders for further movements.

19. In case of an unfavorable outcome, if the yet remaining chances for achieving a victory obviously are no longer commensurate with the disadvantages which a failure of further efforts must have, and if one is forced to evacuate the battlefield, then what counts above all is that the mass of the army distances itself from the enemy.

One will then not be able to avoid engaging the most cohesive units, the last reserves, and exposing them to new, serious, and perhaps costly fighting. This is in order to allow for the others the head start that is unconditionally necessary for maintaining cohesion. One must insert them in the march column to avoid stops and crowding together, which form the basic source of disorder and thus often the beginning of a defeat.

It will be favorable if it is possible to derive profit for the retreat from the approach of darkness, or if a yet intact cavalry unit is ready to be thrown against the pressure of the enemy. By this means, at least the first sections of the enemy force will be brought to a halt. The short span of time that the damaged army thereby wins can perhaps suffice to prevent a catastrophe. Cavalry which accomplishes that will maintain the honor of the day undiminished, even if it does not gain a victory.

It is the job of the artillery to work in the same sense as already mentioned.

20. From this point of view, the cavalry general has to hold his masses as ready as possible. They must not be engaged too early.

In case of a favorable decision, the cavalry commander is obligated to take the initiative in reporting to the commanding general the strength with which he is in a position to begin the pursuit. How far this is to extend and with what intensity it is to be undertaken depend on the circumstances, especially on the attitude of the enemy. But a pursuit must always begin after a victorious engagement, and the earlier and the more directly this happens, the better and the more effective it will be.

The first act of pursuit after a great decision will be to move the entire army forward. But then the mass [of the army] must come to rest and only individual parts may go farther. As long as these latter still have the strength in men and horses to go forward, and as long as the enemy gives way to this pressure, the pursuit may not rest. If the enemy's strength is sufficient for further marching, then so must ours be.

Whatever is consumed by the exertions of a relentless pursuit is compensated for a hundredfold by the daily increasing weakness and disintegration of the opponent.

Often the mere appearance of the advance elements of the pursuit will be sufficient to frighten the opponent again and to produce renewed movement, and will yield new fruits of victory.

In order that the pursuit does not come to a halt in a defile, it will be advisable to advance in multiple columns from the outset. The opponent, who dares not expose himself to a flank attack (*Umfassung*), must then quickly give up resistance at the front.

In the meantime, the victorious army follows on a broad front. It can stretch out to live and to preserve itself. It finds its security in its advanced elements and remains prepared for a flanking attack in case the pursuing units alone are no longer able to overcome enemy resistance.

An indefatigable pursuit advancing in this manner will, unless special circumstances offer the opponent new strong points, produce such a result that a single great decision of arms brings about at the same time the fulfillment of the entire goal of the war.

CHAPTER FIVE
VARIOUS TEACHINGS ON WAR

This chapter stems from Moltke's *Military Works,* volume four, part two, published in 1911. Reducing the 179 pages of that volume's German text to a length suitable for this chapter entailed substantial deletions, primarily from the historical examples appended to Moltke's writings by the General Staff.

The General Staff assembled this material from several sources. The 1885 edition of the *Instructions for Large Unit Commanders* provided material for each of the subsections. Inclusion of some of this material here involves minor duplication, or near-duplication, of a few sections of the previous chapter. The editor has left these sections in place because they seemed integral to the overall text.

A few of this chapter's sections may have been purely Moltke's writing. Others no doubt are a combination of his writings and the contributions of others. Footnotes identify some of the reasons for suspecting that they are not Moltke's. Authorship of the sections on historical examples is more difficult to pin down. Most were definitely not drawn from Moltke's published historical accounts. However, they may well have been taken from essays that Moltke wrote or closely supervised.

The texts printed here shed important light on a number of Moltke's views and on how the Prussian army applied them to warfare in the early twentieth century. Especially important are the texts' suggestions on the form and content of orders, the relationships between the latter and directives, and the role of cavalry in reconnaissance. The section on marching contains some of Moltke's most definite statements on the principle of marching separated and uniting only on the battlefield. Typical for Moltke, however, the text warns that this is not a

procedure to be used in every case. Running as an undercurrent throughout the chapter is Moltke's emphasis on flexibility in the face of the
uncertainties and variations in war.

LESSONS ON WAR (c. 1869–85)[1]

War Organization and Unit Distribution[2]

Under the accepted meaning of the expression *ordre de bataille* we
mean not the formation for battle, but rather the standing organization of an army's units and leaders for the entire campaign. It smooths
the path for the issuing of orders, for the distribution of supplies, and
for the internal administration of the units. It can therefore not be changed
arbitrarily. It is altered neither by changes of personnel nor by temporary detachments.

General von Clausewitz says, "the *ordre de bataille*[3] becomes the
first step and the main foundation for that wholesome method that regulates
the machinery of war like a pendulum."[4] Thus, the *ordre de bataille*
takes proper care that the clockwork is always kept in good order.

In this sense, our "Instructions for Large Unit Commanders" of 1885
state:[5]

The Order of Battle (*Kriegsgliederung*) regulates command and
administrative relationships for the duration of the entire campaign.
It is created when the army is mobilized and can be altered only by
direct command of the king.

---

1. The German title was: *Kriegslehren. Die taktische Vorbereitungen zur Schlacht.*
2. In German: *Kriegsgliederung (Ordre de Bataille) und Truppeneinteilung.*
3. *Vom Kriege*, book 2, chapter 5. The German term used is *Schlachtordnung.*
4. Clausewitz used the term *Werke*, here translated as "machinery" to maintain the
mechanical analogy.
5. Apparently the General Staff took the remainder of this section from the 1885
version of the "Instructions." The editor has been unable to locate a copy of this document, which is available neither in the national military archives nor at the library of
the German army's Military History Research Office, both in Freiburg. It is nearly
the same as the corresponding section from the 1869 edition, which may be found in
chapter four.

The distribution of units (*Truppeneinteilung*), on the other hand, expresses the temporary organization of units for special operational (*operative*) purposes (advance guard, rear guard, flank guard, and so forth). It must conform to the war organization, should disrupt the formations (*Verbände*) as little as possible, and is the more effective when creating very large units.

Existing conditions govern the strength and composition of the individual parts.

Thus, it may be necessary in one case to form an advance guard composed of all arms, while in some other case a very weak advance guard will suffice.[6] Today we may need a flank guard, while tomorrow it may be superfluous. Today's advance guard may become tomorrow's rear or flank guard.

A reserve is first designated at the opening of an engagement. It will remain at the exclusive disposal of the one who designated it.

It is the duty of all units to pay proper attention to cohesion and, where the vicissitudes of operations and engagements cause temporary separations, to overcome them as soon as possible. It is thus the responsibility of a company to maintain close contact with its battalion, and the battalion with its regiment and brigade. The cavalry and artillery of a division keep in steady touch with their division.

Important deviations from the normal organization are justified only in very exceptional cases; for instance, after a victorious battle if we gather together all capable formations for the pursuit, or, in case of a reverse, for the last resistance.

In such a case, of course, all other considerations become secondary to the object at hand. But the general rule is that the order of battle or the momentary distribution of units must be strictly adhered to.

Because of considerations of the proper issuing of orders, of mobility, and of supply, one cannot create individual armies of more than 150,000 to 200,000 men without disadvantage. Experience has shown that, in general, armies of 100,000 men have sufficient strength and powers of resistance to make them suitable for independent operations

---

6. This contrasts with Clausewitz's emphatic point that advance guards of mixed units were always to be avoided.

without impairing their mobility, subsistence, and so forth. An army of this strength is also independent enough to fight for quite a time against superior numbers. We had three such armies until they were united at Königgrätz.

The tactical unit (*taktische Einheit*) of an army in the field consists of that body of units (*Truppenkörper*) of all arms and of such strength that it can independently conduct an engagement for several hours: the infantry division.

Modern engagements will give opportunities to younger officers to act independently. The best results may be expected because of the intelligence of our officer corps. In war, where two cases never will be exactly the same, simple drill procedures are never sufficient. In many cases subordinate commanders must be allowed to act according to their own judgment. This undoubtedly leads to difficulties in the overall conduct of the engagement, which can be overcome only if all subordinate commanders, especially the company commanders, continually endeavor to rejoin their battalions, and if higher commanders continually take care that they do not lose control of their units.

Communications

Issue of Orders and Reports[7]

Continuous communications between headquarters and units is absolutely necessary for proper cooperation of all for a common purpose, that is, for the orderly direction of an army.

This continuous communication is maintained by orders from above no less than by reports and messages from below. The latter form the basis for the former.

Orders must be issued through regular channels as far as possible, not only during operations, but also in combat. Disregarding an intermediate headquarters restricts its activity and makes it appear superfluous. When in individual cases direct intervention of the higher commander is necessary to avoid loss of time, the highest of the bypassed

---

7. The German title was *Verbindung. Befehlserteilung—Meldungen.*

headquarters must be informed of the measures taken, both for their understanding and for that of the others. Such deviation from the regular channel is more justifiable in case of the high command (*Heeresleitung*) than for a subordinate headquarters. This is because time and space are of greater importance to the former, and because it possesses better means of informing the bypassed intermediate headquarters of what has been done. It must never happen that a commander does not know the location of his units or what orders they have.

On the whole, the advantage the leader believes he has attained by continual intervention is, in most cases, only an apparent one. In so doing, he performs the duties of others, more or less forgoes their contribution, and increases his own work in such a measure that he finally will be unable to perform all of it.

The demands made on high commanders are by no means small. It is far more important that the high commander retain a clear overview of the entire situation than that some detail be executed in this or that manner.

To retain a clear overall perspective, the high commander, under heavy responsibility, danger, and exertions, needs his full mental calmness and physical power. He must husband both of these.

To arrive at important decisions, he must evaluate uncertain and unclear messages. It happens only too easily that a greater value will be attached to that which one sees directly and to that in which one personally participates than to the frequently infinitely more important matters that are communicated from far off. On the other hand, these reports may be intentionally or unintentionally distorted. They will more or less always mirror an individual point of view.

From out of such darkness the correct thing has to be felt out and frequently guessed at, to enable the issuing of orders whose execution may encounter unforeseen eventualities and obstacles.

In this fog of uncertainty at least one thing must be certain: one's own decision. "In war everything is uncertain as soon as operations commence, except that which the commander in chief carries in his will and energy." This applies to every commander. He must adhere to a decision once arrived at and will do well not to allow himself to be diverted by the opponent's actions as long as that is not absolutely necessary. The correct way to arrive at a decision is, in every case, to find out what of all the opponent's measures would be most disadvantageous to us. *Then, simple action, consistently executed, will most certainly attain the objective.*

The high commander will do well not to ride around too much during an engagement. Instead, he should remain as long as possible at a point offering an unobstructed overview so that reports can reach him most quickly and with certainty.

In general, one does well not to order more than what is absolutely necessary and not to make dispositions beyond events that one can foresee. These change rapidly in war and any disposition made far in advance and going into too much detail can only seldom be carried out completely. It shakes the trust of subordinates and gives the units a feeling of uncertainty if things happen entirely differently from what orders from higher headquarters had presumed. Since, for instance, the outcome of an engagement can never be foreseen with certainty, one will but seldom be able to make dispositions in advance of an engagement.

But one must also not say, "The units will await further orders." Such an order cripples the independent action of subordinate commanders. The correct moment for action is thus easily lost. It may finally happen that nothing is done. One must always issue definite orders for action and one may, in case of need, send supplementary orders. One should especially give only general directives (*Weisungen*) to commanders of detached units, according to which they can act independently. In such cases one can always send subsequent orders restricting action, if necessary.

One must never forget that if one orders too much, the most important part, that which unconditionally should be done, easily is pushed into the background by minor things and may be carried out only in part or even not at all.

The higher the headquarters, the shorter and more general will be the orders. The larger the main subordinate units, the more freedom must be left to them.

Orders (*Anordnungen*) for higher headquarters usually take the form of directives, which under certain conditions may cover a number of days. Occasionally it may not be possible to issue them in advance to govern any certain day. Theoretically, by "directives" one understands such communications from higher to lower headquarters that do not give definite orders for momentary conduct so much as guiding viewpoints. The latter serve as guidelines for the decisions the subordinate headquarters has to make. In practice this means, "The highest command issues directives to the army commanders as general guides to govern their action for the next goal."

Army commanders also will not always be in a situation to lead their corps from day to day through orders. The reports of what has happened to the corps during the day usually arrive later than the time when the orders for the following day have to be written. In that case the orders can take into account neither the results of an engagement nor conditions of the terrain that are not yet known. The corps commanders must then be allowed independent action within the limits of the directives. Only the lower commanders receive orders from day to day.

Corps headquarters, division headquarters, and all lower headquarters issue orders (*Befehle*) as a rule.

Appropriate composition and correct understanding of both types of commands—directives and orders—are the foundation for agreement in the command of units. Continual practice in this is one of the most important preparations for war.

If one compares the orders for maneuvers and practice rides (*Übungsreisen*) with those issued in actual war, one is struck by the completeness of detail of the former and the brevity of the latter. Above all, time is lacking in war to write or to read much. No one is overly anxious to issue orders where there is great responsibility.

It should be the rule that orders contain everything—but only that—which the subordinate commander cannot independently determine for the attainment of a certain goal.

Orders should commence by stating the results of all reports and the general situation, so far as this is necessary, to place the subordinate in a situation to judge the meaning of his task (*Auftrag*). Next follows the general intent, to the extent that it can be divulged without disadvantage. Then come the special instructions. The paragraphs are to be numbered to facilitate a rapid scanning and to shorten references to certain portions of the order.

If for nothing else than secrecy, which is so important, one does not state any reasons, expectations, or viewpoints in orders.

On the other hand, it is absolutely necessary that subordinate headquarters recognize the object of what has been ordered. This enables them to strive for that object even if conditions make it necessary to act differently than ordered.

Each subordinate headquarters should be informed of only so much of the intentions of higher command as is necessary for the attainment of the object. One reason here is to maintain secrecy. Another is that unforeseen events can change the course of things in a few hours. It will rarely be advisable simply to repeat to subordinate headquarters the instructions received from higher headquarters.

It is the first duty of a commander *to command* and not to allow things to run their course as chance leads them. It goes without saying that he should take care to see if and how his orders are carried out.

For example, the order should briefly and definitely state to the corps (or divisions), and to their advance and flank guards, whether they remain stationary or march off, and in what direction if the latter. In this regard it is also advisable to prescribe as little as possible. There may be many good reasons—unknown to field army headquarters[8]—which make it desirable for one corps to start at five o'clock, another at six; to march in three instead of two columns; to pass through that and not through another village. If the corps are already close together and if contact with the enemy is expected, it will of course be necessary to order the following very definitely for each detachment: place and time of starting, number of columns and special direction of their marches, meal times, the place and time of arrival, and so forth. But all detachments should be left a certain degree of freedom. Being independently organized, they are to execute the will of higher headquarters according to their own understanding under conditions that never can be stated in advance.

An alteration of orders is occasionally unavoidable, but it is always bad. While it looks easy, in theory, to change the direction of march of a corps, the reality is very difficult. In such circumstances the strength of the units is already taxed, detachments have been made, reinforcements are on the way, measures of subsistence have been taken, trains sent off, and an engagement is possibly to be broken off.

---

8. Moltke used the words "*Hauptquartier des Oberkommandos*," which normally referred to army headquarters, just as "*Generalkommando*" usually referred to the corps.

In a march to the front, no mention is made of a retreat. A retreat would have to be preceded by a reverse, and seldom can one foresee to what point we may be able to retreat. That depends in part on the enemy and has to be ordered verbally in accordance with existing circumstances.

Every order must specify the location to which the one issuing it displaces and where he may be found during the march and the engagement. Finally, the hour the order is issued must be stated so that it can be determined under what conditions it was issued—conditions that may have changed greatly because of some important event since that hour.

In order to save time, the order should be the same, word for word, for all participating elements.

It is important that every commander knows what order another commander has. He then sees what roads are assigned his neighbor for the march and which he therefore cannot use. He can also judge where the other units are at a given time.

Special instructions to individual detachments can be added at the end or can be sent separately.

The style of the order should be simple and direct. The expressions "left to your discretion," "try," "if possible," and so forth should be avoided.

Whatever is ordered should be executed, but nothing should be ordered that cannot be executed. This includes, for instance, far-reaching envelopments with isolated, weak detachments along forest roads in the enemy's rear, and other such things.

The more precise is the knowledge of the one issuing the order, the more correctly and appropriately can he order.

All units, subordinate headquarters, outposts, advance guards, detachments, and so forth are unconditionally obliged by duty to inform their immediate headquarters of the situation insofar as possible. The more similar are the pictures that all portions of the whole—the higher and lower commanders—have of the situation, the more easily and correctly will all orders be understood and the better will be their cooperation.

A careful analysis must be made of the contents and composition of each report to ascertain what is certain, what is probable, and what is only possible. Fears and delusions must gain no influence on the estimate of the situation. Correct judgment must distinguish the important from the unimportant. The subordinate commander writing his report may see no value in the fact that his post had no contact with the enemy during a certain time, yet this fact may be very important to the command of the whole army.

At the conclusion of an engagement it is usually of the greatest importance to the high command to know immediately what regiments and corps have opposed it and in what condition the enemy is. The units can best see these things. They should also ascertain the regimental numbers of the killed and prisoners and the names of the hostile corps commanders. They should report the direction of the enemy's retreat.

Just as it is in the interest of every unit, especially an engaged detachment, to inform not only the highest commander but also the neighboring units of the situation, so one must not forget that in times that demand great activity, especially in combat and above all at the decisive moment, the leaders involved often will have no time, and may easily forget, to send messages to the rear unless they believe they need support. In order to keep continually informed of the situation, it is advisable that the high command provide itself with its own reports. For this purpose it should send one of its General Staff officers to the subordinate detachments in contact with the enemy. This officer should be supplied with a few mounted messengers to bring back reports.[9]

This latter method is highly important for cavalry divisions and advance and rear guards. During the engagement, dispatching such an officer is frequently advisable for the purpose of maintaining communications and cooperation with neighboring corps and armies. General Staff officers are to be employed on such tasks in important cases. They remain where they are sent, transmit their reports by mounted messengers, and return to their headquarters only when they believe that a personal report is

9. For one small indication of the influence of Moltke's concepts, one should compare this passage with paragraph 130 of the U.S. Army's Field Manual 100–5 of 1939. Its text stated that "Front-line troops are frequently so closely engaged in combat that they are unable to report as often as desired by the higher commander. Commanders make provision for obtaining prompt information by special reconnaissance by sending liaison officers to subordinate or adjacent units. These provisions do not relieve subordinate commanders from making every effort to keep their superiors fully informed of the situation."

necessary or when the general situation no longer requires their presence at the detachments.

But such measures do not relieve any commander of the duty of keeping the higher commander continually informed of the situation by messages.

Clarity and precision of language are just as necessary in reports as in orders. Notation of place, day, and hour is indispensable. Names must be spelled correctly in both orders and reports, otherwise the worst confusion may arise.

The necessary precautions for the proper transmission of reports and orders must be carefully observed. Highly important orders should be sent in duplicate along different roads, especially if the distance is great and if it is during the night.

Measures taken along these lines will make it possible to lead armies uniformly and to bring to the actions and engagements of small detachments the coherence and harmony upon which the strength of an army essentially rests.

HISTORICAL EXAMPLES

The Campaign of 1859[10]

During the Austrian advance from the Mincio to Solferino, the high command issued orders directly and in excessive detail to the corps, paying no attention to the field army headquarters.

If the high command wished to allow the headquarters of the armies to function in their necessary role, it should have ordered nothing for that advance other than the general direction to be taken, the roads assigned each army, and the objectives of the movement. But this was not done. Orders from highest headquarters assigned the march direction to each corps and army headquarters and were thus merely an impediment.

It would have been much better under these conditions to abolish the army headquarters, the more so as the high command did not appear

---

10. The General Staff extracted this section from Moltke's history of the War of 1859. Moltke wrote most of this study himself.

to have been overworked by corresponding with seven different headquarters—the army corps—or nine, if we count the cavalry and artillery reserves. Corps headquarters of course had to exist. It is very difficult
to lead fourteen infantry and two cavalry divisions, or sixteen units,
directly from a single headquarters. This would require extraordinary
means and very great activity, even if for nothing else than marches
and operations.

The army headquarters proved to be not only superfluous at Solferino,
but actually dangerous to a great degree. During the battle the high
command did not bypass them, but rather adhered to the regular military channels. The corps saw themselves prevented, by the presence
of these army headquarters, from acting freely and independently during
the battle according to their best judgment. At the same time, some
of the French generals did this in a masterful way. The clumsiness of
organization, considering that the fighting strength was only 130,000
men, made itself felt on the Austrian side where the two armies joined.
That, unfortunately, was the decisive point. The old experience again
proved true that not only rapidity of transmission of orders, but also
their clarity, diminishes in proportion to the number of headquarters
through which they have to pass.

It is therefore advisable in the interests of practical issuing of orders to confine the number of intermediate headquarters to the absolutely minimum number necessary. Of course subdivision of an army
into main detachments is of great importance. In the Austrian army it
had a great influence on the outcome of the war.

The Campaign of 1866[11]

The great advantage of disregarding an intermediate headquarters
in the issuing of orders was experienced daily by those divisions that
remained part of a corps and that operated alongside divisions that did
not.

---

11. The precise origin of this section is unclear. Although it draws upon material
from the General Staff's history of the campaign of 1866, the passage does not appear in that volume. It may have been one of Moltke's previously unpublished "critical
essays."

During the march to the front, even divisions not in corps organizations sometimes received their orders only at the last moment, in spite of all efforts of the staff at army headquarters and in spite of the quickness and capabilities of the orderly officers. Thus it was not always possible to give the units march orders at the proper time.

The units within corps organizations received orders even later, as a matter of course. All headquarters through which they passed had no chance for rest until far into the night. The units were compelled to perform excessively hasty marches, could not eat before starting, and when arriving at the rendezvous had no time for rest.

On July 3 the orders for battle were in the hands of Second Army headquarters at 4:00 A.M.[12] The further communication of these orders was from Königinhof through the corps headquarters. In the case of the Guard Corps, for instance, the orders traveled by way of Neu-Rettendorf to the 1st Guard Division and back to Königinhof. A direct communication could have had the orders there at 5:30 instead of 9:00 A.M.[13] In addition, I Corps headquarters received direct information of the intentions of royal headquarters at 5:15 A.M. in Ober-Praussnitz, which the officer carrying the orders to Second Army headquarters, Lieutenant Colonel Count Finckenstein, sent to that headquarters with Lieutenant von Britzke of the Guard Hussars. In spite of this, the corps waited for orders from the crown prince before beginning its movement.[14]

In some instances the orders had to be shortened excessively so that they would get to the units at all.

12. Moltke here refers to the orders for the battle of Königgrätz. See Craig, *Königgrätz,* 81–86.

13. The following sentences of this paragraph were in a footnote in the German edition.

14. Moltke was always reluctant to criticize other officers in public. This statement, implicitly critical of the I Corps commander, Gen. Adolf Karl von Bonin, was about as far as Moltke was willing to go. Craig, *Königgrätz,* has incorrectly identified him as Eduard von Bonin, the former War Minister. The two were only very distantly related. See Kurt von Priesdorff, ed., *Soldatisches Führertum,* 10 vols. (Hamburg: Hanseatische Verlagsanstalt, 1936–42), 6, no. 2005 (for Adolf) and 5, no. 1880 (for Eduard). Their remote genealogical connection may be traced in the *Gothaisches Genealogisches Taschenbuch der Adeligen Häuser* 1902, 132–34.

In all undertakings that had to be started without delay, the head-quarters of the armies had to send orders to the divisions which could be reached directly. Thus it happened that the II Corps's divisions were hardly ever employed in the first line until the battle. This naturally caused a feeling of being slighted among the officers and discontent among the men.

There was no advantage in having the 3d and 4th divisions, fighting alongside of each other, under one command at Königgrätz. On the contrary, the only orders on that day were issued for a retreat, which was executed at 3:00 P.M. by two battalions of the 4th Division crossing the bridge from Sadowa. The men grumbled continuously because they did not want to retreat.

Our organization establishes the division as the first self-contained unit for combat. It should therefore be commanded independently. The division that the corps commander accompanies, however, has two commanders, or at least in addition to the division commander, an inspector who is always a hindrance for the one who has to act. In the forest of Sadowa, besides orders from army headquarters and the division commander, special orders within the division were issued by the corps commander, who was with the division. The units ultimately did not know what orders were to be carried out. A feeling of uncertainty seized them.

One will seldom have available such a large unit as a full corps for attaining a limited goal. One will usually make use of the nearest division. During the campaign of 1866 divisions operating alongside each other usually belonged to different army corps, so that the corps commander did not have a unified command. In each case the command could be temporarily given to a general designated by royal headquarters or the senior division commander, as was the case at Blumenau, for example.[15] There the 7th and 8th divisions and the Cavalry Division Hann were under the commander of the 7th Division, General von Fransecky, the senior division commander.

---

15. This was a minor battle fought on July 22, 1866, after the armistice had been signed. Craig, *Königgrätz*, mentions it only in passing. The Prussian General Staff's *Der Feldzug von 1866*, 532–50, discusses this, the last engagement of the campaign. Each side suffered a few hundred casualties.

The intentions of the respective army headquarters will be carried out by the division commander charged with executing them not only more quickly, but also more completely and energetically, if the orders go directly to him. Six division commanders will more easily understand the will of the army commander and will execute it better if they receive the orders directly from him than if the orders have previously been interpreted by three corps commanders whose views are seldom more precise but frequently are weaker.

But with all the undeniable advantages of a war organization that places independent divisions directly under command of army headquarters, after 1866 such an organization could be recommended for the future only if the above rule could be carried out universally and if the divisions in time of peace could be organized just as independently of corps headquarters in regard to administration as was the case in 1866 with regard to tactics, maneuvers, administration, and military justice.[16]

In the partial, largely improvised organization of independent divisions in 1866, corps had to remain in existence because of administration, which nevertheless ceased in the field in an operational respect. Thus arose a dualism that was not on the whole beneficial.

Some divisions had to bear the burden of providing shelter and security to various elements of the corps then attached to them. Others protested vehemently and successfully against carrying along the war chest. Because of this, III Corps's war chest was brought along far behind the Landwehr marching in the rear.

During the armistice, inquiries concerning the location of this war chest were fruitless. Finally, three months later, it reached the units, then entirely without money, at Brünn. Some divisions received too many supplies, others too few, while all felt the shortage of mail service or oversupply of bakeries.

16. The reader should remember that the corps was a fundamental peacetime administrative unit as well as a tactical headquarters. In peacetime, corps commanders had no superior and reported directly to the king. The position of corps commander was one of the most powerful and prestigious in the army. Abolition of the corps, which was never done, would have brought fundamental changes in the army's peacetime structure for all types of administrative actions, as well as large-scale training.

The lessons of the campaign of 1866 raised the question of forming smaller armies.

In order to hasten routine work and to assure smooth command, not more than four to six infantry divisions and two or three cavalry divisions should be attached to one army. Thus four to six armies would have to be formed if the entire army took the field.

The almost exclusively theoretical command of that number of armies was accomplished by the high command and conformed to the principles adopted in 1859.

The commanders of the peacetime corps, insofar as they were not called to the command of one of the armies or to the royal headquarters, assumed important duties in the home provinces (replacements, police, fortresses, supply and provisions, new organizations), as had been done during the campaign against Austria. In a future war their staffs could be better utilized in better manning of the divisions.

Command in a decisive battle appears not to be greatly more difficult because of divisions being organized without corps, but army headquarters would in the future have to be more completely in control.

Although at Königgrätz discretion had to be left to the Army of the Elbe and to the Second Army in executing their tasks, no dispositions of corps and divisions should have been made in the First Army without orders or reports to royal headquarters. Contrary to the intentions of royal headquarters to conduct the engagement on the Bistritz as a holding action and to wait for Second Army's attack, Prince Frederick Charles— of course under the eyes of the king, who did not object—sent the entire infantry reserve (5th and 6th divisions) at Unter-Dohalitz and Sadowa across the Bistritz to a position behind the Hola Forest.

The prince wanted to commit even these reserves in the attack and had already issued the necessary orders to the corps commanding general, von Manstein.[17] The chief of the general staff of the field army felt compelled at 1:30 P.M. to prevent the execution of these orders.[18]

---

17. This was the father of Maj. Gen. Georg Albrecht von Manstein, the adoptive father of the famous Erich von Manstein (born von Lewinski) of the Second World War.

18. Prince Frederick Charles of Prussia, Second Army commander, ordered his reserves to make a premature frontal attack along the center of the Austrian line. This was

Detaching the Division Alvensleben from the cavalry corps assembled behind the Bistritz at Sucha and the consequent partition of that corps into two parts proceeded without approval and against the intentions of royal headquarters. Similarly, sending parts of the 5th and 6th divisions in the morning into the forest of Sadowa (Hola Forest), which was already occupied in too much force, and the intended offensive from there, were grave errors that could have been avoided had army headquarters previously estimated the situation.

We cannot spare the I Corps commander at Tratenau, General von Bonin, from the criticism that in the evening, under pressure of defeat, he forgot his task in the context of the army and thought only of his corps' salvation. Under the protection of a strong and battle-ready rear guard at Parschnitz, he could have had hope of going into bivouac south of Liebau. The next day he could have counted on the cooperation of the other two army corps, the V and Guard corps, and was close enough to support them in case of need.[19]

If, as has been stated, the corps commander's intention had been to take up such a rear-guard position, then the exhausted and intermingled units should of course not have been designated for this, but

---

contrary to Moltke's plan, which wanted no general advance in the center until the flanking units, especially the Second Army advancing from Silesia, could attack the Austrians in the flank or rear. If successful, an ill-timed attack in the center threatened to force the Austrians into a withdrawal that would save them from the planned flank attack. Craig's account, *Königgrätz*, 97, 111, has some details. The General Staff's *Der Feldzug von 1866*, 355–56, also has a brief account.

19. Tratenau was a corps-sized action fought in Silesia on June 27, 1866. General von Bonin's I Corps, with the task of advancing forward to establish contact with advance elements of the Prussian First Army, suffered a costly though by no means disastrous defeat. General von Bonin, shaken by an unexpected Austrian attack, abandoned his mission and retreated to the position from which he had started the previous day. His retreat exposed other Prussian units to great danger. Fortunately for them, the Austrian forces failed to take advantage of their opportunity. See Craig, *Königgrätz*, 63–64, and the General Staff's *Der Feldzug von 1866*, 118–28. The original text says that the I and Guard corps would be available to support Bonin. This is obviously a mistake, since Bonin commanded the I Corps. Moltke no doubt meant the V Corps. The Second Army's other corps, the VI, was too far away to be of immediate assistance.

rather the ones that were still intact. In any case, it appears that the units did not receive orders to hold. At 9:00 P.M. they were ordered to retreat to their previous camping places at Liebau and Schömberg. All were thoroughly tired. Some of the battalions were completely exhausted after seventeen hours of work. Maintaining strict order in the covered and cut-up terrain was doubly difficult because the somewhat eccentric retreat and the failure of all efforts and sacrifices had to have had a depressing effect.

Under such conditions only a very definite order from above stating a clear objective and going to all commanders could have reassembled the corps for renewed resistance.

This required the iron energy of the commander and the most thorough discipline of the units, as was demonstrated in the simultaneous engagement of the V Corps at Náchod. There General von Steinmetz at once recognized that the only thing for the advance guard to do was to hold the plateau against the main body of an enemy whose strength was unknown until the arrival of the main body, and with the retreat leading through only one difficult defile immediately to the rear. This was unavoidable if the offensive task of the corps was to be fulfilled. On one hand, the directives of the corps commander, who was at the engagement, had as their goal the hastening of the march of the main body especially the artillery. On the other hand, he personally intervened with direct orders wherever it appeared necessary to him. As a matter of fact, he succeeded with 5½ battalions and two platoons of Jägers in holding the plateau for three hours against twenty-one battalions that the enemy had available there. The leading elements of the main body finally arrived at the defile and removed all danger.

The Campaign of 1870–71

The intention expressed after the War of 1866 to do away with the corps organization to facilitate the issue of orders ultimately was not carried out in the next campaign, that against France. The necessity of forming strong field armies prevented the realization of that concept. Only the First Army, consisting of four infantry divisions (13th, 14th, 15th, and 16th) and one cavalry division, would have met the conditions envisioned in 1866 for the introduction of independent divisions.

In its case, only five units would have had to have been commanded by army headquarters. The Second Army, on the other hand, consisted of twelve infantry and four cavalry divisions, that is, sixteen units. The Third Army consisted of ten infantry and one cavalry divisions, or eleven units. In both of these armies the issuing of orders would have been rendered more difficult since they had more than nine units. This was more than a single army command could manage, as was seen from the experiences of 1859 and 1866.

As is known, in critical situations royal headquarters resorted to sending orders directly to some corps, while simultaneously notifying their army headquarters of the action taken. This shortened the regular channels and made success more certain. In one case the chief of the General Staff gave direct orders for a change of direction of march to a division. He did this while riding past the Bavarian 2d Division on August 29, 1870. Royal headquarters, for its part, did not hesitate to give the army headquarters directives lasting for many days. Accordingly, army commanders did not have to send orders to their corps every day, but merely had to provide them with directives covering several days.

General von Manteuffel, commander of the South Army at Châtillon-sur-Seine, was in this situation on January 13, 1871. The directions he received verbally at royal headquarters in Versailles had to be of a very general nature. It was plainly recognized that he could not immediately offer direct support to General von Werder, who was on the march from Vesoul to the Lisaine in order to place himself between Belfort and the enemy coming up for its relief. But it had to produce a very great effect if General von Manteuffel could reach the enemy's rearward communications, when the XIV Corps still held its place in front of Belfort. This operation was an extremely bold one, which might, however, have led to great results. If General von Manteuffel had suffered a reverse, he could not have been blamed. In order to achieve great results, something must be risked. All measures to be taken were left to his own discretion. The army commander, who arrived in Châtillon on the evening of January 12, decided to strike against the enemy's main force, which was assumed to be between Doubs and Ognon. The difficulties that the II and VII corps had to overcome in their advance were by no means small. The march to Vesoul led along bad roads deeply covered with snow across the southern part of the rough Langres plateau. Numerous brooks, originating on the plateau, flow down to the Seine and Saône. They crossed the direction of the march and their deep valleys had to be crossed on steep stretches of road that were doubly difficult because of the slippery footing.

The better roads across the plateau keep to the valleys and consequently run generally from northwest to southeast. Thus they could not be used. Communications between the different columns could hardly be maintained in the extensive forests.

Since from these facts it could be foreseen that there could be no regular issuing of orders for the next few days, General von Manteuffel sent a letter to Generals von Zastrow and von Fransecky to inform them of his intentions. The corps commanders were told that the most important point was to move rapidly to the exits to the plateau and to secure these exits. At the exit, each column was to deploy right and left to facilitate the exit of the neighboring column. They were directed to supply the men with rations for the march. The army commander assumed responsibility for all the exceptional measures taken with that end in view. He had discussed all other details with the corps commanders.

Difficulties in the issuing of orders similar to those of the South Army in the eastern theater of war arose with the Second Army in the west in its march on Le Mans. The center of the hostile position between the Loire and the Sarthe could be approached only on four main roads. Communications between the marching columns, which covered a breadth of twenty-six miles, were confined to a few crossroads that were almost impassable because of the time of the year and the hostility of the inhabitants. Mutual support during the march was entirely out of the question.

Under such conditions, the operations could be conducted only by general directives. Subordinate commanders had to be given discretion to act according to their best judgment. Special orders for each day—such as were issued—could not be executed in many cases. Army headquarters could not see how conditions shaped up in each corps during the daily combat they were engaged in. Reports of these actions generally reached army headquarters only late at night, and orders from army headquarters reached the units only after they had started their movements in the morning. This was due to the shortness of the days.

EXAMPLES OF DIRECTIVES

To Headquarters, First and Second Army:
Berlin, 22 June 1866, P.M.

His majesty orders that both armies invade Bohemia and attempt a junction in the direction of Gitschin. The VI Corps remains available at Neisse.

To Headquarters, Second Army:
Berlin, 22 June 1866

In the recently dispatched encoded telegram of today, orders have been issued from royal headquarters for the invasion of Bohemia.

With regard to distance, road connections and railroads, the direction to Gitschin has been designated for eventual junction of both armies.

By this it is not of course meant that the point must be reached under any and all circumstances, because that will depend entirely on the course of events.

According to all information received here, it is highly improbable that the Austrian main forces can be concentrated in northern Bohemia in the next few days. Seizing the initiative might easily offer an opportunity to attack those forces with superior numbers while they are separated and to pursue the victory in another direction. Nevertheless, the convergence of all our fighting forces for the main decision must always be kept in view.

From the moment they encounter the enemy, the army headquarters must employ their detachments according to their best judgment and according to the situation, but must always properly consider conditions of the neighboring army. Mutual support will be made possible through continual communication between the armies.

Although the VI Corps is presently designated for the defensive protection of Silesia, offensive action is not excluded. An early demonstration in force from Neisse or the county of Glatz against the important railroad line from Pardubitz to Prerau will undoubtedly keep at least one hostile corps away from Bohemia.

The further course of the advance will decide the question of security or reconstruction, respectively, of the Zittau-Reichenberg railroad, as well as telegraphic communications.

To Headquarters, First Army:
Berlin, 22 June 1866

The same letter with the following addition:
Since the weak Second Army has the difficult task of debouching out of the mountains, it will be the duty of the First Army to lessen that crisis by a rapid advance as soon as the first junction has been made with the corps under General von Herwarth.[20]

SAMPLE ORDERS FROM TACTICAL PROBLEMS[21]

At royal headquarters in Pont-à-Mousson reports arrived on August 16 up to 5:00 P.M., according to which the III and X corps were apparently engaged with the French main army west of Metz and were able to maintain themselves only with great difficulty.

Of the Second Army on the evening of this day:

The II Corps got as far as Buchy, nine miles south of Metz, after very long marches;

The IV Corps stood at Les Saizerais, with its advance guard near Toul;

The Guard Corps: Headquarters at Bernecourt; advance guard

---

20. This was Gen. Karl Herwarth von Bittenfeld. His Army of the Elbe was on the right flank of the extended Prussian deployment. In reality his army was a reinforced corps.

21. These orders are samples for training rather than real historical examples.

at Rambucourt; the Guard Uhlan Brigade pushed out toward Commercy–Saint-Mihiel;

The XII Corps was around Pont-à-Mousson, headquarters in Fey en Haye; advance guard at Regnieville en Haye; 12th Cavalry Division at Vigneulles;

The IX Corps was still partly on the right bank of the Moselle, but with its leading units as far as the battlefield.

Of the First Army:

The I Corps had to remain opposite Metz for containment[22] and to secure the communications to the rear;

The VII and VIII corps, on the other hand, had already moved up to Corny and Arry on the Moselle, respectively, in order to cross the river the next day on the bridges existing there, but only after the IX Corps.

Prince Frederick Charles was on the battlefield. His quarters for the night were not known. Those of General von Steinmetz were at Coin on the Seille.

A field telegraph was established to Fey en Haye and Bernecourt.

Problem

On August 17 those corps which can reach the battlefield during the day are to be moved up as early as possible. Above all, the left wing at Mars-la-Tour is to be strengthened. Cavalry is to advance from there toward the roads from Metz to Étain and Briey.

Toul continues to be observed, but in the direction of the Meuse only the Guard Uhlan Brigade remains in position.

The two available corps of the First Army are to be brought up by the shortest road to the right wing of the position at Vionville.

---

22. The German word is "Observation" (*Beobachtung*), in the military sense meaning containing the garrison. Thus "containment" seems a more appropriate modern term.

All intersections and blockages of the corps ordered up are to be avoided. The supply of ammunition must not be forgotten.

Direct reports to his majesty are to be sent to the heights south of Flavigny.

Orders for August 17 will be issued at royal headquarters in Pont-à-Mousson at 7:00 P.M. on the sixteenth, as far as practicable by telegram, and as far as necessary directly to the corps commanders. Communications will be made simultaneously to the army commanders.

At the end of telegrams the number of words (exclusive of address and signature) is to be noted.

Solution

The problem was one of a purely editorial nature. These questions were involved: To whom? What? How? Brevity is herein absolutely necessary, but completeness is the main thing.

To Whom?

Should an order also be sent to the II and IV corps? That would not be a mistake, for one cannot be too strong for the decision. But neither is it absolutely necessary. It was said in the problem that only those corps should be summoned up which could reach the battlefield in the course of the day. If one wished to do so, one division of the IV Corps could, for instance, be ordered up to Thiaucourt, and the II Corps to the bridges at Corny and Arry. The II Corps may not go to Pont-à-Mousson because the covering of the Moselle with its roads, as also the support of the right wing of the Second Army, is more easily effected from the direction of Corny and Arry.

Orders must be sent to the Guard Corps and XII Corps in any case directly from royal headquarters, for if these orders pass through army headquarters they will be too late, especially since the locations of the latter are not known. To the VII and VIII corps, however, orders are not to be issued directly, but rather through headquarters of the First Army, since this is only about five miles away. The regular channels are therefore always to be maintained unless deviation from them becomes an urgent necessity. This is not the case here, since the VII and VIII corps need only to set out the following morning. Neither must the

IX corps be immediately disposed of, since army headquarters probably has already ordered it to close up.

These orders are therefore to be issued in writing to the two army headquarters of the VII and VIII corps, and to the II, IV, and IX corps, respectively, and directly by wire to the Guard and XII corps.

What?

The telegrams must briefly state the general situation. This is necessary in order to explain the change in direction of march. This general information must be identical, if possible, so that everyone is informed of the tasks of neighboring units. The 12th Cavalry Division must not be ordered directly because it is subordinate to the XII Corps and because that corps will have more secure and rapid communications with it.

The general information for the two army headquarters need not be identical. Nor are times to be given for the marches, since at royal headquarters one surely cannot calculate beforehand the marches of eighteen to twenty-two miles of the various corps. One would only unnecessarily increase one's own responsibility by such detailed arrangements. Selection of the various march routes is in any case the business of the chiefs of staff of the armies and of the corps, who can send officers to reconnoiter them in advance. Therefore, definite roads should not be assigned to the Guard Corps and the XII Corps, nor to the VII and VIII corps. Only the general directions, and the objective of the march, are to be indicated.

How?

To Headquarters, First Army, at Coin-sur-Seille (by an orderly officer): Pont-à-Mousson, 16 August 1870, 7:00 P.M.

> III and X corps have maintained themselves today west of Metz against a greatly superior enemy. Guard and XII corps are set in motion toward Mars-la-Tour. The VII and VIII corps are to be moved up the Moselle at Corny and Arry to the right wing of the battlefield at Vionville, but only after the IX Corps, and by the shortest road. The trains remain on this side of the Moselle. Ammunition columns are to be brought up to supply the III Corps.

Reports to his majesty are to be directed tomorrow morning to the hill south of Flavigny.

To Headquarters, Second Army, Noveant-Gorze (In duplicate, by two officers):
Pont-à-Mousson, 16 August 1870, 7:00 P.M.

By telegraph from here, the Guard and XII corps have been ordered up to Mars-la-Tour by Beney and Thiaucourt, the former to the left, the latter to the right; 12th Cavalry Division to advance as early as possible for observation of the roads from Étain and Briey to Metz. The VII and VIII corps cross the Moselle tomorrow after the IX Corps, and move by the shortest road to the right wing of the battle position at Vionville. His majesty arrives tomorrow morning on the hill south of Flavigny.

Telegram to Headquarters, Guard Corps, at Bernecourt:
Pont-à-Mousson, 16 August 1870, 7:00 P.M.

III and X corps fought today west of Metz against a superior enemy. Guard and XII corps will march tonight to Mars-la-Tour by Beney to the left and Thiaucourt to the right. 12th Cavalry Division to be moved forward against roads from Étain and Briey to Metz. Guard Uhlan Brigade remains near the Meuse. Bring up ammunition columns.

Telegram to Headquarters, XII Corps, at Fey en Haye:

Same as above.[23]

---

23. The editors of Moltke's collected works inserted the following sentence at this point in the original text: "For transmission of orders at the present day one would employ modern devices such as automobiles, telephones, etc."

RECONNAISSANCE AND SECURITY (c. 1869–83)

General

In many instances, measures for reconnoitering the enemy's situation go hand in hand with orders for security of resting as well as marching units and will have to be performed simultaneously by the same formations.

Every unit in contact with the enemy is aware of the necessity of providing its own security, and the requirement to obtain intelligence on the enemy makes itself felt to a lesser degree and most probably later.

These conditions require close watching so that reconnaissance, which every unit in the front line needs, is not neglected because of security, and so that the basis on which the high command forms its decisions is not lacking. In any case, far-reaching reconnaissance is the best security.

Reconnaissance is the proper and almost exclusive province of the cavalry. In reconnaissance, cavalry will find a vast field of important activity and the individual rider, as well as commanders up to generals, will find opportunities for distinction. Cleverness and skill, quick perception, and decisive action will be particularly valuable here. Extraordinary efforts cannot be avoided. A high degree of activity is necessary for the cavalry, which will thereby perform important services for the army.

It will always be valuable to take some prisoners as soon as possible. Their sight makes a good impression on the units. From their regimental numbers one can often reach very important conclusions about the disposition of the hostile forces.

In larger commands, and where the enemy is still distant, reconnaissance in the broader sense falls to the cavalry divisions. They set out immediately upon mobilization or even at the declaration of war, under certain conditions. Advancing ahead of the army at as great a distance as possible, they are the best means to gain insight into the general situation. The cavalry divisions' reconnaissance of the enemy situation furnishes the best security for the army, whose movements they conceal at the same time.

The leaders of cavalry divisions therefore must understand not only how to act but must also be able to estimate the general situation. From observed details they must judge the relationships of hostile operations and use this as the basis for further reconnaissance measures.

A cavalry division is independent to the highest degree. Free to move as it pleases, it can easily avoid precarious situations by its mobility and may therefore risk much. It should not confine its activity to the enemy's front, but should extend it to his flanks and rear. There, other important successes—for example destroying railroad and telegraph lines, magazines, depots, and so forth—are to be accomplished along with reconnaissance.

A cavalry division's vehicles must never be an obstacle to rapid and unobstructed movement in important enterprises. In such cases they should be left far behind, under the protection of other units. This is possible because a cavalry division can usually live off the land when moving rapidly from place to place.

If several cavalry divisions conduct reconnaissance alongside each other, each one should be assigned to and assume responsibility for a certain area. The divisions should then maintain permanent and precise communications and must always be ready to furnish mutual support and to cooperate.

Where necessary, insight into the enemy situation must be sought by force of arms. Aside from the *Arme blanche*,[24] cavalry divisions possess a high degree of combat power because of their batteries and carbines, as well as an increased independence and capacity for demolition with the attachment of engineer detachments. In exceptional cases, temporary attachment of infantry may be advantageous or even necessary.

Reconnaissance carried out by divisional cavalry is confined to smaller areas and usually has more limited objectives. For that reason it must extend to the engagement and must never be lacking there. If under some conditions a united deployment of the two divisional cavalry regiments of one army corps appears desirable, then at least one squadron should always be left with each infantry division.

---

24. *Arme blanche* refers to lances and sabers for the cavalry and bayonets for the infantry.

As a rule, one will obtain excellent intelligence on the enemy most easily and economically by employing single riders or smaller detachments (officer patrols).

The cavalry must devote special attention to preparatory training of officers for this purpose. They must possess quick perception and judgment and must be well trained in reading maps and comparing them with the terrain so as to be able to form a clear picture from brief observations of the enemy. They should be well mounted, equipped with good field glasses, and should prepare their messages clearly and briefly after thorough consideration. Officer patrols should be sent especially to the flanks and around the enemy's wings. They may remain near the enemy for a long time and must not be restricted in their action by inflexible regulations (*Vorschriften*). They return as soon as they are satisfied that remaining near the enemy is no longer of any use. In important cases, General Staff officers may be employed on such tasks.

On occasion it will be advisable to have strong cavalry detachments follow such officer patrols at a substantial distance for relays or for support.

Attacks by strong bodies of infantry for reconnaissance purposes are justifiable only as direct preludes to general attacks.

Except for that purpose, bloody reconnaissance fights, accompanied by great loss, are highly objectionable and are usually signs of uncertain leadership and weaknesses in powers of decision.

One best attains security on the march by spreading out and sending the cavalry ahead. The cavalry either overcomes resistance by itself or reports in a timely manner to the commander of the advance guard so that he can take his measures without loss of time. In many cases the simplest and most economical means of attaining security, even in very difficult terrain, will be to send cavalry far ahead. Cavalry sent out at or before the start of the march becomes less tired and brings more consistency into the movement of the whole than if, marching with the advance guard, it is sent out only when need arises, and then usually with great haste.

Providing frontal security for the units on a march is always and automatically the duty of the advance guard, which also protects its own flanks. Special measures are to be taken in case of need for the protection of the flanks of the main body.

The conduct of the advance guard is governed by the general situation, the enemy's action, and terrain. It is also dependent on the main body's condition. Besides reconnaissance and protection of the main body, the advance guard must gain time for the highest commander for the execution of his decision. It will begin an engagement on its own initiative only when its task requires it, or when substantial success may be attained by quick exploitation of favorable circumstances.

The distance between the advance guard and the main body varies. It must be great enough to protect the march of the main body. A strong advance guard may therefore be sent farther ahead than a weak one. The commander will have to determine the proper distance in each case by carefully judging general conditions, his own and the enemy's strength, and especially the peculiarities of the terrain.

All security measures must be so prepared and executed that they do not delay the march of the whole. One must not act with too much punctiliousness in this matter. The main point is to protect the units against serious surprise attacks.

By using correct judgment and some degree of boldness, one will prevent the enemy from influencing the movement of the whole by feigned maneuvers. One should always remember that what flanks will itself be flanked, and that a turning movement is dangerous only to the weaker party.

In a withdrawal, the rear guard must provide the main body's security against minor enemy actions and against every attack. The rear guard will best gain necessary time for the departure of the main body (whose distance must usually be greater than in an advance because of the length of its columns) when it forces the enemy to deploy or forces him to make lengthy turning movements by occupying a position behind obstacles. In extreme cases, the rear guard must not hesitate to gain time by offering serious resistance even against greatly superior forces.

As soon as the main body has gained the necessary head start, the rear guard may march away or break off the engagement. Sacrifices in the latter must be borne for the benefit of the whole. One may most easily evade the enemy by holding one's position until dark.

Security measures while the army is at rest have the purpose of gaining the necessary time for the units to prepare for combat or marching.

They also allow the commander time for the execution of necessary measures. This can be accomplished by resistance or by gaining timely intelligence of the position and movements of the enemy.

The composition of the main body, and especially the general situation, regulates the position of the advance units. The farther forward one sends the advance units and the greater the depth of their deployment, the less will their leading elements be compelled to offer resistance. The lengthy distance the enemy will then have to march allows ample time for the main body to get ready.

As long as we are not in close contact with the enemy, we will frequently gain security more completely and with less expenditure of strength by sending cavalry detachments far to the front. This will give us the assurance that the enemy is still far away and that he needs time to reach us. Infantry detachments, posted in the rear of the cavalry as suitable points for protection if necessary, will secure the cavalry against reverses and enable it to advance farther and more boldly.

One may also preserve the units and make them comfortable as long as advanced detachments hold their own at defiles and crossroads which the enemy must pass. In that case the units farther to the rear have to protect themselves merely by small outposts or, under certain conditions, only by local security.

If one cannot send out the advance units sufficiently far, they will have to fight to protect the resting units against surprise. If the enemy is very close, and especially if a battle ceases in the evening only to be resumed in the morning, or if one is in a lengthy defense of a fortified position, one may be forced to remain under arms while at rest. In that case the first line acts as outposts.

If one wishes to accept battle, one needs only sufficient time to bring the units under arms. If one desires to avoid an engagement, one needs sufficient time to allow the main body to march off without becoming engaged.

The longer one remains at rest at the same spot, the more careful the security must be. If we halt in the evening with the intent of resuming the march the next morning, it will in most cases suffice to occupy the roads leading toward the enemy. In such cases it will be best to extend a chain of individual pickets to the outpost companies, which in their turn send out security detachments along the roads.

But if one desires to remain stationary for a day, one will have to spread out more to the sides. One will also have to establish better cohesion along the line, and will have to take better care for the security of the flanks. Cavalry security detachments will have to be posted to extend the outpost line.

In order to remain stationary for several days or even weeks, one must establish a line of great length that is impenetrable to hostile patrols and detachments.

But many more conditions influence these measures. Taking the proper measures is an art that cannot be confined to definite limits by general rules or by a general scheme. In each case, to attain the assigned objective, the only guides we have to go by are the measures we take ourselves.

In cases where a very long outpost line extends across several main roads or is splintered by obstacles in the terrain, it is advisable to place two or more independent detachments alongside each other.

Cavalry generally provides security during the day. However, those points that absolutely must be held should be garrisoned by infantry. Under certain conditions it may also be advisable to place artillery there.

As a general rule, we relieve the cavalry at night only with infantry, especially when the enemy is near. But that does not mean that we have no cavalry out in front—it should patrol along the roads to gain timely information, especially at dawn.

Independent cavalry divisions must at all times and under all circumstances arrange for their own security. This will be easier because they can know every evening if the enemy is in their vicinity and, if so, where.

Security should never be interrupted by the transition from march to rest and from rest to march. In this sense, and for the purpose of saving the strength of the advance units themselves, it is very important that all security measures be taken quickly. This is far more important than avoiding minor deficiencies in placing the outposts, whose disposition should correspond to the general movement to the greatest extent possible.

When starting the march to the front it is usually better to move with new security formations through the outpost line, and then to assemble that line and insert it in the proper place in the march column, than to use it for the advance guard. This method is also used to relieve the detachments nearest the enemy from their arduous service.

INVENTIONS[25] (c. 1859–68)

We in the military pay due attention to the progress of science and to inventions in other than military matters. But an invention is not what it is in itself; all depends on its further development. The value of any invention rests not only in theory, even if correct, but mainly on its practical application by complete technical development. Our excellent needlegun (1868) had been invented many years previously, but required more than twenty years to become an actually service-able weapon. It will therefore no longer suffice merely to observe what is done in other areas. We must ourselves perfect the invention. Should it be practicable, for instance, to build trucks that transport heavier loads, even if more slowly, than can be done by horse power, they would undoubtedly be quickly adopted universally.[26]

How any invention is to be utilized for war purposes must be left to the military authorities.

It is an error to assume that we can operate against the enemy with trains drawn by trucks.

Railroads are the most effective means for the initial concentration. At the front, railroads can be used just as little as roads if we want to employ trucks. But behind the front, even an advancing one, this new means can be of enormous importance, especially for provisioning the army where railroads are absent or have been disrupted.

If a truck can take the place of forty horses, the advantage is evident. It can travel by itself, consumes but a fraction of its load, and covers greater distances. Military authorities will undoubtedly gain much from the use of trucks when they have been invented [written in 1868].

The balloon cannot be used for military purposes without further development. Its employment as a means of reconnaissance has many limitations. Reconnaissance from a balloon obviously can take place only in daylight when the weather is clear. In wooded terrain or in a culti-vated country like Lombardy, one would, even under those conditions,

25. The source of this essay is uncertain. It probably is a combination of previously unpublished essays.
26. Here Moltke means the primitive steam-driven vehicles of his day, *Strassen-lokomotives*. This translation uses the modern term "trucks" throughout.

not gain a full view. Nevertheless, even given these limitations, one could gain a good view of all positions and movements of the enemy in nearby normal terrain, whether hilly or level. This would be of great assistance the day before and during a battle, but there still are matters that the technique will have to overcome.

Of course the extent of the visible space increases with the altitude. At three thousand feet we can see sixty-seven miles, at one thousand, forty miles—three days' march. But then all elevations in the ground disappear and the ground appears to be level. A correct estimate of the hostile situation can be gained only with the help of field glasses and by study of the map. An altitude of about five hundred feet seems to be sufficient, and more advantageous in most cases.

The observer should be an officer, not the pilot. Since the pilot cannot observe and work the mechanism at the same time, it appears necessary that the balloon should be able to carry at least two persons.

Observation should be carried on for several hours. It is absolutely necessary that the balloon be stationary, like a kite on a string. The technical possibilities of this must be investigated since strong and changing air currents can place the balloon at an angle that halts observation.

If a balloon cannot be made stationary, its entire usefulness disappears. Discounting the fact that in that case it would be impossible for the navigator to bring his balloon back, it is equally important not only that the observer should see, but that he be able to report his observations. The latter might be accomplished by use of weighted messages sliding down the line by means of a ring, but would not be feasible without such means [written in 1859].

MARCHES (c. 1859–83)

The Art of Marching[27]

Combat fills but a moment, of course the most important one, but the movements leading to battle, marching, fill the entire life of an army in the field.

---

27. The German title is *Märsche. Die Kunst zu marschieren.*

A tactical victory is decisive only if won at the strategically correct point. We reach that point, just as the enemy strives to reach it, only if all parts of our army are equally mobile.

An army that could fight at Rossbach on November 5 and at Leuthen on December 5 counts as two armies in its effect.

The campaign of 1809 was decided by marching. Fourteen days after the opening of hostilities, the Austrian army, which had concentrated first and enjoyed numerical superiority, was dispersed and Bavaria was conquered. Seventeen days later the French were in front of Vienna; Archduke Charles was at Stockerau six days after that. And all this without a battle.[28]

Prerequisites for such mobility of an entire army are strong physiques, practice[29] in proper subsistence in the field, and equipment appropriate to all circumstances.

Proper Equipment

An army that marches light will also maneuver light.[30] Thus, every ounce carried by man or horses is important, as well as the method by which it is carried.

Everyone agrees that our pack must be lightened. However, opinions differ about which articles are to be eliminated from the soldier's pack. Marches and bivouacs have been more costly in many campaigns than battles and engagements (Yorck's corps prior to the battle on the Katzbach). A firm yet dry camp, protected from wind and weather, undoubtedly is far superior to one in snow or on a wet plowed field, as our men had to endure for many nights in our campaigns. Tents

28. This version of the early stage of the campaign of 1809 leaves much to be desired. Although the battle of Eggmühl (April 22, 1809) was hardly an epic event, it was a significant encounter. The interested reader should consult Gunther Rothenberg's *Napoleon's Great Adversaries: The Archduke Charles and the Austrian Army, 1792–1814* (Bloomington: Indiana University Press, 1982), 123–39.

29. Here Moltke used the term (ubiquitous in German military literature) *Übung* (practice), a word virtually absent from modern American military literature, theory, and doctrine.

30. *Leicht,* Moltke's term here, could also be rendered as "easily." This translation uses "light" because of the subsequent discussion of the soldier's load.

will ameliorate conditions, for they furnish protection against rain, cold, sun, and wind.

This makes a reduction in the weight of packs even more necessary. Anyone who has not carried a knapsack in the heat of the sun does not know what a burden it is. Cooking utensils increase the load the man carries by the method of carrying, which is made necessary by their weight. We want every individual to cook, but the consequence may be that nobody cooks if the soldier, tired out by an exhausting march, would rather rest and go hungry.

Thousands of cooking utensils require fuel that may not be available in many broad stretches of country. Cooking meals requires several hours. Should the units be alerted during the cooking, the food will have to be thrown away. The advantage of small cooking utensils for detachments cannot offset such disadvantages and must be attained in some other manner. Individual men and small detachments will find something to eat almost anyplace. Even if they do not, that fact merits no consideration when the great question of lightening the burden of the infantryman is concerned.

Rolling kitchens prepare the food on the march.[31] The soldier finds his meal prepared at the bivouac and can rest. Rolling kitchens require far less fuel and are not confined to the consumption of wood exclusively. They follow the units to which attached when the unit is alerted and relieve the individual soldier of weight and work. They keep a company together and prevent straggling. Of course they have the disadvantage of increasing the number of vehicles.

It is possible that a company may become separated from its rolling kitchens, although its greatest interest might be to prevent that very occurrence. In such a case, however, it is no worse off than having kettles and no fuel.

Ammunition carts or wagons can be lost, yet we still should not load the individual down with a reserve supply of ammunition.

Today railroads traverse all countries in which we may conduct a war. It is certainly erroneous to hold that railroads at our strategic front

---

31. Here Moltke refers to the Prussian system of kitchens mounted in wagons, able to prepare meals while the column was on the move.

could furnish the means for offensive operations. But in the rear they offer the incalculable advantage that the burden of war, which formerly crushed individual districts, will now be spread over entire countries and will be borne by them. Railroads permit the transportation of sick and wounded to hospitals far to the rear. They allow movement of rations, reserve ammunition, siege trains, reinforcements, and replacement contingents to the front from even the most distant points of the monarchy. It is even easier to use them to bring clothing and articles of equipment to the mobile units.

This makes it appear advisable not to load down the individual soldier with articles (for example, coats in summertime) that may be issued in case of need at the first lengthy halt of the armies (by means of auto-trucks).[32]

In the case of the cavalry we probably had best look for lightening the load less of the pack than of the man himself. This arm brings about its decision by the violence of the charge in close order. Shock impact is the product of the mass multiplied by the velocity. A horse charging at a high rate of speed with a light rider produces the same effect. The violence of the shock depends, of course, not only on mass and speed, but essentially on the pressure of the second finger of the left hand—which means the will of the rider. One finds decisiveness just as much in the small man as in the large one.

On the other hand, we need hardly mention what a difference there is if the horse, not counting the pack, carries a trooper weighing a hundred forty instead of two hundred pounds. The lighter trooper will not only move more rapidly in an engagement, but will arrive there in better condition. It will be difficult to state whether the larger and stronger or the small and agile man will have the advantage in single combat.

The designation "heavy cavalry" is in itself a contradiction. We will not deny, however, that this arm can be very desirable under certain conditions, especially in case of an actual charge of cavalry against cavalry. But the more rarely that case occurs and the more steadily increasing cultivation of flatlands prevents the employment of large

32. The German word was *Automobillastwagen*. This passage suggests that at least part of the section may have originated after Moltke's retirement.

masses of cavalry, the more will that method of action be limited. The doubtful utility of the shining breastplate need not be referred to here. A man measuring five feet in height is fully competent, all other things being equal, to attend to his horse, to saddle, bridle, and govern him. Thus it may not be paradoxical to hold that the majority of cavalrymen should come from the smallest men and that the largest and strongest men should be assigned to the artillery, which needs them the most. Even infantry requires strong and large men more than does the cavalry.

In the case of the artillery, any lightening of the load rests principally in the guns. The new field pieces have greatly assisted in this manner.

Concentration

Assembly Before the Battle; Assembly on the Battlefield[33]

In most instances, history recounts merely the major events of a war, never the inner circumstances. Everyone likes to read about engagements and glorious deeds. The difficulties of supply, the fatigues of the marches, the privations suffered in bivouacs, the sufferings in hospitals, and the devastation of the country are unattractive and difficult to understand. But they are so very necessary.[34]

Above all, an army must live. It must eat, drink, rest, and be able to move. Hundreds of thousands cannot live off magazines, even if they have railroads to their rear. They cannot bivouac permanently. They therefore will have to go into cantonments in the country, where they remain for the purpose of subsisting and finding shelter, which

33. The German title is *Konzentration. Versammlung vor der Schlacht—Versammlung auf dem Schlachtfelde*. The concept of uniting one's armies only during the battle, rather than a day or two before the battle began, was, in the eyes of many German theorists, the most fundamental difference between Moltke's methods and those of Napoleon. An enormous and sometimes polemical literature grew up on this subject between 1875 and 1939.

34. Here Moltke used an analogy about glorious deeds being points of light and the more mundane events being shadows. This did not translate well and has been rendered for its meaning rather than for a close literal translation.

is even more sparse. Nature itself abhors accumulating great masses in a single place.

The more restricted the space into which an army is crowded, the fewer will be the roads leading to the intended objective. One then has the choice of spreading out again to use several roads or to march on the few existing ones in several daily echelons. It is well known that an army corps with its trains has a march depth of more than thirteen miles. Two corps therefore cannot use the same road on the same day unless we wish to march off the road, which is done at the cost of the strength of the units. Thus, in an advance from a close concentration, one loses by extension of the front or by march depth the very advantage of that concentration, which is, in case one attacks the enemy, to be able to assemble all of our forces on the same day.

Every close concentration of large masses is therefore inherently a calamity. It is justifiable and necessary if it leads directly to battle. It is dangerous to spread out again from a close concentration in the presence of the enemy, and it is impossible to maintain this concentration.

If an army has approached an enemy force concentrated prior to battle, each subsequent division of the forces for the purpose of flanking or enveloping the enemy requires a flank march within the enemy's tactical area of effectiveness.

Conditions are more favorable when the fighting forces can be concentrated from different points toward the battlefield on the day of battle, and when operations can be conducted so that a final short march from *different* directions leads to the enemy's front and flank *simultaneously*. In that case, strategy has performed its best, and great results should be the result. Of course no foresight can assure that the operations of separated armies will actually bring about this final success. That is far more dependent not only on the calculable factors of the size of the forces and time, but in many cases on the outcome of minor engagements, on the weather, or on false information. In short, it is dependent on what in the human sense is designated as chance and luck.

It should also be remembered that the enemy can move while we march. Operations therefore must not unconditionally have fixed points as their object, but must be adjusted to changes occurring with the enemy, of which in many cases we will have no more information than very general suppositions.

But great successes in war cannot be gained without great dangers.

The difficult task of an effective high command consists in maintaining the dispersed state of the masses while at the same time preserving the possibility of timely concentration. For that there are no general rules; the problem in each case will be a different one.

One will be on the safe side to concentrate the units *in all cases* before the battle, and to consider assembling *on* the battlefield the exception. In this, one must firmly realize that under assembly one does not mean the concentration at one point, but that the points of the different columns are directed on a definite point. Assembly should not be confused with deployment (*Aufmarschieren*).

Deployment—Position in Readiness[35]

In order to advance, we need deep march columns. On the other hand, we must deploy prior to battle. If we deploy too early, we make no progress and tire our units unnecessarily. If we deploy too late, the enemy can push our security detachments back and attack us during our deployment. How, therefore, should the deployment be made? There exists no rule for this. One must do in each case what seems to be the most correct. But we have a medium between the march column and the deployed front: the march of columns alongside each other (in that case, tactical deployment)[36] and the position in readiness. This is suitable close behind an intended engagement position as long as we can oversee its proper occupation until the approach of the enemy.

Interior Lines of Operations[37]

(**a**) The indisputable advantages of interior lines of operations retain their value only so long as we have sufficient space to make at

35. The German title is *Aufmarsch–Bereitschaftsstellung*.

36. Here Moltke used the term *Entfaltung*, which German theory typically defined as "transition from the march column or ready position into formations that enable rapid entry into combat within the framework of the plan, but so manageable that the commander can still execute necessary changes and displacements." See Friedrich Stuhlmann, ed., *Wehr-Lexikon. Was jeder Deutsche von der Wehr wissen muss* (Berlin: Carl Heymanns Verlag, 1935), 71.

37. The German title is *Innere Operationslinie*.

least a few marches to meet the enemy, in order to gain time to beat him, to pursue, and then to turn against the other enemy whom we have meanwhile only observed. If this space becomes so restricted that we can no longer attack the one enemy without running the danger of at once becoming engaged with the other, who then attacks us in flank and rear, then the strategic advantage of the interior lines of operation changes into the tactical disadvantage of being surrounded in combat. The latter was the case with Napoleon in 1813 at Leipzig and with Benedek in 1866 at Königgrätz.

(b) In the case of interior lines of operations, everything depends on the distance in relation to the strength of both fighting forces.

If we stand opposed to a numerically very superior but separated enemy, we have a decided advantage if it is possible for us to throw our main forces by two or three marches on the *one* part, while we observe and contain the *other* part. The tactical victory to be expected in that case outweighs all strategic considerations.

If distances are short, it will hardly be possible to hide the movements of large bodies of troops from the enemy. We run the danger of being attacked in the rear during our attack.

If the opponent succeeds in concentrating his forces on the battlefield, then the strategic advantage of the interior line of operations is changed to the tactical disadvantage of being enveloped.

Essay on Sources

Despite Moltke's prominence among the ranks of the world's great military thinkers and practitioners, biographers have generally been little interested in his life and career. There is neither a comprehensive biography in English nor a thorough study of Moltke's impact upon Prussian theory or military thought in a broader context. Of the biographies in English, William O'Connor Morris's *Moltke: A Biographical and Critical Study* is perhaps the best, despite its original publication date of 1893. Frederick E. Whitton's *Moltke* is of only passing interest today. The best introductions in English to Moltke and his theories remain the articles by Hajo Holborn and Gunther Rothenberg in both the original and revised editions of *Makers of Modern Strategy*. These essays are cited fully in the editor's introduction to this volume.

The best biography in any language is Eberhard Kessel's *Moltke* (Stuttgart, 1957). The more recent book by Franz Herre, *Moltke. Der Mann und sein Jahrhundert* (Stuttgart, 1984), adds little if anything to Kessel's study. Eckart von Naso's *Moltke. Mensch und Feldherr* (Berlin, 1937), once enormously popular in Germany, is now read only by devoted specialists. Max Jähns's *Feldmarschall Moltke* (Berlin, 1900) is still useful. Jähns was both an accomplished military writer and Moltke's close associate. Also noteworthy is Friedrich-Christian Stahl's brief biographical sketch in the 1988 *Beiheft zur Europäischen Wehrkunde*.

Several works are available on Moltke's role in planning and executing Prussia's military strategy between 1864 and 1890. Arden Bucholz, in *Moltke, Schlieffen and Prussian War Planning* (Berg, 1991), studies the development of the bureaucratic planning mechanisms and the exploitation of railways. While no sustained analysis of these plans is available in English, Peter Rassow's brief survey of Moltke's planning (*Der Plan des Feldmarschalls Grafen Moltke für den Zweifronten-Krieg,* Breslau, 1936) is a useful introduction. The plans themselves were published in *Die deutsche Aufmarschpläne 1871–1890* (Berlin, 1929). Martin van Creveld's *Command in War* (Cambridge, Mass., 1985) has a fresh interpretation of Moltke's actions in 1866.

A few collections of letters and memoirs are useful for understanding Moltke's views. Most notable among these are Julius von Verdy du Vernois's *With the Royal Headquarters in 1870–71* (London, 1927), Carl Graf von Blumenthal's *Journals of Field Marshal Count von Blumenthal for 1866 and 1870–71* (London, 1903), and F. O. Meissner, ed., *War Diary of the Emperor Frederick, 1870–71* (London, 1927).

Moltke's key role in shaping the German General Staff system emerges in several sources readily available in English. Arden Bucholz's book, cited above, is the most recent. J. D. Hittle's *The Military Staff: Its History and Development* (New York, 1944) is still valuable. The popular book by Walter Görlitz, *History of the German General Staff, 1657–1945* (New York, 1953), is useful for Moltke but unreliable on many other points. Trevor Dupuy, *A Genius for War: The German Army and General Staff* (London, 1977), must be used with caution. Spencer Wilkinson's *The Brain of an Army* (London, 1889) was enormously influential earlier in this century despite its brevity. Paul Bronsart von Schellendorff's *The German General Staff* (London, 1908) is authoritative, although entirely uncritical.

Moltke's political views and his relations with Otto von Bismarck have been the subjects of much discussion. In addition to the standard biographies cited above, one should turn to Gerhard Ritter, *The Sword and the Scepter: The Problem of Militarism in Germany* (Coral Gables, Fla., 1969–73), especially volumes one and two. Gordon Craig's *The Politics of the Prussian Army, 1640–1945* (Oxford, 1956) remains a fundamental source. The standard biographies of Bismarck also have important material on political-military relations during Moltke's era, as do many surveys and special studies of the Second Empire. Otto Pflanze's three-volume study titled *Bismarck and the Development of Modern Germany* (Princeton, 1990) is one of the best.

Although the wars of German unification reshaped the map of Europe and transformed the international balance of power, they have received less attention from military historians than one might imagine. On the war against Austria, Gordon Craig's *The Battle of Königgrätz* (Philadelphia, 1964) is the best single-volume study in any language. Michael Howard's *The Franco-Prussian War* (New York, 1961) is the same for its subject. Though dated, Henri Bonnal's *Sadowa: A Study* (London, 1913) is still useful as a French perspective. Dennis Showalter's *Railroads and Rifles: Technology and the Unification of Germany* (Hamden, Conn., 1975) is extremely important.

Moltke's contributions to the theory of warfare were important but controversial. The best introduction to the lengthy controversy over his methods is Rudolf von Caemmerer's *The Development of Strategical Science During the 19th Century* (London, 1905). Jean Colin's *The Transformations of War* (London, 1912) presents a very different perspective. Few other fundamental works in the controversy are available in English. Stig Förster's "Facing 'People's War': Moltke the Elder and Germany's Military Options after 1871" (*Journal of Strategic Studies,* 1987) is a provocative new interpretation of Moltke's thought and German options after 1871. Dennis Showalter's "German Grand Strategy: A Contradiction in Terms?" (*Militärgeschichtliche Mitteilungen,* 1990) has an equally broad perspective. Jay Luvaas's "European Military Thought and Doctrine 1870–1914" in *The Theory and Practice of War,* edited by Michael Howard (New York, 1966), has useful insights on the relationship between Moltke and Clausewitz. The works of Gen. Sigismund von Schlichting, the key link between Moltke's theories and modern theory, have not been translated. Don Cranz has provided an introduction in his unpublished masters thesis, "Understanding Change: Sigismund von Schlichting and the Operational Level of War" (Fort Leavenworth, Kans., 1990). Edwin A. Pratt's *The Rise of Rail-Power in War and Conquest, 1833–1914* (Philadelphia, 1916) is still a fundamental source. Herbert Rosinski's essay, "Scharnhorst to Schlieffen: The Rise and Decline of German Military Thought" (*Naval War College Review,* 1976 [1942–43]), and his *The German Army* (London, 1939), retain their value.

INDEX

Advanced/rear guards, 181–82, 187, 189–91, 199, 227, 234, 241, 254.

Albert, Prince of Saxony, 85.

Alvensleben, Constantin von, Prussian Gen., 135, 142, 144, 147–49, 241.

Annihilation, principle of, 5, 10, 129, 155, 176, 215.

Artillery, 50, 55, 58–60, 159–60, 191, 204–05; acceptance of loss of, 212–13; commander of, 220, 222; corps structure of, 179, 211; deployment of, 211–12, 213; effectiveness of, 212; tasks of, 164–66, 221–22, 227.

Auftrag (Task), 133, 156, 185, 215, 231.

Balck, Wilhelm, 13.

Balloons, 257–58.

Barnekow, Albert Christoph Freiherr von, Prussian Gen., 144–45, 148.

Battle, importance of, 9–10, 128– 30, 214; when to accept, 51; specific examples of, Gravelotte (1870), 67; Königgrätz (1866), 25, 59–63, 88, 126, 134–37, 237–38, 240–41; Sedan (1870), 25, 39, 85; Spicheren (1870), 41, 81, 140–54; Saint-Privat (1870), 58, 67, 80; Vionville (1870), 84; Wörth (1870), 41, 63–67, 80–81, 137–40.

Bayonets, 48–49.

Bazaine, François Achille, French Marshal, 40–41, 90, 106, 151– 52, 169–70.

Bell, Harry, U.S. Capt., 17.

Benedek, Ludwig Ritter von, Austrian Gen., 136–37, 168.

Benedetti, Count Vincent, 141.

Bewegungskrieg, 54, 201.

Bismarck, Otto Count von, Chancellor, 18, 40.

Blumenthal, Carl Constantin von, Prussian Gen., 80–81, 85–86.

Bonin, Adolf Karl von, Prussian Gen., 134, 241.

Printed in the United States
by Baker & Taylor Publisher Services